"Arriving when new psychoanalytic concerns – narcissism, borderline – were dislodging the hegemony of American ego psychology, but equally consonant with emergent gay, decolonial, and counter-cultural critique, Morgenthaler's deftly subversive clinical lectures for psychoanalysts in Zurich in 1974 create extraordinary space for cultural leverage, now as then. Here is an eye for the needs of outsiders, a psychoanalysis without fixed goals, relational before its time, seeking above all to set an emotional process in motion, one which might, through 'revolutionary psychic turbulence', foster changes that could make all the difference. As Dagmar Herzog puts it, this is not just a tool for psychoanalytic learning, but a manifesto for nonfascist existence."

> **—MATT FFYTCHE, Department of Psychosocial and Psychoanalytic Studies, University of Essex**

"The psychoanalytic contributions of Fritz Morgenthaler, widely admired and idealized in Europe, are mostly unknown in the US. Notably, he was a pioneering contributor to rethinking psychoanalysis' pathologization of same-sex feelings, behaviors and relationships. This new edited translation of Morgenthaler's lectures on psychoanalytic technique is compelling and accessible. *On the Dialectics of Psychoanalytic Practice* should prove a valuable read to historians, students and seasoned practitioners of psychoanalysis."

> **—JACK DRESCHER, MD, Clinical Professor of Psychiatry, Columbia University**

"Fritz Morgenthaler's work is a call for the continued relevance of psychoanalysis to understand not only the self, but also broader social and political phenomena. These lectures and supplemental texts will be essential to anyone interested in the potential of psychoanalysis to offer a systematic critique of social normativity (especially in the domain of sexuality)."

> **—CAMILLE ROBCIS, author of *The Law of Kinship: Anthropology, Psychoanalysis, and the Family in France***

On the Dialectics of Psychoanalytic Practice

Fritz Morgenthaler was a crucial figure in the return of psychoanalysis to post-Nazi Central Europe. An inspiring clinician and teacher to the New Left generation of 1968, he was the first European psychoanalyst since Freud to declare that homosexuality is not, indeed never, a pathology, and in *Technik*, developed revolutionary ideas for transforming clinical technique. *On the Dialectics of Psychoanalytic Practice* offers the first publication in English of this psychoanalytic, counterculture classic.

Those who first picked up *Technik* encountered it at a historical moment when Marxist psychoanalyst Wilhelm Reich, popular New Left cultural critic Klaus Theweleit, and the texts of the Frankfurt School were already required reading. While not a political text in the same direct way, Morgenthaler's *Technik* nonetheless shared many of their preoccupations and conclusions about human nature. It was read as technical guidance for psychoanalysts, but also as a manifesto dedicated to the problem of how it might be possible genuinely to live a postfascist, and nonfascist, existence. Morgenthaler was a protorelationalist who recombined the traditions of ego and self psychology as he retained a commitment to drive theory. Here Dagmar Herzog makes his work available to a new generation of analysts, providing essential source material, annotations, and groundbreaking analysis of the continued importance of the work for historians and therapeutic practitioners alike.

On the Dialectics of Psychoanalytic Practice will interest practicing clinicians as well as intellectual historians and cultural studies scholars seeking to understand the return of psychoanalysis to post-Nazi Central Europe.

Fritz Morgenthaler (1919–1984) was a prominent Swiss physician, psychoanalyst, ethnologist, and painter. Cofounder of the interdisciplinary field of ethnopsychoanalysis, his writings on clinical practice, sexuality, and dream interpretation were essential reading for the counterculture and New Left in Continental Europe.

Dagmar Herzog is Distinguished Professor of History at the Graduate Center, City University of New York. She is the author, most recently, of *Cold War Freud: Psychoanalysis in an Age of Catastrophes* (2017) and *Unlearning Eugenics: Sexuality, Reproduction, and Disability in Post-Nazi Europe* (2018).

The Relational Perspectives Book Series (RPBS) publishes books that grow out of or contribute to the relational tradition in contemporary psychoanalysis. The term *relational psychoanalysis* was first used by Greenberg and Mitchell[1] to bridge the traditions of interpersonal relations, as developed within interpersonal psychoanalysis and object relations, as developed within contemporary British theory. But, under the seminal work of the late Stephen A. Mitchell, the term *relational psychoanalysis* grew and began to accrue to itself many other influences and developments. Various tributaries – interpersonal psychoanalysis, object relations theory, self psychology, empirical infancy research, feminism, queer theory, sociocultural studies, and elements of contemporary Freudian and Kleinian thought – flow into this tradition, which understands relational configurations between self and others, both real and fantasized, as the primary subject of psychoanalytic investigation.

We refer to the relational tradition, rather than to a relational school, to highlight that we are identifying a trend, a tendency within contemporary psychoanalysis, not a more formally organized or coherent school or system of beliefs. Our use of the term *relational* signifies a dimension of theory and practice that has become salient across the wide spectrum of contemporary psychoanalysis. Now under the editorial supervision of Adrienne Harris, Steven Kuchuck, and Eyal Rozmarin, the Relational Perspectives Book Series originated in 1990 under the editorial eye of the late Stephen A. Mitchell. Mitchell was the most prolific and influential of the originators of the relational tradition. Committed to dialogue among psychoanalysts, he abhorred the authoritarianism that dictated adherence to a rigid set of beliefs or technical restrictions. He championed open discussion and comparative and integrative approaches, and promoted new voices across the generations. Mitchell was later joined by the late Lewis Aron, also a visionary and influential writer, teacher, and leading thinker in relational psychoanalysis.

Included in the Relational Perspectives Book Series are authors and works that come from within the relational tradition, those that extend and develop that tradition, and works that critique relational approaches or compare and contrast them with alternative points of view. The series includes our most distinguished senior psychoanalysts, along with younger contributors who bring fresh vision. Our aim is to enable a deepening of relational thinking while reaching across disciplinary and social boundaries in order to foster an inclusive and international literature.

A full list of titles in this series is available at www.routledge.com/mentalhealth/series/LEARPBS.

Note

1 Greenberg, J. & Mitchell, S. (1983). *Object Relations in Psychoanalytic Theory*. Cambridge, MA: Harvard University Press.

On the Dialectics of Psychoanalytic Practice

Fritz Morgenthaler

Edited with an Introduction
by Dagmar Herzog

Translated by Nils F. Schott

Routledge
Taylor & Francis Group

LONDON AND NEW YORK

First published in English in 2020
by Routledge
2 Park Square, Milton Park, Abingdon, Oxon OX14 4RN

and by Routledge
52 Vanderbilt Avenue, New York, NY 10017

Routledge is an imprint of the Taylor & Francis Group, an informa business

British Library Cataloguing-in-Publication Data
A catalogue record for this book is available from the British Library

Library of Congress Cataloging-in-Publication Data
Names: Morgenthaler, Fritz, 1919–1984, author | Herzog, Dagmar, 1961– editor.
Title: On the dialectics of psychoanalytic practice / Fritz Morgenthaler ; edited, with an introduction, by Dagmar Herzog.
Other titles: Technik. English | Relational perspectives book series.
Description: Abingdon, Oxon ; New York, NY : Routledge, 2020. | Series: Relational perspectives book series | Includes bibliographical references and index.
Identifiers: LCCN 2019050791 (print) | LCCN 2019050792 (ebook) | ISBN 9780367337674 (hardback) | ISBN 9780367337681 (paperback) | ISBN 9780429321795 (ebook)
Subjects: MESH: Psychoanalysis—methods | Psychoanalytic Theory | Transference, Psychology
Classification: LCC RC506 (print) | LCC RC506 (ebook) | NLM WM 460 | DDC 616.89/17—dc23
LC record available at https://lccn.loc.gov/2019050791
LC ebook record available at https://lccn.loc.gov/2019050792

ISBN: 978-0-367-33767-4 (hbk)
ISBN: 978-0-367-33768-1 (pbk)
ISBN: 978-0-429-32179-5 (ebk)

Typeset in Times New Roman
by Apex CoVantage, LLC

Printed and bound by CPI Group (UK) Ltd, Croydon, CR0 4YY

Contents

Illustrations

Figure 0.1 Fritz Morgenthaler in Zurich, Switzerland, July 1980, after teargas dispersed protesters at the Autonomes Jugendzentrum. © 1980, Olivia Heussler, Zurich.

Fritz Morgenthaler's *Technik*

Problems, priorities, warnings, metaphors

Dagmar Herzog

> "With psychoanalysis one cannot make any form of progress. There are only transformations."
>
> – Fritz Morgenthaler, *Technik*

Fritz Morgenthaler's *Technik* was never meant to be a book. A version of the text was originally delivered extemporaneously by Morgenthaler as a series of lectures at the Psychoanalytic Seminar Zurich in 1974.[1] These lectures were recorded and later transcribed and edited. *Technik* would finally be published in German in 1978 and Italian in 1980. No portion of it has ever previously appeared in English.

Fritz Morgenthaler (1919–1984) was a Swiss physician and psychoanalyst.[2] (See Figure 0.1.) He was also a prominent member of the International Psychoanalytical Association and – starting at the congress in Amsterdam in 1951 – a frequent invited speaker at its gatherings. In 1952 Morgenthaler joined with Paul Parin and Goldy Parin-Matthèy to open a shared psychoanalytic practice in Zurich. From the mid-1950s on, the three of them, together with Morgenthaler's wife Ruth, took repeated trips to Africa, and in 1960 began fieldwork among the Dogon in just-then-decolonizing Mali – to be followed later by fieldwork among the Anyi in Ivory Coast and (in Morgenthaler's case) among the Iatmul in Papua New Guinea. Morgenthaler is best known to Anglo-American audiences for his collaborative involvement in the invention of the hybrid genre of "ethnopsychoanalysis." Among the important works co-authored by Morgenthaler and the Parins are the ironically titled *Die Weissen denken zuviel* (Whites Think Too Much) and *Fürchte deinen Nächsten wie dich selbst* (Fear Thy Neighbor as Thyself) (Parin et al., 1963, 1971). These two titles in particular put the subjectivity of their informants at their center and became essential reading for the counterculture and New Left in West Germany and Switzerland at the turn from the 1960s to 1970s (cf. Reichmayr, 2003).

The reasons for this fascination among the generation of 1968 with the psychoanalytic fieldwork of Morgenthaler and the Parins in Africa are multiple but can be summarized briefly like this: while at that historical moment, psychoanalysis in the United States was undergoing an abrupt *loss* of prestige within medicine and within mainstream culture, its fortunes were again just beginning to *rise* in post-Nazi Central Europe. This ascent was due not least to the impact of impassioned New Left and women's and gay rights activism. In other words, in West Germany, Switzerland, Austria, and Italy – the countries in which Morgenthaler's work was most fervently received – a renewed interest in psychoanalysis was being carried precisely by those New Left and feminist and gay contingents that had served decisively to crush the conservative version of psychoanalysis in the US (cf. Tändler, 2016; Herzog, 2017; Gutherz, 2019).

However paradoxically and unexpectedly, members of the New Left in post-Nazi Central Europe were in the 1970s urgently captivated by the complex and contradictory legacies of Sigmund Freud. They saw in Freud's writings all sorts of usable tools as they sought – often intensely if not always coherently or accurately – to make sense of their parents' attractions to fascism; to expose the hypocrisies and complicities that marked the postwar era of conservative restoration; to recover the sex-radical (often, though not exclusively, Jewish) inheritance of the early twentieth century that had been destroyed albeit also partially appropriated by the Nazis; and to comprehend their own deepening despair as the political revolutions they had hoped to achieve had, by the later 1970s, been quite evidently beaten back and defeated. For the generation of 1968, psychoanalysis came to acquire a far greater prestige in Central Europe than it had ever received in Freud's own day. (No surprise that the non-German-speaking land in which Morgenthaler was most keenly received was postfascist Italy.)

A book like Morgenthaler and the Parins' *Die Weissen denken zuviel* came to matter to the generation of 1968 in West Germany and elsewhere because it offered the promise of an alternate model for the organization of human community – one based less on competitiveness and more on solidarity. And it was this very concept – that *different cultures could produce different kinds of selves* – which was to become extraordinarily important for the New Left especially in West Germany. Moreover, there can be no question that the New Left's dream of sexual liberation was about more – much more – in postfascist West Germany than the pursuit of pleasure per se. It was very much as well about a major hope that there might be a total remaking of human nature as less aggressive and more free – not least at a moment when the sexual revolution too appeared to have not fulfilled its initial promises.

The years of post-1968 depression and introspection saw widespread critical and reflective engagement with what had been the initially enthusiastically debated post-Freudian lessons advanced by the Marxist psychoanalyst Wilhelm Reich who, among other things, had argued in the 1930s and 1940s that sexual satisfaction and sadism were mutually incompatible. Reich had also advanced the perspective that child sexuality needed to be not just tolerated, but actually celebrated, especially if fascism and neurosis were to be avoided (again). There was in Reich a deep conviction – taken up by the New Left across many European nations as an inescapable truth about human nature – that those who made a lot of love would not, indeed could not, maintain an interest in cruelty toward their fellow man or woman (Reich, 1948 [1933]; Reich, 1946). And yet a further reason for concentrated encounter with psychoanalysis in the New Left was the eagerness to learn from Frankfurt School critical theory – as exemplified in the work of Theodor Adorno and Max Horkheimer – in its grappling with both the psychic sources and the lingering aftereffects of Nazism (Adorno & Horkheimer, 1969 [1947]; Adorno, 1982 [1951]; Adorno, 1998 [1963]). It would have been against the backdrop, then, of a post-Freudian *and* post-Reichian *and* Adorno- and Horkheimer-informed interpretation of the value of psychoanalysis that Morgenthaler would have been widely read – and understood as largely confirmatory – in West Germany and elsewhere in the late 1970s.

So too Morgenthaler's *Technik* would have joined Klaus Theweleit's *Männerphantasien* (Male Fantasies) on a New Left intellectual's bookshelf (1987 [1977], 1989 [1978]). Published at that same moment (1977–1978), Theweleit's sprawling two-volume treatise ostensibly addressed the *Freikorps* – the paramilitary gangs deployed in Weimar Germany and in the Baltics to crush potential popular insurgencies. Read as a study of the protofascist male mind, largely because so many *Freikorps* members later went on to become Nazi stormtroopers and/or concentration and death camp commandants and guards involved in the mass murder of European Jewry, *Männerphantasien* also extensively explored the psychic effects on men socialized into self-discipline, aggression, and hardness. As such, Theweleit essentially proposed that sexual dysfunctionality lay at the core of the most significant and terrifying political event of the twentieth century – arguing that it was crucial to grasp the intimate connections between bodily feelings and the propensity to violence in order to imagine a possible way to a nonfascist future.

Those who first picked up *Technik* when it appeared in 1978 encountered it in a context where Reich and Theweleit and the texts of the Frankfurt School were already required reading. While not a political text in the same direct way that these other works were, *Technik* nonetheless shared many of their preoccupations and conclusions about human nature. Morgenthaler's writings collectively were not just read as guidance for psychoanalysts, but also as manifestos of sorts dedicated to the problem of how it might be possible genuinely to live a postfascist – *and nonfascist* – existence.

Although in many ways a classical, even orthodox, Freudian by predilection and habitus, Morgenthaler's personal and political affinities and solidarities lay with social outsiders – the vulnerable and excluded from respectable European society. He could turn in an instant from an excursus on clinical intricacies to a sensitive and affirmative account of the case of a patient with a cognitive disability. He was recurrently at pains to convince not just his trainee listeners and readers but also his senior confrères that it was counterproductive and morally offensive to attempt to convert the drug addict, failed student, or social misfit into a well-adapted, achievement-oriented citizen. And he was unafraid to compare his own fascination with the luminous colors he saw in such places as the cityscape of Manhattan with the penchant of an avowed fetishist. He was, in sum, a principled and passionate defender of psychoanalytic practice *and* an overt critic of (what he saw as) too many practitioners' tendency to try to adapt patients to normative societal expectations. Morgenthaler expressly noted that useless or damaging technical recommendations filled the extant psychoanalytic literature and, over and over, urged aspiring analysts to maintain a critical antenna vis-à-vis all social expectations of proper performance or conformity.

Relatedly, it was during the years in which he was working out the text of what became *Technik* that Morgenthaler was making a transition from purveying more traditionally stereotypical and prejudiced ideas about homosexuality (evident still in a paper he delivered at the IPA in Rome in 1969) to becoming, in a series of essays published between 1974 and

1984, *the* first European psychoanalyst since Sigmund Freud to declare, resolutely, repeatedly, and without qualification, that homosexual object choice was in no way a defect or a pathology (Morgenthaler, 1974, 1977, 1979, 1980, 1984; Hütt, 2016; Lahl & Henze, 2020). Especially visible in the final two of the supplementary materials included in the appendix to this edition (a letter to the Vienna-born, Chicago-based self psychologist Heinz Kohut in 1977, and an essay published in the widely read West German New Left journal *Kursbuch* also in 1977), Morgenthaler became more generally a stirring and ardent defender of the importance in all lives of the unruly, creative, and undirected force of what he came to call "the sexual" (*das Sexuelle*), in contradistinction to already-formed "organized sexuality" (*organisierte Sexualität*). Morgenthaler came to model a capacious and generous ability not just to sympathize but actually to identify (though never in a presumptuous or appropriating way) across all boundaries of erotic preference and orientation.

For these many reasons, it was not a coincidence that it was with the assistance of Karl Markus Michel, the left-wing West German essayist and publisher (and editor of *Kursbuch* and specialist on Frankfurt School critical theory), that *Technik* made its way into print. (As with so many of his generation, Michel had become intrigued by Morgenthaler's work after reading the book on the Ivory Coast-Anyi, *Fürchte deinen Nächsten wie dich selbst*.) Published by an anarchist New Left press based in Frankfurt am Main, Syndikat, that had been cofounded by Michel just two years earlier, Morgenthaler's *Technik* joined a list alongside works by the West German gay rights activist Martin Dannecker (who had also been directly influenced by Morgenthaler's antihomophobic writings), the French psychoanalyst and antiauthoritarian educator Maud Mannoni, the West German social psychologist Klaus Horn, the Romanian-French-American ethnopsychoanalyst George Devereux, and the West German philosopher and acute critic of the legacies of Nazism within postwar Germany Ulrich Sonnemann. In Italy, *Tecnica* was published by Boringhieri (later Bollati Boringhieri), a press launched by the prominent left-wing activist psychoanalyst Pier Francesco Galli, a press which would publish more than 200 psychoanalytic classics, from such diverse authors as Karl Menninger, Melanie Klein, Anna Freud, and Otto Kernberg in the 1970s through to the relationalists Margaret Black and Stephen Mitchell in the 1990s.

* * *

What of lasting interest do these Morgenthaler lectures have for practicing clinicians, historians of psychoanalysis, and psychoanalysis-interested social scientists and cultural studies scholars in the twenty-first century? Although the lectures were – not least with Michel's extensive help – lightly edited from the spoken presentation, a good deal does still appear unclear and unresolved. Much is not only lost in translation, but remains abstruse and opaque in the original German. There is a level of inscrutability that even specialists in the history of psychoanalysis may find baffling and off-putting.

First and foremost, then, for any adventurous reader who dares to pursue this problematic and difficult text it is critical to keep in mind that Morgenthaler was engaging in what we might call a meditation on the status of clinical psychoanalytic practice as it was then rapidly evolving in the course of the late 1960s and through the 1970s on both sides of the Atlantic and – significantly – as interested members of the New Left within Central Europe were engaging in a highly compressed re-reception of post-Freudian psychoanalytic developments. For instance, texts originally written by US ego psychologists like Heinz Hartmann, Ernst Kris, and Rudolph Loewenstein (or the great systematizer of ego psychology David Rapaport, or ego psychological specialist on child development René Spitz) in the 1940s and 1950s were being read in quick succession with, or jostling alongside, the most recent 1960s and 1970s products of specialists on narcissistic and borderline character disorders by Heinz Kohut or his (more Kleinian) rival Otto Kernberg. Morgenthaler was familiar with the approaches of all these prominent proponents of various schools and attuned to the inevitable insecurities their – very often mutually incompatible – presumptions and recommendations were likely to induce in any novice psychoanalyst.

It is, moreover, equally crucial to keep in mind that the text of *Technik* functions always on multiple levels. On the most basic level it can be read as a riff – an explication and amplification as well as modification – on Sigmund Freud's classic statement on analytic technique, "Remembering, Repeating and Working-Through" (1914, pp. 145–156). Morgenthaler certainly understood himself as experimenting with transference, resistance, and interpretation in unmediated lineage with Freud. Freud's first mentions of "compulsion to repeat" and "working-through" occur in this essay, as does the marvelous and evocative image – a main touchstone for Morgenthaler – of the patient "bring[ing] out of the armory of the past the weapons with which he defends himself against the progress of the treatment – weapons which we must wrest from him one by one" (p. 151). The analysand's resistance to change, in dynamic tension with his or her struggle to change, was a principal focus for Morgenthaler.

Ultimately, however, Morgenthaler was more concerned to call analysts' attention to their unfortunate proclivities to bring weapons of resistance out of *their own armories*. Moreover, and in this respect departing from Freud, Morgenthaler recognized as well a strong tendency, inherent in the analysand's unconscious ego, to counteract his or her resistances and to enable the analyst actually to further the analytic process. Throughout, the text reveals a practicing clinician searching recurrently to find the most apt language (via memorable examples, orienting concepts, and illustrative metaphors) to help each trainee locate his or her own personal-professional style and then adapt this style to each specific patient's (unconscious) needs. For instance, at one point Morgenthaler explains, in discussing a particular case, how a patient used the reporting of a dream – replete with an awakening ejaculation – in order to "arm" himself in the face of an analyst's obtuseness so as to force the redirection of a transference that had gotten confused. At another point, Morgenthaler describes how an analysand (metaphorically) takes a blind analyst by the hand to lead him. And at yet other moments, he describes how the analysand's unconscious is like a theater director, creating a variety of scene-stagings, until the analyst finally understands what is going on. In short, Morgenthaler – unique for his day – emphasized, over and over, that it was very often the *analysand* who assisted and guided the analyst in keeping the analytic process going.

Morgenthaler described his vital foundational message to analysts in training as containing (what he calls in Chapter 2) a "warning" and a "priority." *Technik* is replete with warnings and priorities. The first warning – and it is given repeatedly, in numerous and nuanced variations – is that the analyst should not think of him- or herself as someone cleansed of neurosis or conflict or narcissistic needs. And the first priority is the necessity to understand every new analysis as plunging both the analyst and the analysand ("partners in a deepening relationship") into a continual "flow of emotional movement that characterizes the development of the transference" – one in which the analyst's or analysand's "emotional offer" must be met with an "emotional echo" from the other. Nonetheless, and despite the frequent reminders to the analyst not to assume that he or she is somehow healthier than the analysand, and the repeated warning that every new relationship re-triggers the analyst's own "conflictual inclinations" – though inevitably always again differently – Morgenthaler insists that the analyst is the one responsible for "initiat[ing], maintain[ing], and shap[ing] the analytic process." Thus, on the one hand,

> If as analyst I take the attitude that I can approach the analysand as though I am without conflicts while the analysand, in contrast to me and as a result of his neuroses, seems to be full of conflict, the dynamic is done for.

On the other hand, however, it is definitively the analyst's job to "keep my own conflictual inclinations . . . under control."

Never hesitant to go to the most elemental, primal places, Morgenthaler stipulated that entering into an analytic relationship inescapably involved a mutual "seduction." And although Morgenthaler was writing at a time of dramatic transition within the international psychoanalytic community – as precisely the mid-1970s saw a revival of fierce disputes about whether the typical patient base was changing from one dominated by oedipally challenged neurotics to one characterized more by individuals with preoedipally-determined narcissistic character disorders (i.e. not so much egos at inner odds, as rather weak and damaged selves) – Morgenthaler observed that a mutual seduction with all its dangers became unavoidable whether patients presented a "psychoneurosis" or a "narcissistic neurosis." As he put it tartly, speaking of the analyst's position with respect to the analysand: "Nobody is indifferent toward idealizations, fantasies of omnipotence, and sexual impulses."

In view of the many potential hazards and the abundant anxieties these would cause for beginning analysts, *Technik* issued yet further warnings. All were directed against the (in Morgenthaler's view) all-too-frequent "false suppositions" that "pervade the psychoanalytic literature." Three were particularly significant. First was Morgenthaler's regularly repeated insistence that analysts needed strenuously to *resist the impulse to rush to the analysand's parents* as the origins of all things unwell or in any way to assume that in the transference they themselves were playing the role of "the daddy, . . . the mommy, . . . the siblings of childhood." Although problems with parents (or siblings) were a ubiquitous feature of human life, Morgenthaler urged restraint in presuming in advance where exactly a particular problem had its source. Morgenthaler mocked the tired tendency of many a male analyst, when confronted with a young woman who reported being sexually attracted to older men, to conclude both that this represented a father-fixation and to presume that in the transference she was attracted to the analyst as such a father-figure. (But, characteristically, Morgenthaler remained self-critical. Thus to illustrate his argument he showed how, in one case, the assumption that he was being put by a male patient into the role of the patient's father turned out to be his *own* way of warding off and avoiding "confronting the much more important insight that I was afraid of being homosexually seduced and overwhelmed by my analysand.")

Second, Morgenthaler announced the axiom that *what is conscious cannot simultaneously be unconscious*. Thus, if a patient were to report what behaviors of his or her mother or father had been particularly distressing, these factors could precisely *not* be the source of the individual's deepest troubles because, by definition, these factors were conscious – and any random acquaintance, using empathy or self-comparison, could speculate about how these factors affected the analysand in adulthood. As Freud had before him, so Morgenthaler too dismissively referred to the "psychology of consciousness" (*Bewusstseinspsychologie*) as something anybody could dabble in (cf. Freud, 1912, p. 118) – and which could not possibly help a patient break with the compulsion to repeat that was his or her way of acting out the trouble whose source lay in the depths of the unconscious. So too, for instance, if an analysand became actively reproachful toward an analyst, that by definition could *not* be the underlying dynamic driving the transference.

The third warning concerned the purpose of psychoanalysis itself, as Morgenthaler insisted that *a psychoanalysis should have no goal*. This was both descriptive and prescriptive. In the descriptive sense, it was simply Morgenthaler's conviction that "[p]sychoanalysis never leads us forward. It usually leads to something entirely other than what we thought." Moreover, Morgenthaler was at pains to remind analysts – students and peers alike – that at best an analysis could facilitate a "rearticulation" (*Neuformulierung*) of conflicts, never a disappearance of conflicts. "Most things are what they are, the way they have always been." The idea instead was that the person would develop greater "flexibility and elasticity" (*Flexibilität und Elastizität*) in dealing with his or her conflictual tendencies – would ease up, unclench, formulate things anew, stop needing to repeat, and develop an expanded way of experiencing life (*Erlebnisweise*). The persons stayed themselves as they had always been – and yet everything for them was now transformed.

As a corollary, Morgenthaler cautioned against ever declaring war on a patient's symptoms (cf. Morgenthaler, 1974, p. 1078). This warning was definitely also meant prescriptively, as Morgenthaler underscored how a classic assumption in much of the psychoanalytic literature that the point of an analysis was to provide help to someone restricted in their "ability to work, enjoy, and love" was arrogant nonsense – a sign that the analyst had succumbed to cultural pressures to play a socially efficacious role. Was the point of analysis "getting rid of the symptoms [the patient] is suffering from or making his neurosis disappear? Or does it mean attenuating the difficulties and conflicts he is living through in such a way that he can bear them or so that he can feel good in the kind of social situation in which most people find themselves? Are our analysands to become happy?" (Or, as Morgenthaler sarcastically added, "are they to content themselves with fantasizing that they are happy?") The answers to all these questions were a resounding *no*.

To avoid the various pitfalls within the analytic relationship as it deepened, Morgenthaler proffered a set of additional priorities. The first was to see to it that the relationship with the analysand remained relaxed and de-stressed (*entspannt*); it was of utmost importance that the analysand feel well in the analytic setting. Morgenthaler expressly turned against the (in his time) reigning assumption in psychoanalytic circles (on both sides of the Atlantic) that patients had to experience the "pressure of suffering" (*Leidensdruck*) to enter into, or stick with, an analysis. This also meant – yet a further priority – that it was the analyst's job to ensure that his or her own modalities of cathexis (*Besetzungsmodalitäten*) – in other words, his or her own emotional investments – stayed in sync and congruent (*stimmig*) with those of the patient. The modalities of cathexis needed to "stay oriented in one and the same direction." And it was the *analyst* who needed to adjust to the analysand, and not vice versa – even when the going got rough. It would not be right suddenly to decide that the patient was not analyzable. Here Morgenthaler adduced the metaphor of a journey one has already begun. "It may be the case that the trains aren't running, that the ships are all at anchor because of political unrest, and the airports are shut down." In such instances, Morgenthaler mused: "Perhaps I continue the journey by truck." Above all, a combative situation in which analyst and analysand consciously or unconsciously wanted different things was to be avoided.

This, then, was the basis upon which the next priority, the "actualization" or "reactivation of the transference-conflict, a reactivation that
alone promotes the analytic process," could be set in motion. For, and
this was Morgenthaler's most ardent conviction, an analysis is a process
that "produce[s] revolutionary, intrapsychic turbulence." Thus it should
be a priority to comprehend that analysis is all about the flow of emotionality and the turmoil that ensues in the course of the transference; only
this turbulence could loosen fixations and make new ways of experiencing possible (cf. Binswanger, 2005a; Körbitz, 2020). And while Morgenthaler adamantly endorsed adherence to the framework of the classic
setting – with the analyst sitting in a chair not visible to the analysand on
the couch – and emphasized as well the inappropriateness both of intimate
self-disclosure and of social contacts with a patient outside of the analysis, he radically departed from conventional wisdom in his belief that a
withholding manner and strict abstinence and neutrality were inadvisable.
Instead: "What is expected of me is comprehensive drive-friendliness."
Although every analyst should find the approach that best befit him- or
herself, for his own part Morgenthaler noted that the willingness to make
himself vulnerable to his patients was indispensable.

Undeniably, Morgenthaler was, in all ways, process-oriented. That was
true of his analytic technique, and decidedly true too of his approach as a
teacher. It is no less true of the form and structure of *Technik*. As noted,
Morgenthaler designed the lectures for beginning practitioners struggling
to learn the craft while being bombarded by self-doubt on the one hand
and a welter of (often contradictory) expert pronouncements on how analysis was to be done on the other. But this also meant that almost every
example of a case presented to illustrate a point – whether taken from a
supervision or from Morgenthaler's own practice – included Morgenthaler's sifting-through of various possible approaches that might run through
an analyst's head, allowing the listener-reader to think along, before
Morgenthaler concluded with his own recommendations. Furthermore,
and recurrently, Morgenthaler also left loose ends, only to pick them up
again in later chapters – much as, in an analysis, a topic may have been
broached, only to remain dormant for weeks or months before it rears up
again and takes on new meaning. And at other moments, Morgenthaler
led a listener-reader into a seeming clarity and certainty of perspective
and direction, only then to unravel that certainty and provide relativiza-
tions and qualifications.

Yet in the end, and while "getting involved with each other" (*sich aufeinander einzulassen*), in all the inexorable trickiness that would entail, was indeed Morgenthaler's principal recommended approach to psychoanalysis, this invitation-*cum*-mandate would throughout be held in tension with a quite rigorous attention to formal technical matters. For instance, as *Technik* unfolds, it becomes clear how deeply concerned Morgenthaler was to help an apprentice analyst learn how, in practice, to *distinguish* different kinds of resistances evinced by analysands (Do they come from the id or from the ego? Should they be respected or dismantled?) and how, again feasibly and concretely, it would be best to *time* various kinds of interpretations. Morgenthaler evidently assumed that interpretations of the transference would be provided fairly early on – and that these, in turn, would affect what he called the "coloring" of the transference (cf. Pomeranz, 2005; Binswanger, 2012). But he also gave pragmatic advice on how an analyst might recognize the moment when he or she would experience what he named a "summation effect" – the moment when the accumulation of quantitative information gleaned from the analysand's reports would flip over into a sudden qualitative comprehension of a deeper set of connections. And he demonstrated in an accessible, step-by-step way, why it could be important to delay (longer than most of his peers did) what analysts called "reconstructive interpretations."

Perhaps the most innovative and lastingly practical suggestion made in *Technik* has to do with Morgenthaler's insistence on *redirecting the analyst's attention from the contents of what patients are saying to the form in which they are saying it* – not just the nonverbal cues that accompany all talking, but specifically the *sequentiality* (*Sukzession* or *Abfolge*) in the course of associations. It is exactly at moments when the analyst feels most perplexed that the best move, Morgenthaler proposes, is a seemingly hypertheoretical and abstract one: to attend, very precisely, to the order of what is being brought forward. Crucially, moreover, it is not the sequence in which something happened that matters, *but the sequence in which it is reported* (which may not be at all the same) – for this is what provides traces of the unconscious motivations.

This was a concept that Morgenthaler had initially developed in the context of dream analysis (cf. Binswanger, 2016). He had found it useful to assume not only that a dream – both the remembered dream and the told dream (again: two different things) – were part of the ongoing unconscious conversation with and relationship with the analyst, but also that the trajectory and directionality of the dream (in other words: its movement), and the sequentiality of details in and around the dream's telling, were more important evidence for what was going on unconsciously than any latent symbolic content one might try to decode out of it, project into it, or rationalize around it. It was this shift to the *formal* aspects of the analysand's reports – no matter how nonsensical the ensuing sequence might initially seem to be – that helped the analyst regain footing:

> From a technical point of view, this attitude has top priority. I must not shy away from realizing that, at this very moment, I do not understand more than the analysand does. Moreover, I must not be afraid to formulate what might seem like completely absurd coherences, solely because they have presented themselves specifically in this and not in any other way.

A distinct added value of this approach, moreover, was that summarizing the sequence, in all its seeming incongruity or even preposterousness, back to the analysand was a nonconfrontational way of extricating the analyst from being potentially ensnared into either shared acting-out or further muddling. Not least of all, doing so prompted the analysand's curiosity and helped him or her begin to identify with the analyst and see connections and new perspectives where previously there had only been confusion or repetition. To make these ideas tangible, Morgenthaler presented various case examples: a young woman torn between her husband and her first love and disappointed in both (as she seemed always to be disappointed in everyone); a young man who manifested the need to think the analyst was hard of hearing (not because this made the analyst be like his father but because it showed the need to take a threatening rival down a notch by ascribing a weakness to him); and a man who compulsively and masochistically took care of all his family members and a wide circle of friends (while resenting them all) but also constantly feared being disapproved of by his boss. Through these examples, Morgenthaler showed how following the seemingly absurd sequentiality of the patient's utterances can give clues to the unconscious, which is (as Morgenthaler rarely tired of reminding his listeners and readers) also never rational.

Finally, what Morgenthaler urged was modesty of aims – and sustained capacity to tolerate *a not-knowing*. Yet in accepting and bearing that ongoing nonknowing, not only an attitude of attentiveness to that which is not yet understood becomes possible, but also an openness to new ways of experiencing – for both analysand and analyst. Among the many luminous metaphors adduced in *Technik* is one that describes the analyst as "the belated guest" at the untidy and memory-and-forgetfulness-laden table at which the child, which the patient had once been, had sat so long ago:

> I do not sit down with my analysand at a table set for us both where we could now enjoy together the meal we've ordered. But neither is it the case that at this table we're being served, instead of well-cooked dishes, nothing but trash, refuse, or pebbles. I am always the belated guest of my analysand, and I sit with him among half-empty bottles long after the meal has been served and eaten. No one has been sitting at the table like this before. It is a new experience for us both.
>
> With this metaphor, I'm describing nothing other than the emotional content that so lastingly characterizes the analysis. In the analytic relationship, the emotional offer of the analyst always prompts an emotional echo on the part of the analysand. This emotional echo contains the leftovers and bears the traces of the guests who have convened, dined, gorged, raged, fasted, scorned, devoured, spat, stolen, and imbibed at the once freshly laid table of the child that the analysand once was. That all is now submerged in the past. As analyst, I am the belated guest who knows nothing and understands nothing of all that once took place there.

And so with this, the analysis could now begin.

* * *

In all of these respects, Morgenthaler anticipated the relational turn that would soon after his death come to prominence internationally, as also in the US "the Hartmann era" of ego psychological predominance gave way, over the course of the 1970s–1980s, to the – in the meantime apparently quite durable – ascent of intersubjective and relational approaches (cf. Aron, 1996; McLaughlin, 1998; Bergmann, 2000). In his unwavering adherence to the idea that what matters most is *the quality of relationship* between analyst and analysand and in his commitment to understanding analyst and analysand as *two partners who are both conflicted*, Morgenthaler was quite evidently a proto- or incipient relationalist – even though the term, and the movement to which it referred, were just being developed at the very moment *Technik* was being published (cf. Deserno, 2005, pp. 107–109; Hamburger, 2017). And although the language to name his methods in this way did not yet exist, Morgenthaler would certainly have recognized himself in the category. In an interview given in Munich in 1977 – as he was just presenting the about-to-be-published text of *Technik* to professional peers and in the context of rebutting the accusation that he was providing only an "anti-technique" and that for something to qualify as a guidebook for "technique," it would need to include a "system of rules" – Morgenthaler not only contended that, on the contrary, "of course . . . it is desirable to desist from fixed rule systems. . . . Fixed rules would block the emotionality." He went on directly from this claim to elaborate that what mattered most was that

> as an analyst one must build on one's own capacity for relationship with the analysand. One of the crucial attributes that an analyst needs to develop is the ability to create an intensive relationship with people with very different personalities and to sustain that relationship within the spatially and temporally restricted situation of the analysis.
> (Morgenthaler & Kilian, 2017 [1978], p. 11)

Another way of putting the point is to say that Morgenthaler was already fashioning – in his clinical practice and in his supervising and teaching – a new way of "doing" psychoanalysis at a moment when the relationalist school was just coming into existence and did not yet have any access to participation in the then most influential circles of either the American Psychoanalytic Association or the IPA.

But Morgenthaler was always also a selective recombiner of psychoanalytic traditions – and he understood himself as standing primarily at the intersection of ego and self psychology. Morgenthaler's writings on clinical technique – and *Technik* was no exception – provide a distinctive mix of conservatism and radicalism. From ego psychology, Morgenthaler took an unshakeable conviction in the reality of drives, most especially libidinal drives (in all their compound variations, including "drive-impulses," "drive-wishes," and "drive-vicissitudes") – a notion that would have been anathema to contemporaneous relationalists (who were far more interested in objects and attachments than in drives). He retained from classical Freudian thought the idea that every human being in infancy and toddlerhood went through stages of libidinal development. These arced from the oral (incorporative) through the anal (variously defined as retentive, sadistic, or passive) and the phallic (associated with exhibitionistic self-display) to the genital. Revealingly, and although Morgenthaler did occasionally write about orality (especially in his ethnopsychoanalytic texts), in his clinical writing he was notably more preoccupied with the tensions within Europeans – and in European men especially, of whatever sexual orientation – between the passivity he (like Freud and like all ego psychologists before him) associated with the anal phase, on the one hand, and, on the other, the activity and comfort with joyful competence and self-display, without shame or shyness, that he associated with the phallic phase. The genital phase – so vaunted as the acme of maturity by most of his predecessors and peers – interested him markedly less (Reiche, 2005; Heinrichs, 2005b). Meanwhile, and unlike most ego psychologists, he was dubious about the possible existence of an aggressive drive (cf. Parin & Morgenthaler, 1969; Morgenthaler, 1984, pp. 25, 28).

In retrospect, however – and tellingly – it is apparent that the specific pieces he plucked from leading ego psychologists were among the most empathic and noncondescending bits one could find in the otherwise all-too-often rather more austere writings of those individuals. Good examples would be Morgenthaler's espousal of Ernst Kris' idea of "regressions in the service of the ego" (Kris, 1952, pp. 253–254; cf. Loewenstein, 1963, p. 471) or – in an innovative discussion of a perversion as also a kind of self-healing attempt – his adoption of Heinz Hartmann's remark that while a particular symptom, if it were viewed "laterally," would be deemed "pathological" and "be attributed to certain deficiencies at particular stages of development," it might well "present the best solution for an optimal interaction between the mental systems and the self when viewed longitudinally, i.e., in terms of the total development of the personality" (Hartmann, 1954, pp. 31–36; cf. Morgenthaler, 1974, p. 1079).[3] In his idiosyncrasy, in short, Morgenthaler was in his own way quite precise.

The incipient "relationalism" was no less apparent in Morgenthaler's intensive grappling with the work of Heinz Kohut. Strikingly, Morgenthaler was drawn both to Kohut's recommendations for clinical work with patients evincing narcissistic character disorders (patients "who present a profound disturbance in their narcissistic development") and, crucially, also to Kohut's whole-hearted endorsement of the benefits to *all* people of a vigorous and supple sense of self-esteem. Morgenthaler was, in addition, uniquely able to manage Kohut's own sensitivity to slights and need for narcissistic nourishment, both in individual interaction and in public settings (for instance at the IPA in Paris in 1973, when Kohut was stung by some of his peers' greater interest in the work of borderline specialist Otto Kernberg, and Morgenthaler rose to Kohut's defense). But it was precisely in what turned out to be a strong duality in his engagement with Kohut – the affection and genuine admiration, on the one hand, and, on the other, the resistance and challenge to what Morgenthaler was increasingly coming to see in Kohut as an at once entrenched and unpsychoanalytic adherence to socially normative sexual conservatism – that Morgenthaler was able to work out his own views with greatest clarity.

Morgenthaler was especially impressed, already in reading Kohut's first major book, *The Analysis of the Self* (1971), by the new strategies Kohut had developed which demonstrated that patients with severe early damage to their emergent selves could, nonetheless, develop a "stable narcissistic transference." And he loved the idea that all people, for robust early development, needed both (in Kohut's terms) a "grandiose and exhibitionist image" of themselves and an admired, omnipotent "idealized parental imago" – and also that it was good if these phase-specific phenomena could be integrated into an adult personality as a joyful, ambitious, positive sense of self, and as the capacity to formulate and to pursue ideals of one's own devising. He was intrigued as well by Kohut's proposal that, especially for patients with damage to their sense of self, an analyst might need to serve, for long stretches, more as a *function* (even an extension of the self) than as an *object* in the proper sense of that term. By the time Morgenthaler read the second volume by Kohut, *The Restoration of the Self* (1977), he was even more enthusiastic – but, and simultaneously, also far more sharply critical (even as he embedded his criticism in warm and effusive praise).

In his letter to Kohut of September 1977 at the occasion of the publication of Kohut's second volume, Morgenthaler gingerly attempted to point out the awkward but unmistakable fact of Kohut's adherence to normative notions of appropriate sexual behavior. Morgenthaler averred – in the context of commentary on Kohut's discussion of a patient he had named "Mr. M." – that he, Morgenthaler, for his part believed it was not at all acceptable to be "simply stamping out whatever seems to be pathological so as to postulate some kind of 'healing' through an illusory disposal." For Morgenthaler, the point of an analysis, *if* there was such a point, would be to achieve a "relaxation" of what had hitherto been "irritating" to the patient about his own desires and activities. Morgenthaler reproached Kohut for "stay[ing] with a polar opposition in your observing and assessing of sexual strivings and permit[ting] the reader to feel confirmed in his prejudiced, moralizing, unarticulated attitude toward homosexuality." Instead, Morgenthaler suggested, the ideal outcome would be for a patient with homosexual desires "to become reconciled with his homosexuality."

By the time he wrote the essay for the New Left journal *Kursbuch* in 1977 (in the context of a special issue dedicated to "Sensualities"), Morgenthaler had honed his critical perspectives on what he saw not only as the "hypocrisy" rampant in an "achievement-oriented society" (in fact, "a hypocrisy that covers over a profound helplessness") but also the damages such a social organization did to *everyone's* capacities for fulfilling interpersonal interactions and senses of themselves. The essay covered several topics, among them: the blur, rather than the clear distinction, between those labeled by society as perverse and those who thought themselves "normal"; the problem with a psychoanalytic guild that had become "ever less capable of recognizing the absurd within itself the more it adapted to the roles society assigned to it" and the "elitist, condescending consciousness" the guild promulgated; and the profound yearning of all people to develop a "beautiful and whole" image of oneself such that one's self-esteem could "be so strong and resistant that it can bear the reality of life and the reality of the society in which one lives." But the essay additionally made the at once sarcastic and absolutely earnest point that

> thanks to their socially-adequate role behavior, it may seem easier for banking experts, car salesmen, bicyclists, psychoanalysts, vegetable merchants, film distributors, heterosexuals, husbands, antiauthoritarian pedagogues, and policemen to develop a good, balanced sense of self. . . . Perverts, homosexuals, rent boys and whores, drug addicts, and juveniles who refuse to take on a role offered by society have a much harder time fashioning and also holding onto a complete, beautiful image of themselves.

Imperfectly phrased though it may have been, Morgenthaler here offered arguments that still have their resonances.

* * *

Though there had been prior efforts to systematize psychoanalytic technique – among them works by Edward Glover and Otto Fenichel – the most widely read technical guidebook of the era was the prominent Los Angeles-based psychoanalyst Ralph Greenson's *The Technique and Practice of Psychoanalysis* (1967), which appeared also in German translation in 1973. Of necessity, there was substantive overlap between Greenson's and Morgenthaler's explications of the basics of psychoanalytic practice. How could it be otherwise? Anyone hoping to become an effective analyst would need to have a basic grasp of concepts such as free association, ego functions, transference (including eroticized transference, with all its possible snares), resistances, interpretations, and working-through. Yet there were subtle and not-so-subtle distinctions. Greenson had been arguing steadily already since the 1950s that, in an analysis, a "troubled and unknowing" analysand met with a "relatively untroubled and expert" analyst. He believed that the use of interpretations – "the making of the unconscious conscious" – was the analyst's "most effective and final lever in influencing his patient." Moreover, he baldly declared: "Our objective is to make possible the birth of a mature adult" (Greenson, 1958, pp. 200–201). And there was something else: through all his many clinical case essays as in the enormously readable, almost chatty style of his guidebook, Greenson's account of his patients' sexual predilections, masturbatory or day-dream fantasies, and concrete sexual activities was consistently salacious, almost pornographically so (e.g. Greenson, 1967, pp. 19–22, 40–42, 185–187, 302–303) – and simultaneously, the tone made it clear that the doctor himself was largely inured to such troubles.

The contrast between Greenson's and Morgenthaler's approaches could not be more evident. Morgenthaler disapproved heartily of the goal of "maturity." He was aghast at the condescension to the patient apparent in the predominant form of psychoanalysis – which "wants to distinguish the healthy from the sick, wants to help the one who suffers by realizing goals, wants to cure everything that appears to it to be ill." He could not have been less interested in salacious voyeuristic intrigue. Morgenthaler in the *Kursbuch* essay went beyond the repeated claim made in *Technik* that also the analyst inevitably has "conflictual inclinations" to argue forthrightly that any analyst also has "perverse inclinations." And in an aside, Morgenthaler even observed that this was much like the way "we all are perverse without really knowing it." Most importantly, however, Morgenthaler wanted to insist that critique was not enough; there were other ways to live. "Things don't have to be the way they are." Human beings could – often in the most unexpected ways – initiate transformations in each other, both inside and outside of psychoanalytic encounters.

The text of *Technik* is demanding. But it rewards close reading. A perspicacious comment made by Morgenthaler in his letter to Kohut, in response to Kohut's second book, observed that the book was challenging not least because "the reader himself changes in the course of the reading." Or, as he put it even more forcefully: "That which one read in an earlier chapter was read by a different person." The same or similar might be said of the careful reader of Morgenthaler's *Technik*.

Notes

1 The Psychoanalytic Seminar Zurich, growing out of a postwar initiative led by Morgenthaler and his closest associates, was founded in 1958 and was throughout the 1960s and most of the 1970s an influential component organization within the (IPA-affiliated) Swiss Society for Psychoanalysis (*Schweizerische Gesellschaft für Psychoanalyse*, SGP), although in 1977, the Seminar would formally split from the SGP, mostly over selection and training of candidates (cf. Kurz, 1993, pp. 50–53). The – highly respected and democratically organized – Seminar remains the single largest training institute for psychoanalysis in Switzerland today. In 1974, Morgenthaler's audience would have been a lively mix of all generations, from beginning students to senior analysts.

2 Morgenthaler's complicated, iridescent personality is especially well captured in memoirs and correspondence (Heinrichs, 2005a; Fehr, 2005; Reichmayr & Reichmayr, 2019; Parin, 2019; Zweifel, 2019). Tributes to his significance as a clinician clarify the singularities of his writings especially on clinical technique, dream interpretation, and sexuality (Körbitz, 2003; Binswanger, 2005b; Deserno, 2005; Knellessen, 2005; Pomeranz, 2005; Reiche, 2009; Binswanger, 2016).

3 Certainly Anna Freud's *The Ego and the Mechanisms of Defence* (1937 [1936]) was an important text for Morgenthaler. Further explicitly cited ego psychological points of orientation for Morgenthaler included essays on: the systematization of psychoanalytic concepts and Freud's structural theory, including insights into the co-production of egos and ids – rather than sequential emergence of egos out of ids – as well as on processes and functions of identification (Hartmann et al., 1946); the limits of analysands' capacities for free association (Loewenstein, 1963); and the idea that Freud's distinction, developed in *The Interpretation of Dreams*, between "primary-process" mental activity (associated with the unconscious, the id, and the pleasure principle) and "secondary-process" mental activity (associated with the conscious and the preconscious, with the ego and with the reality principle) could be extended beyond dream interpretation to all aspects of life (Lewy & Rapaport, 1944; Rapaport, 1960).

Part I

Technik

Chapter 1

Theory of technique and analytic process

When I tell an aspiring analyst who is putting his first analysand on the couch, "Sit down and wait for what the patient tells you," I have told him something that may be correct – but it might be of no use to him because the relationship of the one person with the other, of the analysand with his analyst, is different in each particular case. It is a very specific, individual, unique relationship determined simultaneously by what is going on within the analysand and what is going on within the analyst.[1]

There are analysands who act in a relaxed way and freely recount what is going on inside them. Others feel inhibited and develop anxieties that are linked to the expectations analysis prompts in them. Curiously, however, one and the same analysand may, with a specific analyst, speak openly and freely about himself from the very beginning of the analysis while with a different analyst, as the result of inhibitions and anxieties, he has difficulty saying anything at all. In such situations and similar ones, questions arise that everyone answers in his own way. For example, in French psychoanalytic circles for a while the question played a certain role whether a certain analysand ought better to be analyzed by a woman or a man. A young man who feels so inhibited toward women that he wants to go into analysis would, according to one side, be sent to a male analyst as a matter of course, whereas from the vantage of others, a female analyst would be much more suitable precisely because of this inhibition.

It becomes clear here that such points of view are not binding criteria at all. We will never see the end of it if we try to clarify and fix what, in a situation within the analytic process which a specific analyst has entered into with a specific analysand, is to be, may be, or ought to be interpreted or not interpreted, what must be avoided, what is correct, what is orthodox, what is right or wrong, in short, what works.

Because what is going on within the analyst facing an analysand differs from person to person, each and every one will behave in such a situation as befits him. This can be neither predicted nor codified. In other words: the use of the psychoanalytic method cannot be grasped in mere concepts. That is also why it cannot be taught. But there is, nonetheless, a foundation for the use of the psychoanalytic method. It is: the theory of technique.

We can trace over the course of the development of the science of psychoanalysis a tendency to bring out generally valid laws and to reify particular concepts. Starting from clinical experience – the experience, that is, that analysts have gained in applying the psychoanalytic method – two large areas have, in the decades since the emergence of psychoanalysis, been theoretically charted: on the one hand metapsychology and on the other the theory of psychoanalytic technique.[2]

Metapsychology and theory of technique are two systems for theoretically conceiving and consolidating psychoanalytic knowledge, and they stand in a dialectical relationship with each other. This means that the contradictoriness which is inevitably inherent in every theory about life-processes is here once again reflected, and this time in a more precisely graspable way, in the concepts of the two theoretical systems. On the one hand, the two theories are inseparably connected with, depend on, and supplement each other. On the other hand, they diametrically oppose each other. Metapsychology as it develops tends toward an ever more complete clarification and transparency of human psychic life. It aims for an all-encompassing, cohesive whole. The theory of technique as it develops, in turn, tends more toward locating and conceptually grasping specific positions or vantages in a way that comes as close as possible to how human beings actually relate to and engage with one another. Its concepts are related to each other but only very loosely, since uniformity would destroy the possibility of using them. They can be applied only in the context of specific situations. They are aids to orientation – signposts in the flow of the emotional movement that characterizes the development of transference.

We might compare the analytic process of interpretation with a phenomenon of spherical optics and consider the conditions that apply in the emergence of a virtual image, an image I cannot see and whose distorted projection becomes comprehensible only when I reconstruct it abstractly using physics and mathematics. Metapsychology and a theory of technique trigger in our thinking wholly different ways of cognitively grasping connections, as if these were rays with different refraction angles that nonetheless, taken together, compose an image. Only, this image is a virtual image, in complete analogy with the invisible virtual image in spherical optics. As an analyst, I can abstractly articulate this virtual image of a psychic process for myself if I know the metapsychological theorems and am familiar with the theory of technique. Only then will it be possible for me to reconstruct and rearticulate in a new way the distorted picture that my and my analysand's consciousness reflect of that which is invisible and unconscious. The derivation of a practicably implementable interpretational step is only ever possible for me after this rearticulation. It is these circumstances that make learning the psychoanalytic method so especially difficult.

The preconditions for being able to apply the psychoanalytic method of course depend on numerous factors. One of the most important of these is the prospective analyst's own analysis. This personal analysis, however, is certainly not a precondition in the sense that the analyst will then, as a non-neurotic personality, be able to help a neurotically ill person. Such a way of looking at things, which has, after all, been advocated in the past, contains the unspoken idea that only a person relatively free of conflicts would be in a position, in an (as it were) elitist attitude, to help a psychically troubled person, full of conflict, resolve the problems he confronts. This conception has actually been put forward in some phases of the historical psychoanalytic movement, but it was never advocated by the pioneers of psychoanalytic science.

At the time of the great discoveries of psychoanalysis, the initial researchers were violently attacked for their conviction that human psychic life is determined not by consciousness but by the unconscious. Because they were able in the course of time to prevail and psychoanalysis became a science to be taken seriously, psychoanalysis and psychoanalysts achieved great social prestige. This prestige was often illusorily interpreted to mean that those who know the way to the unconscious were above being conflicted in their own psychic life. The expansion of one's own experiential range obtained in an analytic process was understood as having refined and purified one's own person. In reality, matters are entirely different. The role the analyst assumes in the society in which he lives forces him to more or less meet the demands society addresses to him. At least he is inclined to take such societal expectations into consideration when he treats an analysand who finds himself in grave conflict and who, from the point of view of the society, is restricted in his ability to work, enjoy, and love. The analyst then easily feels called to lead his analysand, with the help of the analytic process, toward the goal of becoming able to work, enjoy, and love again. In adopting such an attitude, he consciously or unconsciously follows the performance principle that in our society is considered to show the way to success, psychic health, and nonneurotic behavior.

Such a model of thought suffices for positivistic thinking, but it contradicts analytic thinking, which is dialectical.[3] A dialectical model of thought includes contradictions within itself and recognizes that the task is not to remove or resolve contradictions in any form in the realm of experiencing or in social relations. All people, psychoanalysts too, are shot through with inclinations toward conflictedness that reactivate each time a relationship really deepens. All people can influence other people. This certainly is not the quintessence of the analyst's function. The task, rather, is an expansion of the experiential domain both in the analyst and in the analysand, which leads to flexibility and elasticity in assessing one's own conflictuality. Only with this newly gained flexibility is it then also possible to find rearticulations of the conflictual inclinations that put things into perspective, expand ways of looking at things, and allow for a different understanding of what has previously been fixed. The experience of one's own analysis is primarily the experience of limits, of how restricted the scope is of what can be changed. Most things are what they are, the way they have always been.

When I take someone into analysis who obviously seems unable to work, enjoy, and love, my goal will not be to in some way make him able to work, enjoy, and love. Rather, in my relationship with him, I will adjust myself in such a way that precisely this conception of what the goal is can be put into perspective and that the largely socially conditioned structuration of experiences he has had with himself and his environment can, through the uncovering of the life-historical background, find a rearticulation that lets the disturbances of which he is conscious appear in a fresh light. Then it might, with time, happen that the analysand is capable of taking a different attitude toward his conflicts. Possibly, thanks to the newly gained flexibility in assessing his conflicts, he will then also be able to confront the contradictions he encounters in the social milieu in which he lives in a different way than before.

The question that poses itself, then, is less how the personal analysis puts the future analyst in a position to perform with his analysands a socially efficacious analytic activity but rather what preconditions must be met for him to become able to initiate, maintain, and shape the analytic process with another person.

Insofar as his own analysis was a real analysis, the future analyst has had an important experience in himself. This experience is in no way one of passing a test, even if in most training institutes everything, it seems, is being done to give candidates that impression. Nor is the experience at issue restricted to greater awareness of what is going on in one's self and a better understanding of one's conflictual tendencies. The real experience the personal analysis brings is due to a process that has produced revolutionary, intrapsychic turbulence. Thereby the conflicts in which everyone finds himself and which everyone recognizes or feels in his own life have, in a particular, individually specific way, received a new articulation. I would like to emphasize especially that the rearticulation of conflicts in the course of the analytic process does not consist in the disappearance of these conflicts. Nor does it mean that they can henceforth be effortlessly resolved when they do appear. Rather, the conflicts everyone carries with them in their lives are given a new significance within the interaction with objects and the relations with the environment. If the personal analysis is a training analysis, it creates the precondition for the analyst later to be able to encounter the analysands who come to him – and expect him to initiate an analytic process with them – as partners in a deepening relationship, partners in whom he, as in other personal relationships, experiences the rearticulation of his own conflictual inclinations. The analyst does not just observe the analytic process into which his analysand is drawn but uses it in order to understand his own unconscious reactions.

The second precondition for being able to apply the psychoanalytic method is based not so much on the emotional experience of one's own analysis but on knowledge. In that respect, the analyst's profession in no way differs from other professions that are also founded on knowledge and experience in dealing with the instrument of their specific activity. One of the psychoanalyst's instruments is metapsychology, that is, the theory that contains all those concepts that give us a picture of how the psychic development of the human being is to be understood. Within this metapsychology, we can make out different systems: the theory of the development of the drives, that is, of the development of libido; the theory of the development of the ego and of narcissism; and the theories about aggression. We could add a series of other concepts. What I am after here, however, is the following: for me, the entire scientific system of metapsychology, viewed from the theory of technique, is always justified only insofar as, on the one hand, it comes from the clinical experience we gain in working with analysands and, on the other, it serves to articulate the laws of the theory of technique and thereby to develop the foundations for the practical application of psychoanalysis.

After all, it was through experiences that psychoanalysts were forced to learn that there is no easier path, or that we as yet do not know any easier path, to develop the theoretical formulations that belong to psychoanalytic technique. In that endeavor I, at least, have to rely on metapsychology. I could also say, inversely, that for me, metapsychological concepts prove to be untenable or improbable whenever I see that they cannot be reconciled with concepts of technique. New technical aspects or guidelines are always based on untenable theoretical suppositions wherever the interpretive technique derived from them proves to be insufficient or wrong. The literature contains many examples. Indeed, we could say that such false suppositions pervade the psychoanalytic literature. That is one important source of the difficulty in orienting themselves that students and analysts experience as they try to find their way through the psychoanalytic literature.

Concepts like that can only be recognized as misleading when adverse experiences are repeated with different analysts. I'd like to mention as an example the notion, quite generally promoted in the 1920s, of activating aggressions in obsessional neurotics. People thought that outbursts of aggression during the analytic session could effect a kind of catharsis. There were analysts back then who believed that it would help a patient who was displaying coprophiliac tendencies to gain insight into his unconscious impulses if they asked him to sit in a bathtub and play with his feces. Those analysts who prided themselves on flower vases and other objects frequently flying through the room because their analysands developed such violent outbursts of rage belong to this group as well. This misunderstood concept of aggressive impulses has a certain meaning in the theory of libido. For, undoubtedly, as people develop, instinctual impulses fall prey to repression because aggressive impulses could find no expressions in the social relations of the child with its parents and its wider surroundings; fury, hatred, and intolerance of frustrations had to be repressed. Here is a likely situation for the formation of symptoms. Every time a patient ought to, for example, feel anger, he might instead scratch himself behind the ear or feel an itch. In that case, we may very well say that lying behind these symptoms are the repressed aggressions that now express themselves in a kind of conversion. In most cases, however, we are dealing with substitute activities, in other words with reaction-formations such as, for example, constantly re-counting money or compulsive washing. As long as metapsychology was still entirely built on the theory of libido it was in a way understandable and obvious to suppose that all that mattered was to give the analysand in the analytic relationship the freedom of expressing what was going on in him. Accordingly, in this view, if the analysand suddenly has the courage to insult the analyst with swear-words as he once would have wanted to scream at his father, then conditions are met that make the analytic process progress. These conditions, of course, are met only if, in the development of transference, relationships have indeed evolved in which the analysand repeats attitudes and emotions that once existed toward his father. That is why, first and above all, it is decisive to consider more closely the precondition of such a transference-development. Leaving it aside amounts to applying a kind of short-circuit technology and seeing only the inhibitions of the patient that are now to be broken through. On a patient so inhibited that he is not saying anything, one could, for example, put stress by remaining silent until something, albeit something unpredictable, happens. One could also choose a different form and interrupt the patient when he is saying something or again and again draw attention to things of which one already knows that he cannot bear them. In such a way of proceeding, a simplification has taken place in the application of a system of rules one has read or heard about. The decisive point here is that the conditions of the analytic process have not been understood in their true essence or have not been taken into consideration.

If in such cases a negative therapeutic reaction develops and the analysand breaks off the analysis, it is easily said that the patient probably was not suitable enough for analysis or was not at the intellectual level required for meaningfully experiencing an analysis, or that the analysis was too stressful for the patient. In fact, however, things are exactly the other way around. The analyst was insufficiently suitable. It is he who was not up to the stress because he was incapable of doing justice to the needs of his analysand.

Although these examples exaggerate a little, I note that in the course of the development of psychoanalytic theory, there have been numerous deviations and deformations, attempts by our colleagues from days past and present to conceptualize their experiences with their analysands while failing to consider extremely important aspects. This has given rise to many individual theories that cannot be generalized. In the curriculum for prospective analysts, one important task is helping students to find, in reading psychoanalytic writings, those points that deserve priority. We often take things from the literature that seem particularly cogent to us, perhaps for reasons that have to do with our individual conflicts. That is why it takes a certain experience to find in the literature those approaches that are significant for the elaboration of the theory of technique. In the psychoanalytic literature, it is notable that theoreticians tend to give pride of place to metapsychology and to the development of concepts connected with it. The concepts thus developed are then often illustrated with case descriptions. By comparison, the theory of technique proper is given only limited space. This is not by chance, for it is not that easy to formulate concepts of technique and in so doing avoid the danger of founding a metapsychology of technique that is rigid and useless.

Before I examine how one may formulate concepts of technique, I want to turn to the question of what it really means to get an analytic process going with an analysand. Does it mean getting rid of the symptoms he is suffering from or making his neurosis disappear? Or does it mean attenuating the difficulties and conflicts he is living through in such a way that he can bear them or so that he can feel good in the kind of social situation in which most people find themselves? Are our analysands to become happy or are they to content themselves with fantasizing that they are happy? No, neither the former nor the latter. An analytic process effects something completely different.

Speaking of the future analyst's personal analysis earlier, I already mentioned, in its essence, what the analytic process is: the decisive task I have as an analyst when an analysand comes to me is, by all means, to set an emotional process into motion; that is to say that a relationship will develop between analyst and analysand that is primarily borne by forces which maintain the analysand's self-esteem and the coherence of the image he has of himself. The essence of analysis consists in directing this process in such a way that it does not trigger those consequences it could have were it to be taking place outside the analytic situation. Such consequences would in all cases be a grave regression.

The concept of regression describes psychic occurrences that, under the pressure of anxieties, or threats issuing from unacceptable drives, or excessive external strain, push the individual's modes of experiencing and behavior back to an earlier stage of psychic development. Such regressions are usually accompanied by a relative loss of specific important ego functions, a diminution of internal and external autonomy, and an inclination toward undifferentiated reactions and emotions that, taken together, restrict the capacity for acting and experiencing.

In psychoanalytic theory, regressive processes can be discussed from quite different perspectives. One can for instance look at regressions that only concern ideational contents and do not disrupt the organization and structure of the psychic systems. Not only are such regressions not dangerous, they are very much welcome in the analytic process because for the analyst and the analysand they reveal unconscious tendencies that lie at the root of certain conflictual inclinations. Through insight into such connections, the analysand's ego can experience an expansion and strengthening insofar as it now becomes capable of confronting the conflictual propensities differently and more adequately than before. One can also talk about regressions that occur in a deepening relationship, because drive-impulses are being permitted to express themselves that allow attitudes, emotions, and reactions to arise that are not typical in everyday life. This happens normally in almost all love relationships, where we see, for example, longings for tenderness that bear infantile traits. We might then say that the intensification of a relationship has, by regressive means, activated infantile desires for tender care. Such regressions no longer refer only to ideational contents but also to emotional impulses and modes of experience. In such a case, too, regressions are not only not dangerous but welcome in the analytic process because, again, there is the possibility to recognize connections between earlier experiences, often from childhood, and current inclinations toward conflict and to make these conscious through interpretations such that the ego can deal with specific emotional impulses and modes of experience differently and more adequately. Such and similar regressive processes we designate as regressions in the service of the ego.[4] With this we express the fact that the regression does not lead to structural impairments in the organization of the libido and the ego functions of the personality. However, regressions that lie beyond what could still be called a regression in the service of the ego are not welcome in the analytic process. They are dangerous and can block the analysis, lead it into confusion, or even make it impossible altogether.

The task is thus to structure and maintain a relationship with the person coming into analysis in such a way as to make an emotional movement possible without regressive processes seriously and durably impairing the functions of the ego. This is the frame within which the analytic process develops. As an analyst, I thus face the task of establishing a relationship in which the analysand's emotionality comes to involve his entire psychic constitution and yet also to take care that the autonomous functions, the structures within the ego, and the image the analysand carries within the self of his own person and of his body, are not damaged. This requires respecting those libidinal cathexes and ego functions that are working well.[5] That is why, as a matter of principle, I approach every analysand – no matter how ill he might seem to be – as a partner who, to be sure, stands in conflicts, displays symptoms, and brings with him whatever concomitant issues there might be but who, from the point of view of his ego functions and his libidinal vicissitudes, is as healthy as he can possibly be and not as ill as possible.

Let me take as an example an analysand who suffered from an obsessive-compulsive disorder.[6] He was afraid that while driving, a part of his car would detach and cause a serious accident for the car behind him. The anxieties spread to many of his activities. When, for example, he reached into the freezer in a supermarket and noticed that he had chosen mocha rather than raspberry ice cream, as he had wanted, he barely dared to put the mocha ice cream back and take the raspberry ice cream for he was tormented by the idea that germs sticking to his hand could get into the freezer and contaminate all portions of ice cream such that later buyers of these ice creams would get sick. Yet despite this grave symptom of compulsive ideas I have to position myself carefully. I tell myself: even if the patient does have such extremely serious obsessive-compulsive notions, he must first, as a matter of principle, prove to me his mental illness, his nonfunctioning. For, at the same time, he is the father of a family, has three children, leads a satisfying life in the family and in his profession, pursues numerous different interests, and is politically active. If he is an autonomously thinking person in all these respects then I cannot foreground his compulsive symptom too much, even if in the analytic situation the patient almost exclusively talks about his compulsive ideas, which constantly occupy him.

With this example, I also want to show that in such a situation my empathy would be obviously insufficient to establish a psychoanalytic attitude toward my analysand. I cannot count on empathy alone here, on feeling my way into the other person. In such cases, without concepts that can orient me, I fall into a process of which I do not know where it will actually lead me. The difficulties in which I find myself with such a patient then easily collude with the difficulties the analysand himself has. Then all that remains is the hope that the conflict that finally results from these two difficulties will solve the problem that I, for all intents and purposes, no longer even see.

In this context, I ought to highlight in particular one tendency of analysts that can cause distortions in applying the psychoanalytic method or lead to interpretive steps that head off in the wrong direction. Psychoanalytic theory describes the role of the nuclear family in the emergence of neuroses as particularly important. As is well known, neurosis centers around the Oedipus complex. This Oedipus complex is the result of the disturbances that occur in the experience of the child when its all-encompassing wish to possess the object of its love is disrupted by the appearance of a third party. Since this usually plays itself out in relation to father and mother, the child's all-encompassing wish corresponds to an incestuous one. The disrupting third is the father when the child is a boy, the mother when a girl's wish for love is directed at the father. A competition breaks out with the disrupting third that leads to anxieties because the rival is experienced as all-powerful. These anxieties are referred to as castration anxieties. In a normal, healthy development, the Oedipus complex dissolves, whereby the superego is formed and protects against the return of incestuous desires.

This foundational concept of infantile sexuality, which so eminently clearly and correctly characterizes the development of libido – it is perhaps Sigmund Freud's greatest discovery – has caused much mischief in the application of the psychoanalytic method. Fully aware that such metapsychological knowledge could be useful to his work, the analyst tends to feel pressed early on into a specific transference-role. He then supposes that he is father or mother to the analysand because traits the analysand describes from his childhood or traits of his current behavior (toward authority figures or toward women, for example) seem to be very similar to the feelings the analysand experiences in the relationship with the analyst – or very similar to the feelings we as analysts believe he experiences. When, for example, a young girl reports being sexually attracted to older men, one immediately thinks of a father fixation. If the analysand then adds that she is particularly shy toward such men and if in the analytic sessions, too, she shows herself as shy and reserved, the conclusion on the analyst's part that a father transference is taking place very much suggests itself. Interpretations of this kind, which the analyst initially formulates just for himself, may indeed by correct. What I am interested in here, however, are the situations where they prove to be incorrect because the emotional dynamic in the relationship between analysand and analyst has not been considered and because the assumption about a specific transference-role has been based not on unconscious motives but on conscious ideas on the part of the analysand.[7] In such cases – and they are by no means rare – the analyst fends off a particular development of the relationship in the analytic process by means of the cliché transference-role he ascribes to himself. This is an example of how one can circumvent little difficulties that arise in the development of a relationship by dragging in the biggest life problems.

All analysts have difficulties in entering into a relaxed, congruent relationship with their analysands. It is often overlooked that what counts, fundamentally, is that the analysand can feel well during the analytic session, that he can express himself in an unclenched and unhampered way. I say it is often overlooked and I add: this is so even though we know exactly that the basic rule of free association is founded on it. Nonetheless we analysts speak of the pressure of suffering that allegedly compels the analysand to cooperate.[8] But we thereby overlook that we are all subject to a certain pressure of suffering that in turn compels us to have something in mind for the analysand, to analyze him with a goal – be it admitted or unconscious. These difficulties must not be underestimated, all the more so because we all tend to circumvent them, bridge them, indeed, resolve them by taking recourse to the very greatest problems of human experience, to the problems with the daddy, with the mommy, with the siblings of childhood. But where, I ask, are problems with the parents *not* the root of all later conflicts? Is the recourse to the parent figures thus ultimately only a convenient evasion? Indeed, the actualization of a transference-conflict is most conveniently handled when the conflict is kept away from the person of the analyst, in other words, when it is rationalized in a "family" role he assumes.

The difficulties we encounter, however, do not lie so much in our analysand establishing one or another kind of relationship with us but, rather, are based on seduction. We cannot take any analysand into analysis without the analysand attempting to seduce us, and we cannot set in motion any analytic process if we do not admit to ourselves that we seduce the analysand to do so. The libidinal cathexes I invest in my patient and my patient in me arise unavoidably whenever I am consistently producing an analytic situation. In the case of a psychoneurosis, these processes are reflected in a developing object-love or in derivatives of repressed impulses of some kind. In the case of a narcissistic neurosis, these libidinal cathexes initially show up in the form of precursors. Be that as it may, nobody is indifferent toward idealizations, fantasies of omnipotence, and sexual impulses.

It took a long time for me to realize that I knew very well how to evade conflictual tensions that may arise in the relationship between the analysand and me by assuming a specific role. I remember an analysand, about fifteen years older than me, who wanted to do a second analysis with me because his first analysis, which had taken up many years, had (in his view) failed. I was still relatively young then and accepted the task. After a few months, difficulties set in because the analytic relationship threatened to degenerate into a combat situation. The analysand had given me an exhaustive account of his life story and above all his conflictual relationship with his father. In so doing, he had also, time and again, stressed erotic feelings and sexual particularities so as to help me understand him. He finally began reproaching me with prematurely having given, after only a few weeks, an interpretation that represented a capital and fundamental mistake. This capital and fundamental mistake consisted in an intervention that, the analysand said, could have come from his father. I was unable, he continued, to understand that in his analysis he did not desire to be exposed anew to the same conflicts he had always suffered under so much. The analysand had managed to push me into the role of his father, and I myself was convinced that in the transference I had become a paternal figure. With this conviction, I found an inner calm and assumed a neutral expectant analytic attitude by telling myself that the projections the analysand directed at me were precisely an expression of his neurosis that now was taking shape as a transference-neurosis. I had overlooked that by supposing myself to be the father I had evaded confronting the much more important insight that I was afraid of being homosexually seduced and overwhelmed by my analysand. With his graphic descriptions and the intrusive curiosity with which he encircled me, he tried to catch me off-guard and force me to reveal myself. Without realizing it, I started acting as though I was being persecuted. The analysand enjoyed this and got ever more obtrusively close to me, meanwhile pretending to despise me for my incompetence and to have as low an opinion of me as he once had of his father.

What happened to me with this analysand is not a rare exceptional case but rather something that occurs with relative frequency. One woman analyst, for example, had her analysand in analysis for three years and said in a particular phase: "This shows very clearly, doesn't it, that I have taken on the role of the mother." And yet actually she had constantly refused the patient's transference. The idea, however, that she herself was the inadequate mother had helped her overlook what she was massively fending off. She never understood her patient's offer of transference. Of course, social conditions are also to blame for the way we, as analysts, get ourselves into specific roles all too easily. When we are the father, when we are the mother, the sister, the aunt, when we are the good grandfather (if we have already reached a certain age), the beloved brother (if we are still young), then the nuclear family in Uhland's sense is all together in harmony.[9] This allows the analysis to develop in a direction in which it is possible to evade the actualization of the transference-conflict. In other words, wherever the transference-conflict is on the horizon we have an interpretation at the ready that refers the analysand to his childhood or to this or that vicissitude of his drive-wishes without ourselves noticing that the "looming" transference-conflict, which actually should be set in motion here, is being suppressed with rationalizations.

In such situations I can then tell myself, with a touch of concern:

> It's now eight months that I have my analysand in analysis. Something is not moving forward. It is so difficult. This probably has to do with my not having enough experience, not knowing enough about metapsychology, not having read enough, not being able to interpret dreams correctly. Perhaps I should go and see a more experienced supervisor and accept help.

All this indicates that I do not feel up to my function as analyst.

In such developments I may also, however, take a different attitude and be especially cautious and reserved. In that case, I am emphatically respectful toward the patient, let him do what seems right to him, hold back, and do not intervene. If in a given session the patient wishes to sit facing me rather than lie down, I take a passive attitude and leave the decision to him because I want to respect the autonomous functions of my partner.

The one like the other, the feeling of not being up to the analytic function and the emphatically respectful demeanor toward the analysand, are two extremes that have a similarly detrimental effect on the analytic relationship. In seeking to retreat to what he has learned or in behaving with emphatic respectfulness, the analyst avoids getting involved in the relationship and yet promotes everything that may cause his partner to turn to him. This amplifies regressive propensities, and the analysand's autonomous functions are endangered and affected in an adverse way.

In the case of such developments, polar opposite attitudes toward the analytic process emerge. The cathexes of the analyst and the analysand are no longer congruently oriented, and the consequence is that often, unwittingly, a relationship evolves in which it looks as if analyst and analysand are pursuing goals in opposing directions even though they are supposed to lead to the same result. Suddenly, then, questions of procedure become ever more important. The analysand doubts whether it is right to begin a session by reporting events from his daily life and only then his dream, or to express a thought that seems to have little to do with his current problems. He sits there silently doubting and tries to solve these questions by himself or he confronts the analyst with his questions in order then to receive directives on how to proceed. The analyst gets into similar difficulties. He asks himself:

Should I remain silent when the patient is silent, or should I say something to encourage him? Should I interpret a dream when it is told or should I wait until the analysand begins interpreting the dream himself? Should I confirm my analysand's view and thereby reveal myself or should I not say anything and be for my partner simply the mirror of his unconscious?

The retreat into questions of psychoanalytic procedure, however, merely expresses a kind of fatalistic watchful waiting. The motto is: we'll see.

I ask: what will we see?

One would need to understand that the analytic relationship is established between two partners, neither of whom is unconflicted. Both partners stand in conflicts even if these conflicts are differently situated. If as analyst I take the attitude that I can approach the analysand as though I am without conflicts while the analysand, in contrast to me and as a result of his neuroses, seems to be full of conflict, the dynamic is done for. Once the psychoanalytic process is on this track, the analyst all too easily takes recourse to the role interpretation. Rationalizing and intellectualizing increase and inhibit the subsequent course of the analysis.

Such a development in the analytic process means that the analyst's imaginative worldview has come to replace reality. The positivistic model of thought that is adapted to the societal conditions in which analyst and analysand are living takes the place of dialectical analytic reflection. Specific wishful ideas lose their character as fantasies because they conform to societal demands and therefore seem adapted to reality. This happens with such notions as wanting to help the patient, to let him experience one thing or another, to remedy his sexual disorders – for example to turn a homosexual into a heterosexual or a fetishist into the father of a family, or to guide a delinquent drug addict toward an apprenticeship in a bank – in short, in all cases to do something in order to achieve something. But where fantasy replaces reality, I usually also no longer see what I want to achieve and can achieve. Interpretations and insights then correspond to agreements between the demands of the superego, my own and those which the analysand and I share. As time goes on, we become an ever better match and outdo each other in proving our nonneurotic behavior. In this way, a vicious circle of rationalizing ensues. The analytic process is being blocked because the whole thing primarily serves a defensive position, one that has become invisible or can no longer be tackled.

When I get into such a situation, I cannot simply say that it is a defense the analysand has built up against me because there exists an antipathy or because certain personal traits of mine are unbearable for the analysand. Inversely, I also evade the real facts when I say, for example, that I can only treat analysands I find likable. I must be aware that the defense at issue here is quite obviously and in all cases a defense against seduction. I must have no illusions on this point: no analysand who comes to me can completely escape the influence I exert over him. It is alarming and it weighs on the analytic relationship if I do not recognize this. For in that case, my influence leads to a reaction in my patient that prompts in him the sensation that his consciousness is under my control. That, however, would constitute for him the most severe loss of autonomous functions.

It is certainly worthwhile to formulate some concepts of psychoanalytic technique that indicate the directions in which it is possible to recognize – and thereby escape – the snares and dangers in the interpretive process.

For me, the analyst's aids are in the first instance those that help me to keep my own conflictual inclinations – the ones that inevitably reactivate in the analytic relationship with my analysand – under control. Among these aids, I count: the adherence to the analytic situation, the so-called "setting"; the knowledge of metapsychology; and the concepts of the theory of psychoanalytic technique. The reflective thinking I apply in the framework of analytic labor serves the maintenance of my own deconflict-ualized ego functions.

Notes

1 Despite Morgenthaler's more classically ego psychological belief in drives and defenses, he was also protorelationalist in his conviction that in the analytic encounter there are *two* partners who are *both* conflict-filled, and two uncon-sciouses in dynamic interaction with each other.

2 Here as elsewhere, Morgenthaler distinguishes between psychoanalytic "meta-psychology" – the body of ideas used by analysts to describe mental-emotional structures (like the id, the ego, and the superego) or mental-emotional processes (like cathexis or transference) – and a psychoanalytic "theory of technique" which he wanted *Technik* to provide and which, he believed, was no less sci-entific but which above all needed to be oriented to concrete clinical practice. While for him, metapsychology was often associated with rigidity and fixity rather than the adaptability and flexibility he called for in clinical technique, he nonetheless showed intermittent respect for metapsychology. At one point, for instance, he will note in defense of metapsychology (Chapter 7) that "often the oldest and most conservative tools are the most useful."

3 Morgenthaler will several times in the course of *Technik* contrast a "dialectical" approach – also a key-term in the book's subtitle – with what he dismissively refers to as "positivistic" thinking. "Positivism," for him, is *not* meant in the generic sense as a form of simplistic, undertheorized empiricism. Rather, for Morgenthaler, it is associated with social conformity and conventional morality. As he put it: "Positivistic thinking, in our society, is the basis of economic suc-cess, the ideology of performance-conscious man, the instrument of the domi-nant class, of power generally. Positivistic psychoanalysis wants to distinguish the healthy from the sick, wants to help the one who suffers by realizing goals, wants to cure everything that appears to it to be ill" (Supplement 3). Whether literally inspired by insights or turns of phrase in the works of Engels or Lenin or Mao or, rather, creatively and forthrightly repurposing for his own use reso-nant ideas more generally in the air in the 1970s, a "dialectical" approach meant, for Morgenthaler, as he says here, a "model of thought [that] includes contra-dictions within itself and recognizes that the task is not to remove or resolve contradictions in any form in the realm of experiencing or in social relations" (cf. Engels, 1877; Lenin, 1927 [1915]; Mao Zedong, 1954 [1937]; Binswanger, 2003; Parin et al., 2003). Or as he put it in a 1977 interview, the dialectical approach "includes the immanent contradictions that all life contains. Instead of trying reductively to eliminate them, or treating them as something ancillary and unimportant, it tries to integrate and incorporate them as part of a genuinely successful way of experiencing" (Morgenthaler & Kilian, 2017 [1978], p. 11).

4 "Regression in the service of the ego" is a concept first formulated in a paper delivered at the IPA in Lucerne in 1934 by the ego psychologist Ernst Kris to distinguish between beneficial and pathological forms of regression (Kris, 1936, cf. Kris, 1952).

5 "Cathexis" is the common English translation for Freud's concept of *Besetzung*. When John Forrester translated the seminars of Jacques Lacan, he chose instead to use the word "investment" – colloquially comprehensible in the phrase "emotional investment" (Forrester, 1988, p. vii).

6 In the German original, Morgenthaler – for reasons that cannot now be clarified – used the word *Wahnvorstellungen* (delusional imaginings) instead of *Zwangsgedanken* (obsessive-compulsive thoughts), but it is clearly the latter that he meant.

7 Here is the first mention of one of Morgenthaler's key axioms: that what is conscious cannot simultaneously be unconscious. It will recur throughout the text of *Technik*.

8 A concept regularly promoted among analysts on both sides of the Atlantic in the 1950s–1960s was the idea that an indication that a psychoanalysis would be appropriate for a particular patient was the presence of "sufficient suffering" or "urgent suffering" (as the noted Los Angelean analyst Ralph Greenson put it in his standard textbook, *The Technique and Practice of Psychoanalysis* [1967, pp. 54, 356]). In addition, Greenson asserted that it was the patient's suffering that would "enable him to endure the rigors of treatment" and "impel[] him to work in the analysis, no matter how painful" (pp. 54, 98). This is precisely one of the main reasons Morgenthaler's *Technik* was experienced as so revolutionary: he was dubious about the entire idea of "pressure of suffering" and was most concerned for the patient to feel well and de-stressed in the course of analysis.

9 Morgenthaler intended sarcasm when he mentioned the nuclear family as being "all together in harmony." In the 1974 audiotape rendition of this lecture/chapter, Morgenthaler quotes a passage from a nineteenth-century poem (actually by Gustav Schwab, misremembered here as Ludwig Uhland). The passage is not a happy one at all – in the poem, the whole family dies when their house is struck by lightning.

Chapter 2

Sequentiality in the course of associations

A patient has been in analysis for quite some time.[1] The relationship to his analyst remains emotionally distant. He is convinced he has been telling the analyst whatever he can think of. The analyst does not agree. Whenever he carefully tries to point out the analysand's difficulties in expressing his feelings, the analysand becomes defensive and declares that he has always told him everything. He does not wish to be reproached. If what he provides does not suffice, this means that he must be incapable of undergoing analysis. The analyst tries to explain to the patient that he is in a state of resistance, constantly tense and – at just that moment, at the beginning of the psychoanalytic session – has been unable to say anything for a while. The analysand responds that he just could not think of anything and that is why he did not speak. A feeling of emptiness had come over him. The analyst responds by saying that it was precisely this issue, which he, the analysand, did not want to talk about. Now, the patient becomes agitated and accuses the analyst of being presumptuous. The analyst notes that the patient has become agitated and quite angry, and that there must be a reason behind this.

In the next session, which takes place on a Monday, the analysand reports the following:

"I had a dream in which I explained the particular case of the Latin word *agricola* to a woman. We began a dispute about the importance of the dative *agricolae* versus the accusative *agricolam*. I wanted to discuss the accusative form first. The woman could have been you. In the dream debate the woman insisted on considering the dative form first."

Here, the analyst wants to refer to the transference, but the analysand does not give him a chance to speak and resumes: "I must tell you that I woke up from this dream ejaculating."

Without pausing, he continues: "Yesterday, on Sunday, I visited an old friend. I was very disappointed, because this friend, with whom I used to be able to talk about all sorts of things and who would share everything candidly with me, had become a square. He has changed for the worse. Upon my arrival, he immediately wanted to have a beer at a pub. As if he thought I would enjoy sitting in a noisy restaurant, drinking beer and gloomily sharing trivialities – like the other guests. This really disappointed me very much."

The analysand stops speaking.

The analyst interprets: "Aside from being disappointed, you must have felt somewhat satisfied and triumphant."

For a moment, the analysand seems skeptical, but then answers that though this might be so, the feeling of disappointment was clearly more important.

The analyst: "But I really believe you grew apart from your friend, or, in any case, that you felt he didn't match up to you anymore. Maybe your friend had always behaved the way you experienced yesterday. You realized it now because it is you who has changed."

The analysand: "I don't think you're right."

The analyst: "However, maybe the reproach directed toward your friend is a reproach you have always wanted to express, which – as we know – in fact applies to your father."

The analysand: "You're definitely right. I have always wanted to reproach somebody, and it was you I blamed for not really understanding me. But every time, you always had the upper hand, I mean you always had the last word."

The session ended there.

First of all, this example clearly depicts how a relationship between the analyst and the analysand can develop unfavorably. And why is this the case here?

We could, of course, dismiss this question and merely try to understand the above dialogue between the analyst and the analysand.[2] We could also point out that it is not permissible to single out one analytic session and then deliver a premature judgment without having considered the wider context. Why not first think about the meaning of this dream? Is the relationship between the analysand and his analyst good or bad? Admittedly, these questions aren't easy to answer.

In the first place, with everything he tells him, the analysand is challenging his analyst. We might interpret this challenge as the expression of an aggressive impulse. But it is even more important to consider another viewpoint first.

The analysand is obviously struggling to be heard and understood. This is because he has strongly cathected with his physician. The cathexis is determined by libidinal strivings, which inflect the development of the transference. Even without looking closely into the contents of this transferential development, I can observe that the analyst is somehow failing to take note of what the analysand is offering him. There is no doubt that the patient's wishes directed at the person of the analyst play a role here, and which can be described in the context of a positive development of the transference as a "wish to be loved."

What justifies such a conclusion?

It follows from the succession of the thoughts the analysand expressed in the course of the analytic session I have reproduced here. He begins the session by reporting a dream and immediately adds that he had woken from the dream ejaculating. In the first instance, this means that something has stirred in him erotically when he dreamed the dream in the night after the meeting with his friend. In the manifest dream content the Latin word *agricola* turns up.[3] This word, peculiarly, has both masculine and feminine connotations. The idea of the farmer – in contrast to *poeta* for example – involves a mental link to a manual laborer who works with somewhat simple devices. If the analysand were to associate any corresponding ideas, the analyst will assume deeper connections related to certain drive-vicissitudes, which are not insignificant if one wants to understand the transference in all its manifestations.

This perspective shall not be pursued here, however, because we must first understand a much more evident and surface feature of the analysand's behavior: his definitely conscious reproachful attitude towards the analyst.[4] We are by no means dealing with a very agreeable conversational partner; rather, this is a person doing his very best to unsettle the analyst. The analyst's reaction to this reproachful attitude is defensive, not merely with respect to the analysand and his demands. He is defensive above all because he is counteracting his own fears, which he hardly recognizes.

It is completely understandable that analysts may develop anxieties in their work with certain analysands. They cannot be blamed for this. However, seen from a psychoanalytic point of view, it is of great significance how an analyst deals with these anxieties. He must be conscious of them and not deny them, because only the awareness of such emotions can prevent blindly succumbing to them in the analytic process.

I should now like to return to the motives which evoked the analyst's anxieties. It immediately becomes evident, considering the analysand's remark that the woman in his dream might very well stand for the analyst, that a massive transference-content is at the forefront. Moreover, the analysand repeatedly expresses quite candidly how often he had wanted to – and actually had – reproached the analyst. The analysand's detachment and the tense atmosphere during the sessions are further evidence of his reproachful attitude. Thus, the assumption that the aggressive tendencies directed toward the analyst are the cause of the analyst's fears might seem logical. But such an assumption is misleading because a reproachful attitude, aggression, and provocation in fact belong to ideas which the analysand is very well able to become conscious of and the analyst's interpretations along these lines have been largely ineffective. They thus cannot be the unconscious motives. My fundamental insistence is that conscious reactions of both the analysand and the analyst can never simultaneously be unconscious, even if, with regard to my example, such a conclusion seems almost to force itself upon us.

In fact, on the contrary, the patient wishes to turn to the analyst lovingly, and the entire emotional process that is underway here is based on this wish. And it is the love of the analysand – admittedly, a love cloaked by neurosis – which is permanently provoking the analyst's anxiety. With the dream, this love story has reached a zenith, which is marked by the ejaculation. By his vehemence, and then not least also by producing an ejaculation, the analysand has drawn far too near to the analyst, who reacts with an unconscious fright.

In this context, it is important to understand why the analysand does not give the analyst a chance to speak, but immediately goes on telling him about his disappointment in his friend. He does not give the analyst a chance to speak because he must remain active and avoid being passively subjected to him. If I were to settle for the assumption that, herewith, the analysand is actually expressing his disappointment in the analyst, I am simply practicing consciousness-psychology, because it is evident – and has been well known to both the analysand and the analyst for some time – that the transference has been characterized by this kind of disappointment. Undoubtedly, it has been interpreted repeatedly. Should the analyst try to interpret that the analysand was actually expressing disappointment in his analysis and his analyst, he could simply answer that, while this might well be the case, on that particular Sunday, he had not been disappointed by his analyst, but rather by his friend. This too would be justified, because both the analysand's and the analyst's assumptions refer to perceptions of which they have become conscious. Both assumptions express rationalizations. The analyst and the analysand are both right in their own way of understanding the meaning of "being right."

I should like to emphasize once again which of the analysand's affects are especially important in this situation: in some kind of way, he loves his analyst. He reveals needs in his own specific manner. On the other hand, he does not feel understood. Now let's have a look at the analyst. Is he really so unapproachable? The analysand mentioned as much. When it comes to discussing his reproachful attitude, he believes the analyst to have the upper hand each time.

Is this accusation justified? I do not think so, because, of course, the analyst is doing what he can. He is neither incompetent, unreasonable, nor clumsy. It's not that simple.

As to the transference, I find it predominantly ambivalent, or, in other words, we are dealing with a positive transference with strong negative contents. I could recognize idealizing tendencies, suspect a latent homosexual inclination, emphasize the competitive power play or the substantial problem of aggression. But in this case, the transference does not tend in the one or other direction either qualitatively or quantitatively but is most strongly defined by confusion. During the above-mentioned two sessions, the transference is confused, chaotic. It is unstructured.

Of course, in every transferential development, confusion might occur now and then. How could this be avoided or prevented at any rate? In fact, we are faced with such a situation more often than we think or admit to colleagues. What can the theory of technique contribute in this case?

Here, the theory of technique offers two concepts. One is a warning and makes the analyst aware of what should not happen. The other focuses on the priority of dynamics.

The warning is based on the metapsychological concept of the unconscious not only encompassing the area of impulses, i.e. the id, but also parts of the ego. Not only drive-impulses, libidinal stirrings, wishes, tension due to needs must be considered as the expression of unconscious tendencies; attitudes, availabilities, certain priorities of the ego are under the pressure of unconscious impulses as well. In order to reinforce resistance, the unconscious parts of the ego are lying in wait for nourishment, so to speak. This occurs because the confusion in the development of transference promotes anxieties and uncontrollable regressive motions. In the case of a confusing transferential offer, the warning serves to stop the analyst before he rushes to make connections to the analysand's biography or to his current experiences with the analysand, with which, because these would be rationalizations, he would be able to construct an artificial whole. Insights enforced in such a manner cannot be understood as insights in a psychoanalytic sense because they are, rather, rationalizing cognitive processes reinforcing defense mechanisms, which intensify unconscious conflictual ideas and reactions. Consequently, at such moments, I would refrain from interpreting the relationship to the analysand's father, mother, or childhood, or to his tendency to idealize, to his homosexual inclination, or to power play, rivalry, or aggression.

The second concept suggested by the theory of technique is based on the metapsychological ideas developed in psychoanalysis to describe the primary process. Freud's insights, mostly gained from the interpretation of dreams, are crucial for integrating what goes on at the primary-process level into the theory of technique in a sensible way.[5] The rule of free association, which is such a decisive element in psychoanalysis, is based on the modus operandi of the primary process. It implies that the sequence of *what follows what* during free association – and which from the perspective of conscious processing often seems incongruous and strange – is linked and related in a distinct way. This internal connection corresponds to the unconscious in the given situation of the current area of experience. Thus, the *sequentiality* in the associative process is not only crucial if, for example, the analysand offers associations to one of his dreams, or if he follows the request of the analyst to say everything that comes to mind. Sequentiality is generally valid in the analytic situation, or, in other words: everything put forth by the analysand, what he talks about, and at what point and in which order the succeeding ideas are expressed, contains the determining dynamic factors on which the unconscious motivations rest.

Sequentiality in the associative process is important in order to reach a psychoanalytic comprehension. If I am faced with the task of redirecting a transference-development that has led to confusion onto a more favorable track, the technical concept of attending to sequentiality of associations, i.e., categorically following the analysand's words, will be orienting. From a technical point of view, this attitude has top priority. I must not shy away from realizing that, at this very moment, I do not understand more than the analysand does. Moreover, I must not be afraid to formulate what might seem like completely absurd coherences, solely because they have presented themselves specifically in this and not in any other way. The difficulty of this approach lies in the aversion resulting from both my self-criticism and the analysand's own critical faculty, as well as in our need to arrange ideas and cognitive functions in such a way as to achieve a meaningful whole.

As a technical theorem, attention to sequentiality in the associative process could be applied to our example in the following manner:

The analyst might tell his patient: "I noticed that you reported your dream before telling me about the experience with your friend on Sunday."

Such an interpretation is based simply on the formal aspects of the sequence and refers to what the analysand told us during the session. Therefore, we can deduce that the analysand needs the dream – that he arms himself with it, as it were – so he can begin by reporting it to the analyst and thereby dispose of it *before* he speaks about the disappointing experience with his friend. The analysand will not be able to reject this simple summary sequence of facts or dismiss it as speculative. Without a doubt it was just so. Only the interpretation can be discussed.

Usually, it is the analysand who criticizes the interpretation. He might say: "I really don't know what you mean." In doing so, he is following his intuition because he is unable to understand what the analyst is trying to tell him. He does not yet realize that, in fact, the analyst is in the same situation as he is and could just as well say to himself: "I don't really know what I am telling my analysand."

In the analytic situation, at this point, neither of the partners acts according to his or her empathy or intuition anymore. A purely formal perspective is applied, aimed at discovering an unconscious tendency leading to confusion. I must admit that here, both the analyst and the analysand find themselves adrift on a similar sea of uncertainty. This is because the analytic relationship basically develops between partners who each have internal conflicts of his or her own, rather than between an enlightened, nonneurotic analyst and an analysand who is troubled by internal conflicts and neurotic reactions.

The analysand has every right to respond to the analyst's absurd remarks with caution and doubt. But the analyst must hold on to his concept and further elaborate his statements. He continues and says:

> What I mean is that you were not able to speak about your disappointing experience with your friend before having told me your dream. Consequently, what affected you most is contained within your dream. I understand that you don't know what this is all about. You cannot know it because it's unconscious. It must be so; if this were not the case, you would not have had the dream, you would either have forgotten it or not have told me about it at the beginning of the session.

Of course, such an undifferentiated statement of a sequence of simple formal aspects without any inner connections must initially appear disconcerting and alienating, because things that just happen to appear in sequence are being presented, in an artificial way, as causally linked and mutually dependent. The disconcertedness and the resistances that arise in all of us originate in our secondary-process thinking and reacting, because the principles I just described are characteristics of the primary process – in other words, of the mental-emotional motions which we identify with the unconscious.

It is now important to continue along this path and draw conclusions from our previous deductions.

What exactly is the analysand attempting? Does he want to be loved? Does he want to express his unconscious homosexual tendencies? Does he feel compelled to win the competitive power struggle he has engaged in, or does he want to release his aggressions once and for all and direct them towards the analyst? I don't think so. Primarily, the analysand longs for emotional unclenching, for relaxation. He wants to feel comfortable when he arrives for his session, lies on the couch, and begins to speak. For months, his attitude at the beginning of his sessions has been extremely tense, detached, apprehensive, anxious, aggressive, reproachful, or sexualized, rivaling, and combative. What does he wish for? Among psychoanalysts it has become more and more common to say: he wishes to be understood. Sure, but what's the point of our feeling understood, if we nevertheless cannot relax?

I therefore deliberately repeat: the analysand wants to be able to relax. Above all he wants this. What follows from this emphasis is that it is up to the analyst to facilitate this relaxation and to make sure that the pressurized feeling with regard to the transference is reduced. The analysand is not capable of taking on this task. He has agreed to undergo analysis. If he arrives for his sessions regularly and fulfills the requirements of the psychoanalytic setting, he has done everything he can. But this also implies that something in him has been set in motion. Freud describes this intrapsychic turmoil in "Remembering, Repeating and Working-Through" with the image of the analysand who, piece by piece, brings out his weapons from the armory of the past, weapons with which he tries to defend himself against the continuation of the treatment.[6] Such defenses and struggles will always lead to tensions that will appear in the evolving transference and that are connected to reactivations of conflictual tendencies. The analyst must make sure to interpret these reactivations of conflictual tendencies in each phase of the analytic process in such a way that de-stressing will occur because only the achievement of this particular affective relaxation will enable a reformulation of the conflicts which have become established and fixed in the course of the analysand's past. Only when this reformulation, this re-constellation, has occurred will a new experience in the analytic relationship be possible, one which can become the wellspring of that emotional revolution that is the actual point of the analytic process.

From a practical point of view, it is therefore essential, in our example, to explain to the analysand that during the session, he was not able to share with the analyst the emotional upheaval unleashed by the conflict with his friend. The affects that had been provoked on the Sunday by the visit of the friend were displaced into the dream. This brings us to a new view, one which uncovers what actually took place within the analysand; the pollution following the dream acquires a new meaning.

What did the analysand actually experience during the meeting with his friend on Sunday, in the night with dream and pollution that followed, and in the session on Monday?

When he was with his friend on Sunday and noticed his own disappointment, he felt an intense wish to tell the analyst about it in the following session. But the ongoing tension and distance he experienced in his analytic sessions deeply shaped his expectations about the prospect of being able to fulfill his wish. He recognized – painfully – that he could speak candidly only if he could make sure that he would not immediately, and in a self-depreciating way, get into a very tense encounter with his analytic dialogue partner. It becomes clear here in what a stereotyped manner the patient's relationships develop again and again, because the tension-filled relationship with his analyst resembles almost completely the impaired relationship with his friend. Indeed, at this point I assume that the patient, in the sense of a repetition compulsion, will apparently always and with all people get into a tension-laden relationship.

In short, the analysand feared that, if he were to tell the analyst about his frustrating experience on Sunday, he would trigger a reaction leading to tension because he could anticipate that the analyst would relate the experience of disappointment with the friend to himself and to the ongoing analysis. I also would like to mention that with his attempt at interpretation, the analyst himself was subject to repetition compulsion. The patient had the dream precisely in order to *avoid* having to anticipate such an outcome in the subsequent sessions. In the dream, both – the meeting with his friend as well as the upcoming analytic session – are contained in a condensed way. The tension in both relationships is mirrored in the manifest dream content regarding the discussion about the Latin word *agricola*. In order to understand what is involved in the meaning of the grammatical term *accusative,* it is important to add that the analysand spoke French, was a French teacher at a high school, and was very interested in linguistics. Because in French, the grammatical term *accusative* involves the phonetic association with *accuser* (to accuse), the use of this word in the dream contains the symbolic meaning of an accusation. This is the expression of a tendency to eliminate what is reproach-filled and accusatory in the psychoanalytic relationship and resituate it within an experience beyond the analytic session, i.e. in the dream experience. The dreamer's waking up due to polluting implies the fulfillment of his wish to be engaged in a relaxed relationship with his analyst before telling him about the experience with his friend on the following day. In this context, to interpret the sexual meaning of the pollution would be secondary and neither appropriate nor sensible at the moment.[7]

We are clearly dealing with a transference-dream here. The unconscious wish is determined by the patient's hope of being able to speak within a relaxed, conflict-free analytic relationship, thus enabling him to express what had touched him so profoundly when he became conscious of the disappointment in his friend.

It is only here at this moment that I may assume that unconscious, or maybe even conscious, homosexual feelings towards his friend, which he had perceived for a long time, were experienced in a somewhat altered way, be it because the analysand became aware of feeling empty, or, alternatively, of experiencing a stronger sexual attraction – or that similar feelings for his analyst were emerging more and more clearly. Seen from this vantage, we might be able to elaborate on the dream together with the analysand and trace deeper, unconscious ideas. This could make it possible to shed some fresh light on the entirety of the emotional upheaval in which he had found himself on Sunday.

It now becomes progressively clear why the analyst's interpretation that the patient was in a state of resistance vis-à-vis the analyst or the analysis, and that his disappointment was a disappointment about the analyst, must remain ineffective and could not penetrate the analysand's detached attitude. It is simply impossible to set the analytic process in motion before having freed what is happening in transference from confusion. Upon finding myself involved in such a confusing transference, I must not rush to provide interpretations of the analysand's behavioral patterns or his fantasies and ideas, because at this point, all such interpretations will only increase his resistance. I must instead, at first, limit myself entirely to a description of the order and the connections in the sequentiality of the associations.[8]

Notes

1 This chapter is based on a case that Morgenthaler supervised, so the analyst in discussion is not himself but someone he knew.
2 The next two paragraphs are a typical example of Morgenthaler's habit of walking his readers through possible alternative psychoanalytic approaches. One by one, he considers other plausible (but in his view inappropriate) options, before finally explaining what he recommends.
3 One of Morgenthaler's main recommendations with regard to dreams told in analysis is to postpone, or even eschew entirely, any attempt to decode their symbolism and instead, in a first move, attend to the role of the dream-telling in the analytic relationship. As becomes evident later within this chapter and is elaborated on in subsequent chapters and other writings specifically on dreams (cf. Binswanger, 2016), Morgenthaler takes the view that both the remembered dream and the told dream are part of the unconscious conversation with the analyst and that the trajectory or directionality of the dream and – again – the *sequentiality* in the dream, as in its telling, are more significant than any decodable latent symbolic content one might project into it.
4 As in Chapter 1, here too, Morgenthaler insists on one of his key propositions: whatever is conscious can by definition not *simultaneously* be unconscious. He will say this directly a few paragraphs further on, but it is already germane here. The point is that it would be a mistake to provide an "interpretation"

which suggests that the "deeper," unconscious dynamic at work is the patient's annoyance at and hostility to the analyst. Although that is true, both partners in this analytic pairing are conscious of it, and thus it cannot be what is really most significant.

5 Throughout *Technik*, Morgenthaler will recurrently refer to a distinction between primary-process and secondary-process psychic activity. James Strachey, in the introduction to his 1938 translation of Freud's *The Interpretation of Dreams* (1900), declares "the most momentous of the discoveries given to the world in *The Interpretation of Dreams*" to be "the distinction between the two different modes of mental functioning, the Primary and Secondary Processes" (1938, p. xv). Generally, primary-process mental activity is associated with the unconscious, and especially with the id and with the pleasure principle, while secondary-process mental activity is associated with the preconscious and the conscious, with the ego and the reality principle. In an essay on "dream diagnostics" published posthumously, Morgenthaler elaborates, citing Freud's coinage of the terms, not only that Freud "called that which in the formation of dreams is an expression of unconscious drive-stirrings of the id the primary process and that which shows itself in the manifest dream the secondary process," but also noted that "to the primary process belongs the experiential quality of the dream which arises from the tendency of the unconscious motivations that are contained in the dream, but remain hidden. To the secondary process belong those ideational contents of the manifest dream, the dream-situation, and the associations to the dream, which are able to enter consciousness" (2004, p. 65). Crucially, although the distinction had first been formulated by Freud in relation to dream interpretation, and certainly was extended by Morgenthaler also for that particular purpose, the distinction had far broader relevance for Morgenthaler in all of his clinical work as well as in his later theorizing about sexuality. While maintaining adherence to many ego psychological precepts (and in the same essay Morgenthaler invoked the renowned systematizer of ego psychological theory David Rapaport who already in 1944 had extended Freud's dreamwork-based distinctions between primary and secondary processes to other kinds of mental functioning, including memory), Morgenthaler could also be said to have resuscitated aspects of earlier id psychology in his emphatic commitment to revaluing "undirected drive-stirrings," "emotional movement," and "experiential quality."

6 Although Morgenthaler here is directly invoking Freud's image of the analysand defending himself against the continuation of the treatment (Freud, 1914, p. 151), he mentions this iconic image only to go on to highlight other priorities entirely – above all, the analyst's responsibility to ensure the maintenance of a de-stressed atmosphere. Moreover, Morgenthaler precisely does not want to focus on the analysand's resistances, but on the contrary, and crucially, the assistance that the unconscious of the analysand is giving the analyst in furthering the analytic process.

7 One of Morgenthaler's persistent fascinations – one he shared with Kohut – was the phenomenon of (seeming) sexualization of actually nonsexual impulses.

8 Morgenthaler deliberately leaves the case incompletely resolved at this point, returning to it in Chapter 8.

Chapter 3

Setting priorities – and relativizing them

Considering the great variety of possible interventions or interpretive steps, it is not easy to perceive priorities that, from the point of view of technique, could advance the analytic process. When I try to orient myself as to what I believe I have understood, I am constantly torn back and forth. In other words: there is no straight path to figuring out what I will want to say to an analysand. Perception, conception, understanding, and processing in thinking and combining continually oscillate around different, interconnected models of ideas that come to mind and finally result in a summation effect.

With the expression *summation effect*, I try to describe a process characterized by impulses and impressions that accumulate in such a way as to steer attention in a very specific and determined direction and toward a very determined content. The analyst listening to his analysand and, in so doing, putting himself in that state Freud called free-floating attention is not really in a state but rather in a constant movement, which he follows.[1] This movement has a dynamic and a content. The dynamic is determined by the emotionality, the content by the succession of ideas that come to mind; both parts work together and, in the course of an hour, a week, or in the course of just a few minutes, they produce a summation effect of certain ideas that gives me the impression I could or should now say what I then, in fact, do say.

It is in no way the case that I know from the beginning what I ought to do, for example, when an analysand remains silent for a long time and then says, tensely, that he has been unable to work before coming to me. He had become angry for once again having to leave work to keep the appointment for his analytic session. It bothers him, he adds, that he always sneaks out, as if he felt guilty for doing something unsavory. Confronted with such a situation, I do not at first know how to adjust. Am I dealing with a resistance? Might it be that he fends off positive feelings in this way, or do his remarks call into question the analysis as a whole? Perhaps, however, the analysand simply expresses that it is easier for him to say what he is saying than it is to say something else, for example, something embarrassing he has noticed about me, which he remains silent about. I don't intend to go into the motives in detail that prompt the analysand to express himself in this way but rather stress how little sense it makes to think about it if we fail to pay the greatest possible attention to the sequentiality of that which the analysand now goes on to put forward. Only then can we expect to gain insight into what is really going on.

And so I wait.

Such waiting is often misjudged. Waiting is not the polar opposite of intervening, interpreting, encouraging, or saying anything-at-all, in order therewith to render the atmosphere in the analytic situation friendlier again. On the contrary, there is a highly volatile dynamic in waiting. In a very short time, different conceptions of what is going on in the relationship between analysand and analyst are oscillating. While I become aware of this or that perception or attitude of my own, I can also trace where I want to give in to an urge to interpret the one or other aspect. But it is not only the analyst who is having thoughts and shifts from one conception to another. The analysand does the same. Only the motives of each of the partners are different.

From this point, we can articulate a priority of great significance from a technical point of view: in this specific phase of the analytic process, the actualization of the transference-conflict is the highest priority. But what am I to do to actualize the transference-conflict in a manner appropriate to each phase?

It might sound paradoxical now for me to note that this priority I speak of involves the deep, unconscious connections that, in a critical hour or phase, are lying at the root of the analysand's complex, incomprehensible mode of experiencing.

The task, initially, is not to elucidate these unconscious connections. In my discussion of the pitfalls we confront in orienting ourselves in the analytic process (Chapter 1), I already pointed out the dangerous tendency, in approaching the unconscious, prematurely to home in on the great figures of childhood and the greatest life-problems connected with them. In the actualization of the transference-conflict, linking up with such contents, memories, or any ideas associated with them is not the primary point. Rather, a purely quantitative factor among the modalities of cathexis that appear in the analytic relationship stands front and center. To illustrate this point, let me go back to the two examples I already cited.

In the analysis of the man who, after a disappointing meeting with his friend, recounted the dream in which a linguistic dispute occurred, what seemed so complex and incomprehensible about it was nothing other than the expression of the deep connections that had led to the confused transference-development. In the case of the other analysand who, after a long silence, voiced his annoyance about the obligation to come to analysis, the deeper connections that provoked this behavior are connected with an affective overtaxing of the entire psychic economy.

In the first case, it is an increasing confusion, in the second, an increasing overtaxing that has caused a tension-filled atmosphere to arise in the relationship between analysand and analyst. Such a tension has its source in a gradually or suddenly developing polar opposition in the modalities of cathexis in the psyche of the two partners in the analytic relationship. Almost imperceptibly, this now gives rise to a psychic tug-of-war because the interests of the two partners oppose each other. The analysand who, of course unconsciously, is advancing the confusion encounters an analyst who, again unconsciously, resists this tendency, tries to check it, seeks to prevent it. The analysand, who is constantly overtaxed but only gradually begins to manifest this overtaxing in some form in the course of the transference-development, confronts an analyst concerned with attenuating, neutralizing, cushioning, and compensating for this overtaxing.

I have to insist once more that I am not talking about conscious intentions here, neither on the part of the analysand nor on that of the analyst. When I speak of polar opposite attitudes, I mean those within the emotional movement that leads both partners in the analysis to get involved with each other.

The most important aspect of these entire reflections is the reactivation of the transference-conflict, a reactivation that alone promotes the analytic process. Moreover, in no way does a tension that derives from a polar opposition in the modalities of cathexis of the two partners in the analysis lead to a reactivation of the transference-conflict. A tension-filled relationship between analyst and analysand can no doubt be filled with conflict, but such conflict is one that belongs to the domain of the psychology of consciousness since the unconscious motivations connected with it remain obscure. The transference-conflict can be reactivated in the analytic process only if the modalities of cathexis, both of the analysand and of the analyst, are oriented in one and the same direction. These, then, are the conditions deserving of supreme priority.

To do justice to this priority, it is the analyst, not the analysand, who must adjust accordingly. But he can adjust accordingly only if he is aware of his task, only, that is, if he knows what's important. Empathy helps me in all situations in which I do not face difficulties and is of little use to me as soon as I do.

It is a wise old saying about psychoanalytic procedure that as analysts, we should follow the analysand; that we should serve as the mirror of his unconscious; that it is the analysand who must become capable of talking about what moves him, rather than the analyst being moved by what comes into his mind.

But how is that to happen? What does it mean to adjust oneself in such a way that one is in sync with the analysand's modalities of cathexis when the motivations for all this lie, unfathomably, in the realm of the unconscious?

I admit there is no technical concept for this. But I also do not need a technical concept for it. The demand that I adjust to the analysand, and not the other way around, is at bottom not a demand but a fundamental element of psychoanalysis itself. If, then, I engage in psychoanalysis, I bring this attitude to the analytic relationship in any event. But then, difficulties and obstacles can arise. I would like to compare the conditions that appear here with a journey into an unknown country. As an analyst, I am always already on the move and possibly encountering obstacles, finding myself in difficulties, or temporarily getting stuck somewhere. I am on the move and not at home, no longer just busy with travel brochures and maps and dealing with all the questions that might then be answered by deciding to undertake the journey. The difficulties and obstacles that always appear when I am in doubt whether or not to tackle a great undertaking are difficulties that I must very consciously distinguish from those other difficulties that arise when I am on the move.

With this comparison, I've merely tried to clarify that the analyst is not only on the move with his analysand once the analysis begins but already when he sees or talks to someone for the first time who might undertake an analysis. Whenever I take an analytic attitude, I am already on the move. This aspect is of foundational importance for me when it comes to creating or, precisely, not creating an analytic situation with an analysand, the way, already on a journey, I have to clarify, for example, whether I keep advancing by boat or train or whatever other means. It may be the case that the trains aren't running, that the ships are all at anchor because of political unrest, and the airports are shut down. Perhaps I continue the journey by truck. I as analyst have encountered many people this way with whom I encountered obstacles that made an analysis impossible. We just have to see one thing very clearly: we must not compromise. We must not dissimulate about what is and what is not. That really sums up everything analysts like Willi Hoffer mean when they say that analysis is indivisible.[2]

I have given so much space to this aspect because this foundational attitude toward analysis creates a starting position that in the further course of the analysis allows a myriad of problems and ostensible difficulties with psychoanalytic technique to appear in a different light, to be differently articulable.

How might we sketch such a rearticulation?

I want to see the situation as realistically as it is. The difficulties I encounter show themselves in exactly the same way all difficulties I cannot avoid in my life show themselves. In dealing with a person I do not understand I must, just as in other situations, examine where I stand. To be able to delimit this location, I need signals. These come from the outside and the inside. I must first recognize how the partner, in this case the analysand, reacts to me. What is the echo I produce in him? Nothing must keep me from grasping and understanding this. It is decisive for everything that follows and has nothing at all to do with my revealing myself or acting-out in the countertransference. The misunderstandings that still persist in this area confuse matters. They have their source in the difficult conditions that define the social role of the analyst in the society in which he lives. In any event these misunderstandings are the cause of confusions that often arise in analysands' transference-development. They arise because the analyst feels unsure in his social role and because he subordinates himself to false demands that prevent him from doing what suits him. The relationship I create with my analysand must in every case suit me, it must fit, which by no means contradicts my following the analysand, adjusting to him accordingly, and not letting myself be manipulated into assuming a polar-opposite position, for example.

This is exactly the same as when I go to eat in a restaurant, for example. Once I have arrived, I adjust in such a way that I feel good, I order what suits me, what fits. I do so, of course, taking into consideration everything I am offered: kitchen, service staff, ambiance, the other guests, the prices. If in such equilibria disproportions arise, I quickly feel a tension and a discomfort. In that event, I can expect the disruptive conditions outside of me to change only to a very limited extent. It is I who must readjust, and if I am not disposed to do so, I cannot do anything but leave the restaurant and go to one that appeals to me more.

What is important in dealing with an analysand is that I know what I want and that I also say what is unavoidable for me to exercise my function without tension. That alone, however, is not enough to guard against grave mistakes. We must be mindful of the limits that protect against shared acting-out and against detrimental reactions in the countertransference. These limits are all the more clearly visible the more we take the following aspects into consideration and all the more blurry the less we do so:

(1) The analytic process is in no way linear. It is complex and never structured in such a way that the simpler points of reference would appear first and the more complicated ones only later.

(2) The analysand – and even if he were to have cognitive deficits – always has very differentiated modes of reacting that do not allow us to simplify the psychic processes that move him or to codify them according to some sort of schema.[3]

(3) There is no hierarchy in people's capacities to deal better or worse with inclinations toward conflictedness, even if it might sometimes seem that way. We are always inclined to judge people we do not know either too optimistically or too pessimistically when we compare them with ourselves. The greatest danger the analyst finds himself in lies in his inclination to feel himself disposed, in elitist fashion, to being able to help other people in dealing with their conflicts. But all people have a certain influence on others. That is not the property that makes the analyst what he is.

When I talk about psychoanalytic technique, it is not by accident that I choose examples that present very problematic situations or point out an irresolvable tension in the analytic relationship, for such examples are much more meaningful than those that allow me to show how everything unfolds coherently and without conflict. When everything fits, we always find the right thing to say. It is just these conditions that the theory of technique picks up on. It formulates concepts that are really only applied when I have to take recourse to them because I encounter difficulty in the relationship with my analysand and in my task of getting the analytic process going. The concepts of technique by no means encompass everything taking place between the two partners in the analytic process. Most of the movements that come out in the affective and cognitive relation do not need to be described in more detail by the theory of technique. The theory of technique is a collection of models that need to be put to use when the analyst, due to his own conflictedness, runs the risk of losing track of what is going on in the analysis. It is then his task to make use, from among what the theory of technique has to offer, of those concepts he now needs to make the analytic process advance. In every situation and with every analyst this will be different. What is important, however, is that such a situation is clearly recognized.

I would like to describe the function of the theory of technique and its concepts by way of two comparisons.

(1) The theory of technique can be compared to our pharmacies, its concepts with the medicines to be obtained there. When we feel healthy, we hardly pay attention to the pharmacies, because medicines do not interest us. The moment we are sick, however, we seek them out and choose the ones that help us become healthy again. The drugs are arranged on the pharmacy's shelves in bottles, boxes, and tubes, in alphabetical order, perhaps, or according to groups of diseases, like heart problems, digestive troubles, and the like. Now no one would get it into their head to study all drugs in a pharmacy in order to get a picture of the makeup of the human body and how its organism functions. It is just the same with psychoanalytic technique. The study of technique and the most comprehensive memorization of its concepts will never lead the analyst to a better understanding of what is going on in his analysand.

(2) When I set out in my car to go to a large city I do not know yet, I follow the signs along the roads, and the distances marked on them allow me to get a sense of how long I'll still have to drive. Signs and distance markers are useful. They have the character of symbols. They usually are simple signs that are easily understood. Nobody could wish that

these signs be replaced with images or films about life in that city, its architecture, and its history that would, for example, present themselves as ever larger, more mobile, and more impressive the closer one got to the city. That would be absurd and would greatly increase the risk of accidents due to distraction. It is just the same with the theory of technique and its concepts. These are limited to signs and signals as along the side of a road. One cannot gain insight from them into either the general or the particular makeup of the object we are trying to reach with the help of these signs and signals.

I expect from the technique of psychoanalysis neither a better understanding of the psychic structure of my analysand nor the satisfaction of my curiosity, for example by discovering through the application of technical concepts how my partners feel, react, love, think, fantasize, in short, how they shape their lives.

The overestimation of technique in this or any other sense is, to a very large extent, responsible for many forms of shared acting-out and adverse countertransference reactions.

The so frequent stereotypical application of the famous basic rule furnishes a simple example for this point. Analysts have almost gotten used to communicating the basic rule to their analysands at the beginning of the analysis, as if it could be obtained like a train ticket from a counter before getting on the train.

The analyst explains to his analysand, for example: "When you now begin analysis, it is best if you simply say everything that comes to your mind."

The analysand answers: "Okay, I will do that."

What we have here is an abuse of the technical concept, for the analysand simply cannot follow this rule. This is what [Rudolph] Loewenstein realized thanks to the development of ego psychology in psychoanalytic studies. In his article "Some Considerations on Free Association" he says that, at best, one may allow but one can never prescribe that an analysand give voice to what comes to his mind.[4]

The view that the analyst ought to prompt the analysand at the beginning of the analysis to say everything that comes to his mind can be explained historically by the fact that the psychoanalytic method derives from the employment of hypnosis and the pressure technique. During a certain period of time, when he had already foregone hypnosis but not yet discovered the efficacy of free association, Freud employed the method of the pressure technique. He laid his hand on the patient's forehead and prompted him immediately to divulge what came to his mind. This procedure naturally has something demanding and influencing about it and is closer to hypnosis than it is to psychoanalysis. Today, in turn, communicating the basic rule at the beginning of an analysis is an anachronism that has something rigid about it and belongs to the unanalytic tendency to shower an analysand in the process of turning toward analysis with directives:

> You are to be on time for the session and to cancel sufficiently in advance, or else you'll have to pay for the missed session, and when you go on vacation, you pay for the sessions anyway, or else [in the case of some other analysts] you don't need to pay for it. You should also know how we do things here. When you come in, you are to close the door and lie down. If the window is still open, it will be me, not you, who closes it.

There are even analysts who direct the analysand to bring along a small white cloth, either to protect the cushion on the couch or to have the analysand lie on a small cloth that belongs to him such that the intimate and familiar will arise in the analysis. Once the analysis is completed, the analyst then sends the cloth back to his former analysand in the mail. All these are not fantasies; rather they are things I know to have actually happened.

Another tendency to abuse technical concepts is apparent in certain ascetic conceptions of purity. One analyst, for example, boasts that his analysis room is entirely neutral, painted light grey, no pictures on the wall. Everything is consciously dull and uninteresting to allow the analysand freely to associate without being influenced, without being distracted, and thereby to make insight, all in all, come more easily. This also includes the conception that neutrality enhances the patient's capacity for fantasy and that the fact of the analyst sitting invisibly behind the analysand makes it easier for the latter to relax and let himself go.

What is remarkable here is that the significance of this setup of the analytic situation for the analyst himself is relegated entirely to the background. Yet every analyst is aware of how much more freely he can move if he remains unobserved by the analysand. This greater freedom may also refer to the inner freedom for the analyst all the better to be able to follow his own associations, but we must not ignore the fact that it especially concerns external matters. The analyst, unobserved, does a series of little things he would never do if he felt observed by a partner sitting across from him. With this setup of the analytic situation, he puts himself in a position that in some respects removes him from socially significant control functions. He thereby makes his task, to turn to the analysand in a way that is attuned to what the analysand himself is, easier.

It would be making it too easy for oneself, though, to deduce from all this that what I am suggesting is that the analyst should have the courage to announce everything he is doing behind the analysand's back, because this is not the point. Rather, the crux lies in the attitude of the analyst toward the freedom he allows himself in his role. For he easily develops unconscious guilt feelings. These feelings, however, are in no way due to the secret little activities – thinking so would be mere rationalization. Instead, the guilt feelings are of a societal nature. The analyst suddenly observes his own behavior and fears being caught if the analysand were unexpectedly to turn around. In most cases, these feelings of the analyst, which occur much more often than one thinks, are presented as being of no consequences or simply passed over in silence. Nobody wants to recognize them for the substitute acts they are, acts connected with a difficult to grasp conflict of conscience that almost always forces the analyst into a compromise between the goals of the analytic process and society's unwritten demands. The compromise usually develops quite gradually and invisibly. It is difficult to generalize this: everyone experiences it in his own way. For me, it was often the case that a discomfort set in when, listening to the analysand recount promiscuous or delinquent actions, I suppressed inner demands from my superego and then caught myself straightening up in my chair and sitting in a "well-behaved" manner, as it were, as if I had to "make a good impression." I noticed that my discomfort then abated. What I then said I said in a benevolent pastoral tone of voice. Only once it had become possible for me to reflect on these conditions was I able to regain my relaxed, deconflictualized way of being. I finally understood that my analysand was seducing me to enter into a compromise between the analysis and societally relevant demands.

Multiple aspersions have in recent years been cast on the analytic "setting." Therapists who prefer direct confrontation, group therapy, and open exchanges to the rigid analytic situation criticize the hierarchical status of the invisible analyst, unchecked by any oversight, who, while constantly making evaluations, acts benevolently disposed toward the vulnerably exposed analysand. This point of view persists, no matter how much analysts insist that this is in no way their attitude. The analysts and the flawed theories they advocate, anachronisms that are not to be touched, have only themselves to blame if the analytic way of proceeding is experienced by ever more people as something unsocial, reactionary. To blame the fees of analysts for this bad reputation and to say that psychoanalysis is just something only for rich people is to evade the problem. The decisive point is the abuse of analytic technique, in the widest sense, for moral purposes. These habits, however, are largely unconscious, and where they are conscious, they are obfuscated to protect the vested status interests of the clan-profession.

Now, as far as the analytic process is concerned, I think that all these seemingly external things that touch on the analytic situation play a great role. The setup I as analyst choose in order to create an analytic situation is nothing other than a consciously sought-for construction. Now, this construction is in no way sought for primarily to promote in the analysand some kind of regressive, magic-symbolic modes of reaction and series of associations. The analytic situation, instead, is a precondition that allows me to keep pursuing the analytic process within an intermediate area. On the one hand, one avoids dangerous emotional breakthroughs, on the other hand, a regression can be prevented – namely the kind of regression that exceeds what is called a "regression in the service of the ego."

Emotional breakthroughs in the sense of a great acting-out, like the kind of psychic upheaval that provokes the analysand into violent threats toward the analyst or leads to erotic or sexual outbursts, are as undesirable and perilous as are those deep regressions in which the analysand relinquishes his autonomous functions and is no longer even in a position to give direction to the analytic process and to understand what is going on within himself.

Before the analyst decides on the analysis, he must have become equally aware of both the dangers and the possibilities. This is as true here as it is for the profession of the physician in general. But once we have begun the analysis, we must also continue it. We can do so only if the analytic situation has been set up on the broadest possible basis. It is not enough for the analyst to adjust in such a way as to say, for example, "You know, I feel that for you, an analysis would really be advisable," and, given the analysand's agreement, for the analysis to begin. After two or three weeks, one gradually realizes that serious obstacles appear that have neither been discussed nor considered and now throw the entire analysis into question. These are always indicators that the preparations for producing a sustainable analytic situation were insufficient and not undertaken seriously enough. From the start, there must be the prospect that the analysand can accept the setting and stick with it.

The setting, the analytic situation, is thus of great significance for every analytic process above all because it represents a safeguard for the analyst. It is impossible for me sufficiently to follow what the analysand is expressing, in order really to understand what is going on within him, if I maintain more intense contact with him outside the analytic framework. Suppose I go to dinner with my analysands, go to the theater with their friends, receive flowers brought over by their child playing with my child or my dog – all these are events my analysands might possibly deal with quite well. I, however, would be unable to handle it, and especially if I were not to notice that I am being influenced by it.

On the other hand I must also be aware of what it means when I put too much stress on the analysand with outsize demands. This could take place almost unnoticed, if for example I conducted tests prior to the analysis, a Rorschach test, say, to get a better picture of the gravity of the neurosis. More harmless interventions, too, such as reading an analysand's diaries from earlier years or looking at childhood photographs and reading the letters of a past love story gone awry, signify an overstraining of the analysand that he may perhaps welcome and in fact offer but that in many cases leads the analytic situation into confusion at the very beginning of the analysis.

The analytic situation is the result of a most definitely conscious agreement between two people who do not know or hardly know each other to create an intense relationship in an artificial, constructed way – artificial precisely because it is intentionally initiated. It thus differs quite essentially from an encounter with someone I am immediately fascinated by and whom I would like to see again. Yet it also differs from a chance relationship I am unable for some reason to interrupt although I would like to, being rather indifferent to my partner. Such a relationship might arise on a ship, for example, where I might have to share a cabin during a longer journey with someone to whom I find no access. The analytic relationship is of an entirely different kind. Neither fascination nor indifference but my psychoanalytic interest leads me to create the relationship with my future analysand. Every relationship motivated by a delimited interest has something artificial and constructed about it. But the psychoanalytic relationship differs from other interest-driven relationships in that the analyst's motives are not connected with advantages he personally expects from this relationship. This also means that the relationship is already getting on an unanalytic track when, for instance, financial considerations come to play a role in the sense that the analyst needs an analysand in order to make a living. Similar disturbances also arise if and when the analyst approaches the analysand with certain resolutions. This could be the case when he strives to "cure" a homosexual or when he seeks to help guide a young woman, who seems work-shy to him and shows herself inclined toward prostitution, "onto the right path." Yet if the analyst adjusts himself in such a way that neither personal advantages nor moral or other intentions constrain him, the developing analytic relationship soon loses its artificial, constructed overtones. What it means for the analytic relationship to be a construction is thus limited to the setting itself, that is, to the external framework for the unfolding interaction and the external conditions of individual sessions.

Many analysands do indeed for a long time experience the analytic situation as something artificial. They talk about it. The critical objections they raise also make it easy to recognize the reactions of disappointment connected with these. They assert, for example, that the analyst is interested in the analysand only because he is a patient or because he is paying for the sessions. Fundamentally, they say, there is no real human feeling of sympathy because the analyst stops thinking of the analysand the moment the session is over.

In situations of this kind, the analyst should be clearly aware that, to a certain extent, his analysand is right but also that this relationship is one of the necessary preconditions that belong to the analytic situation. There is not much sense in regretting this or toning it down and covering over it or signaling silent agreement that, unfortunately, it is the way things are, bad luck for our fellow human being who, as everyone knows, in the course of life has to get used to such painful experiences, in keeping with the reality principle. Here, too, the analyst likes to take recourse to the "pressure of suffering," which allegedly belongs to the preconditions for successfully entering into an analysis as well. And the demand, so often misunderstood, that analysis has to take place in conditions of self-abnegation offers a handy excuse for avoiding what one really ought to understand.

It is not good if the analyst at the end of his workday spends the entire evening brooding over the analytic sessions and, to try to understand more, searching the literature for information to help him along. Nor is it good if a particularly difficult situation with an analysand occupies him so intensely that he seeks out a colleague to discuss the case extensively. Matters are different for the supervision of an as yet relatively inexperienced analyst by a supervisory analyst. In such a case, the analyst who is undergoing his training regularly reports to the supervisory analyst on the course of the analysis quite independently of whether he is encountering particular difficulties or not. If, however, we have such discussion only whenever we are unable to advance, it is in most cases not exactly beneficial for the analysis we are conducting, even if we must admit there can be certain advantages – when, for example, thanks to such an outside "affair," an analyst whose relationship with his partner is disturbed, regains a state that is less conflictual.

The most important thing in such situations of inner tension is that the analyst finds within himself possibilities for understanding why all analysands, or a very specific constellation in one analysis, take such a toll on him and reactivate his inclinations toward conflictedness in a very particular direction.

Conversely, the fact that an analysand repeatedly declares how much the analysis preoccupies him, also outside of the sessions, is not necessarily proof of his collaboration and his readiness to recognize or change something about himself. Analysands, too, have a propensity to research in books about what is taking place in their psychic life and to discuss the analytic sessions with friends to clarify, for example, whether an interpretation was correct or not. It also happens that an analysand in such a situation of pressure goes to see, even regularly visits, a second analyst to hear a confirmation or a criticism of the way his own analyst proceeds.

We must not simply put down such events to our analysands' neuroses. More often, they are the result of an unconscious readiness to react to the inclinations toward conflictedness that by no means exist only in the analysand but also, and to no lesser an extent, in the analyst. We must thus always take into account our own inclination toward conflictedness when we as analysts sit behind our partner. Only then will we also understand what advantages we have when we take the analytic setting seriously: advantages that make it easier for us, or indeed allow us at all in the first place, to piece together disharmonies – as in modern music – in such a way that in the transference that develops they sound out harmoniously. This is the essential foundation for the actualization of the transference-conflict.

Notes

1 In a productively revealing instance of misremembering, Morgenthaler rede-scribes Freud's call (in his 1912 "Recommendations to Physicians Practic-ing Psycho-Analysis") for "evenly hovering attention" (*gleichschwebende Aufmerksamkeit*) by the analyst as "free-floating attention" (*freischwebende Aufkmerksamkeit*) – only then to go on to underscore the importance of this greater freedom by emphasizing the idea of "constant movement."

2 By referring to psychoanalysis as being "indivisible," Morgenthaler means that it is always and only an all-or-nothing proposition. Physician and psycho-analyst Wilhelm (Willi) Hoffer (1897–1967) was one of Anna Freud's closest associates and staunchest supporters in London. He served as editor-in-chief of the *International Journal of Psycho-Analysis* and was from 1957–1960 presi-dent of the British Psycho-Analytical Society. He also served as Morgenthaler's supervisor at some point in the 1950s.

3 Morgenthaler did have experience with at least one patient with cognitive defi-cits, and found that he had a rich interior life and that he was able to work effectively with him. The case is described in the essay, "Modes of Interaction in Perversions and Perversion of Modes of Interaction" (1977), in the Supple-mentary materials at the end of this book.

4 Rudolph Loewenstein (1898–1976) was a Polish-born psychoanalyst who practiced in Germany, France (where he was Jacques Lacan's training analyst from 1932/33–1938/39), and the United States (where he famously became, together with Heinz Hartmann and Ernst Kris, one of the main figures in ego psychology in the 1940s–1960s). Loewenstein's "Some Considerations on Free Association" appeared in the *Journal of the American Psychoanalytic Associa-tion* in 1963.

Chapter 4

The actualization of the transference-conflict

The emotional movement that characterizes the analytic process leads to a reformulation of neurotic conflicts through the development of the transference. Expressed differently: the neurotic fixations the patient suffers from are being reactivated as a gradually developing transference-conflict actualizes.

I remember a seminar on technique that featured the presentation and discussion of the analysis of a young woman who, shortly after the beginning of the treatment, displayed a series of reactions and attitudes that almost all participants in the seminar saw as a disappointment in the person of the analyst. I was of a different opinion and thought I saw that the main problem of this analysis consisted first of all in the fact that no transference-conflict had developed and that for precisely that reason the patient's disappointment reactions were unable to actualize in the transference. In the first sessions, the young woman had rather animatedly reported her entire life story and presented the difficult situations that had ultimately led her into the analysis. From that point onward, however, she was often silent and could hardly ever be brought to participate in a meaningful way.

She had for some years been married to a young man who loved her, but his love – it seemed to her – gradually withered because she felt incapable of reciprocating this love. The husband was of a different opinion. He claimed his love was as it had been on the first day. The patient could not believe it and separated from him. She moved in with a childhood friend with whom she got involved in an intense love relationship. After some time, she once again had the impression that this childhood friend no longer loved her. She felt attracted by her husband again and visited him often. The husband wanted to talk her into coming back to him. The woman was at a loss and sought out a psychologist, but her impression of this psychologist was that he did not understand her and was thus unable to give her advice. She was generally disappointed by all people, she said, and had come to realize that she had to help herself. That's what she did, and she decided no longer to visit her husband and to stay with her childhood friend. Soon afterward, severe conflicts arose. With the beginning of the analysis, she felt better because the conflicts with her friend diminished. It seemed obvious that the disappointments the woman experienced with her husband and her friend had transferred onto the person of the analyst already after a few analytic sessions.

The analyst interpreted this connection and linked it with experiences from her life story to show her that she had doubted already in childhood that her father's attention was genuine and directed toward her. The patient accepted the interpretation. She was aware that she distrusted the father's love. Her doubts were realistic. There was no reason to see in these doubts neurotic reactions or an expression of fantasies. The analysand voiced concerns about the purpose and value of the analysis. She said she must be a boring case for her analyst but that she would make an effort to understand what he meant. She remained silent for a long time, and when she told something, she smiled at the end of her little narrative in expectation of what the analyst was now going to say. In the course of more than fifty analytic sessions nothing changed in this picture, even though the analyst tried to interpret, from every possible angle, the defense he observed in his analysand. Her identification with the cool, strict, rather ascetic mother, whom the analysand despised; her envy of the successful older brothers; her protective concern for the younger, sickly brother; the open penis envy, of which the patient spoke; her phallic features; her scorn and ridicule for the men who loved her; and the meaning of her frigidity: all this was interpreted and placed in connection with her defensive manner in the analytic relationship.[1] Time and again, the analyst pointed to the serious reaction of disappointment the analysand experienced with him and tried to understand with what in particular this disappointment might be associated. The patient usually averred that the physician's views were correct. She usually said that nothing impressed her anymore because she was constantly being disappointed by everyone.

As the case was being presented, it seemed to me that the disappointment-reaction had appeared very early and very suddenly without my being able to identify any faulty approaches or inadequate interpretations on the analyst's part. That is why I did not agree with the seminar participants' general impression that the issue was a disappointment-reaction the woman was experiencing with her analyst. I tried to show that in this case very probably the issue was not a disappointment-reaction and that what counted most was understanding how important it was that a disappointment-reaction really was actualized and experienceable.

In my view, the patient had an inhibition about exposing herself. She was unable to show that she was not really disappointed. At most, she was disappointed in herself, namely in not being able to show what she really felt in the relationship with the analyst. This is what had led to a diminution of her sense of self-worth. She was looking to compensate by talking about herself in the way a psychiatrist talks about one of his patients. The woman was really suffering from a stereotyped assumption that she was always disappointed, and this restricted her feelings and destroyed her relationships with others. The disappointment-reaction the analysand displayed was thus undoubtedly not the expression of a transference-development that had led to the reactivation of an inclination toward conflictedness but a fixation that blocked the analytic process.

It is important to note that our analysands sense this. They feel it when something in the analysis isn't right, even if they cannot say what it is. All our analysands have an unspoken expectation that the relationship between them and their analyst will get underway and that thereby something unexpected, something special will happen in their experiencing. The palpable reciprocal affective cathexes and the emotional movements that accompany these cathexes lead analyst and analysand to have the impression that their relationship is right or that it isn't, that the analysis gets underway or constantly is moving in circles that restrain them and block what is essential. In this context, it is initially not necessary to know precisely what is meant by the feeling that the relationship is right or what the essential matter is that is blocked by some restriction. The peculiar thing about these situations is not, however, that agreement and peaceful togetherness accompany the feeling that the analytic relationship is right. Rather, it is the expectation that a conflictualization will appear in the development of the transference. This conflictualization reactivates the fixations that stand in a causal relationship with the analysand's symptoms and psychic disturbances but also with the resistances that have formed within the transference.

The emotional movement is always the primary thing. It is from here that the development of the transference begins. Everything that is going on in the analysand, his reactions, feelings, attitudes, resistances, and defense manifestations can, as a matter of principle, be meaningfully interpreted and worked through only if their significance is understood within the transference.

The development of transference and the analysis of resistances accordingly stand in a very specific relationship with each other, one that we must always keep in mind in the psychoanalytic process. They should be neither applied too expansively nor should cause and effect be inverted. We might speak of an expansion if we assume, for example, that the transference had developed for a specific analysand under the pressure of suffering or that the transference had got underway despite intense resistance. We would have to speak of an inversion if we supposed that a transference-development has not been possible for a long time because of resistances that were just too great or because very particular defense-reactions, such as stubbornly holding on to intellectualizing objections, have one-sidedly influenced the evolution of the transference.

I would like to repeat that the transference develops along the lines of the emotional movement that arises in the relationship between analysand and analyst. The pressure of suffering can, at most, distort such a relationship, but it can never determine it. We must also distinguish between resistances and obstacles, for – at most – the development of a transference encounters obstacles. Resistances are always the effect of a transference that has already arisen. One could of course introduce another terminology and interpret differently what psychoanalysis understands by resistance. Psychoanalytic technique, however, relies on clearly delimiting the concept of resistance from other concepts. For that very reason, it is absurd to speak of resistances that render a transference-development impossible. Resistances, as a matter of principle, are the consequences of a transference-development. Nor is a transference ever in any way influenced only one-sidedly or incompletely by defensive processes. What appears as partial or incomplete is nothing but an expression of the transference itself, a transference that has developed to such an extent that, for example, specific forms of defense appear.

Before we may speak of resistances in the analytic process, we should always have obtained a picture of the development of the transference. The transference can be discerned in the actualization of specific conflictual inclinations in the analysand's relationship with the analyst. The actualization of the transference-conflict encompasses the modes of experiencing of both the analysand and the analyst. The domain of experience in which the conflictualization shows itself is the domain of the analytic situation. This domain is new for both partners and cannot be compared to other experiential domains. For the analysand, this domain also fills up with new contents, new demands, and new restrictions on these demands, whereby the reactivation of the conflictual inclinations stemming from early childhood happens under the influence of all these new experiences. The effect of this influence on the analysand is that he develops an insight that allows him to experience a contrast between fantasy and reality. The fantasies have to do with the ideational contents associated with the person of the analyst while reality is expressed in that which constitutes the genuine relationship with this analyst.

Many years ago, I had a young man in analysis who talked to me quite normally. In a certain phase of the analysis he began, almost imperceptibly, then increasingly conspicuously, to speak more loudly until he was almost shouting what he had to say. I asked him why he spoke so loudly, to which he answered: "Because you're hard of hearing."

I said: "Since when do you believe that I'm hard of hearing?"

He answered: "You've always been hard of hearing. I have always spoken loudly so that you can understand me."

In our further conversation about this fantasy, the analysand reported that since his early childhood his father had been hard of hearing.

Such information from an analysand by no means allows for concluding that as an analyst, one had become the father in the course of the transference. Such an assumption would obfuscate the much more important insight that something new and alien had entered into our heretofore relaxed and deconflictualized real relationship in the analytic situation, something that in no way befitted us; I mean, it befitted neither my young patient nor myself. The sense of disconcertedness my analysand felt when he realized that I was by no means hard of hearing would never have transmitted the impression of absurdity in its full impact if I had for example offered as a rationalizing stop-gap the interpretation that since the beginning of the analysis he had experienced me as a representative of his own father. The astonishment and disconcertedness the analysand felt proved to be a first, decisive experience, namely that something from his psychic past had entered into our relationship as a foreign and strange body. As a consequence of this insight, the analytic process deepened. The analysand had understood something decisive about what was going on in him. The analytic process had shaken something in him, had moved him emotionally. He had taken notice of his unconscious without initially understanding it. After this analytic session the relationship, which at the time bore the traits of a certain distancing and was characterized by a tendency toward rationalizations, changed in a quite conspicuous way. While previously, at the beginning of almost all analytic sessions, he had stopped at the door of my analysis room to let me enter first, he from now on led the way without inhibitions and let me close the door. Only now did we notice that the frequent questions he had asked me in the previous sessions, which had always aimed at reassuring himself that I had understood what he meant, went back to concerns I might not have properly understood him acoustically whereas I had surmised he believed me to have shown little understanding of what was important to him. The experience that something from the distance of his childhood had shown itself with almost hallucinatory certainty, something that did not accord at all with the reality of our relationship, had led to a relaxation in the transference. The distancing and polite reserve disappeared. However, thereafter the analysand did not by any means act inconspicuously. Instead, he showed excessive reactions. He almost ran down the corridor to the analysis room and already lay on the divan when I entered the room whereas earlier, he had only lain down when I had already taken my seat behind him. His attitudes seemed inversed, as it were. It was as if a new foreign body had intervened in our relationship. Yet this new foreign body should not be interpreted before a situation evolved in which these traits in the analysand's experiencing and behaving could themselves become conscious as something foreign and strange. To that end, other impressions and memories from his past would have to present themselves, beyond those of the hard-of-hearing father, so that a contrast-experience to the analytic relationship could be actualized.

I must add at this point that I do not advocate the view that one mustn't speak of the father because of the potential danger that this would be a rationalization. On the contrary, I would like to highlight how important it was, following the analysand's insight into the transference-dynamic, to interpret the transference-contents for him as well. Here the emphasis lay less on the interpretation that the analysand had experienced me as a father figure than on which unconscious wishes he was attempting to fulfill when he hoped to find in me a figure that would correspond to the figure of his father in at least one respect, that of hardness of hearing.

The interpretation that in the analysand's projection, the analyst represents the father is, at bottom, no interpretation at all because such a statement is inflexible and nondynamic. An interpretive step requires a relative completeness that is only given when the competing desires on which such projection is based are made conscious.

In my analysand's case, the unconscious wishes aimed in two directions, which were the directions of the gradually actualizing transference-conflict: the first wish corresponded to the tendency to indulge passive strivings that resulted from a negative-oedipal drive-vicissitude – and in the analytic relationship, too, because anxieties blocked the analysand from getting involved with me in a phallic-narcissistic rivalrous exchange. The other wish aimed at eliminating or denying the disturbing and inhibiting effects of an over-powerful authority figure by assuming a physical affliction – hardness of hearing – to substantiate the impotence of a partner who otherwise appeared threatening.

This example was meant to show the importance of the correct sequentiality: awareness of emotional movement always comes first. Only after that does a comprehensive interpretive step make an insight meaningfully possible.

Observing and following these phenomena finally leads to what I call the summation effect, which results on the one hand from a multitude of such observations and on the other hand from remembering what the analysand has already reported earlier and which allows for interpretive steps that, with assistance from certain concepts, advance and deepen the analytic process.

Such a summation effect, however, will arise for the analyst only if he pays special attention to it in his associations and in so doing refrains from focusing on his own difficulties. It is not good, for example, if in the analytic labor he is constantly occupied with reminding himself that he does not know enough, does not have sufficient experience, and needs the help of other analysts who are better equipped for this difficult task than he would say he is. Such self-reflections disturb the readiness to draw on certain aids from the theory of technique that allow an analyst to relax again when a situation has developed in which one believes one has lost sight of the big picture.

Accordingly, when I get ready for a summation effect that might arise, the most important thing is that I always assign greater significance to what the analysand shares with me, what comes to his mind, and what he narrates, than to my own difficulties. As analyst, I of course constantly reflect on both sets of thematics. But, as I said, it is not good if, as a summation effect starts to push its way into view in my train of thought, it so strongly foregrounds my own problems that I decide, for example, to give the analysand interpretations concerning the countertransference. Interpretations that concern the countertransference may in very rare cases be appropriate and right, but it is better to say that in most cases they are wrong.

But am I really, as an analyst, constantly torn back and forth? Am I as exposed to the summation effects that impose themselves in my trains of thought as a sailor in his boat is to the wind? In other words: are there in the analytic process quiet and tumultuous phases comparable to a lulling calm of the wind and the greatest alertness during a storm at sea? I do not think such an assessment does justice to the psychoanalytic situation. What I call a summation effect cannot be considered detached from other factors, such as, for example, sequentiality in the course of associations. The inner connection that exists there, however, is difficult to describe in theoretical terms. I would rather trace it in a practical example. For me, psychoanalysis only makes sense if its concepts can be verified in the living example of the relationship that develops between analyst and analysand.

I'd like to cite an episode from an analysis that had not yet progressed far but in which it had already been possible to uncover essential parts of the analysand's conflictual inclinations. Most prominent were conflicts that resulted from the 28-year-old patient's attitudes toward his family members. He behaved as if he was the one in his family who was responsible for constantly ensuring that the members of the family more or less got along with each other, in order to avoid greater conflicts. He was a kind of guardian angel for the father, for the mother, for the brother and sister. Regular visits at home and frequent telephone contact occupied him so much that in the relationships with his own friends and acquaintances, he always reacted as pressured and rushed. These difficulties were not the cause of his wanting to enter analysis. The real motive lay in disorders of his sense of self-worth that very much tormented him, and he also displayed compulsive restrictedness with numerous reaction-formations. He was extraordinarily diligent in his job and had an independent position as a merchant that came with a lot of responsibilities.

Once it had become possible for him to see that his protective stance toward the members of his family derived more from a difficult-to-control inner compulsion than it did from the genuine demands arising from his family's life-situation, nothing initially changed in his calm, measured attitude toward the analyst and toward the task he set himself in his analysis. He gave a relaxed impression and talked about events that affected him personally, not his relationship with the members of his family.

In the following session, he reported that something very remarkable had happened: he felt enormously disturbed in his work before coming to the analytic session. He had chosen the time of his sessions in such a way as to interfere with his work as little as possible. Nonetheless, he always had to leave work early, even if this fact had caused him no difficulty since he was so independent that he could plan his work however he wanted. The intense feelings that accompanied the current disruption of his work produced a fury in him that was directed at the upcoming analytic session. Yet what was remarkable was that, during the session, the patient was able to talk about it openly and calmly, without particular tension or anger.

As analysts, we should never be so ambitious as to want to understand instantly the unconscious background of such situations. We should, rather, ensure that the analysand's good relationship to the analyst is maintained. When the analysand reports these experiences to me without bringing a tension or disturbance into the relationship, I for my part must ensure that during this analytic session no tension arises from any sense of provocation. If, for example, I were to point out to the analysand that I understand his feelings very well but that they are a sign for something new having now entered the analysis, something whose effects create quite a disturbance, it might easily happen that the patient will react with an irritation or fall silent because my statements would bring nothing new at all and merely give the analysand the provocative impression that I opportunistically adapt to him so that he might feel solidarity with me.

It makes much more sense in such a situation to share the disconcertedness he feels. Because initially, I am not in a position to understand how a young man who is usually so productive suddenly gets into such a state of tension for which, for the moment, there is no evident reason – even if I can confidently surmise that it has something to do with the analytic situation. I must not underestimate my analysand. He surmises the same thing and could say it out loud just as easily as I. If he himself says it, that is always better than me making a preemptive pronouncement.

In the following session, something peculiar and surprising happened. The patient said:

> This morning, the trouble I had working was even stronger than two days ago. I was supposed to dictate some letters but I found it impossible to do anything. All morning long, I was thinking about the analytic session and waited for finally being able to leave the store.

The analysand then reported how relaxed and cheerful he felt strolling through the city on the way to the session. Then he fell silent and lay quietly on the divan. Finally he said that nothing was occurring to him. He had a feeling of emptiness, he said. After a few minutes, he became restless. I had the impression he was looking for a topic he could talk about. At last, he laboriously and haltingly reported events that had unfolded the night before. He described conflicts with friends of his who had come over. Many of his acquaintances would visit his apartment to prepare dinner and spend the evening together. The patient was used to buying the necessary groceries, and he was always glad to be able to prepare the meals. He liked cooking. Dinner seemed a success, for everyone was cheerful and content. Having finished eating, they carried the dishes to the kitchen together. The friends urged not interrupting the nice evening with washing dishes and cleaning up but postponing that work until the next day. The analysand was of a different view. He wanted things to be clean and organized. Slight tensions arose. The analysand withdrew to the kitchen and took care of washing, drying, and putting away the dishes by himself. He was very annoyed and had the feeling of being exposed, without defense, to his friends' inconsiderateness.

I will now try to work through the two analytic sessions recounted here according to the concepts of the theory of technique derived so far. On the one hand, I follow the associations put forward by the analysand; on the other hand, I pay attention to what is going on within me when I try to understand the connections. The questions I ask myself are: Will a summation effect occur in me or not? And in what direction do the emotional fluctuations move to which the analysand is subjected?

For this way of looking at things, my empathy does not suffice. In order to get the right perspective, I must assume an analytic attitude, that is, I must follow the sequentiality in the course of associations and simultaneously track the possible occurrence of a summation effect in my own thoughts. In so doing, I employ a tool of psychoanalytic technique. It helps lead me to the following observations:

> At first the patient is unable to work, and consciously he associates this disruption of his work-ability with what he is expecting, that is, with the upcoming analytic session. Thanks to the good, relaxed relationship he maintains with his analyst, he freely and openly recounts these experiences without any suppression of affect, instead of, for example, remaining silent about his anger. I do not intervene but ensure that the disturbances that have occurred do not break into the analytic relationship and create a tension-filled atmosphere. The experience of the analytic session must not create an additional pressure of suffering in the analysand.

We had evidently succeeded in keeping the analytic session in question free of conflict. In other words: in precisely this session, we had succeeded in avoiding a polar-opposite cathexis in the relationship between analysand and analyst. It was avoided because I had refrained from affirming the obvious rationalization the analysand had put forward in believing that the trouble he had working stood in some direct, causal relationship with his upcoming analytic session. Such an assumption would merely be an expression of an unanalytic tendency to allow the disruptive factor of consciously accessible pop-psychological associations to intrude into the relationship. From all these reflections results a first summation effect that indicates that a confusion in the transference-development was in this session happily avoided. To say more about it is as unnecessary as it is dangerous. There is no need to think any more about it. We can wait for what the next session will bring.

Before the following session, the disruption of work is rather more intense. Something new is visible. The analysand no longer feels any anger but a longing for the upcoming analytic session. We may therefore say that the analysand comes to the following session with an attitude that quite obviously advances and deepens the analytic process because the emotional movement in the transference has been amplified. Had the patient not shown up for work at all that morning and had gone, instead of to work, to the analyst's apartment intending urgently to speak with him, his behavior would have displayed an emotional decline that no longer advances but, as a result of acting-out, inhibits the analytic process.

The analysand, in any case, comes to this second session with a greater emotional offer than he did to the first. The greater emotional offer normally also brings with it a greater offering of associations that come to mind. Instead, nothing came to the analysand's mind. He has, instead, a feeling of emptiness. This gap in associations shows that the analysand is unable to say something that has come to his mind because certain feelings he senses in the relationship to his analyst prevent him from doing so. They may be embarrassing or bashful feelings because the contents of his ideas seem too intimate or too hostile or offensive or otherwise inappropriate and not articulable. Yet the gap in associations could also be conditioned by a genuine repression of certain ideational contents. In that case, truly nothing comes to the analysand's mind.

How are we to evaluate the gap in associations my analysand showed in this situation? We may wonder whether it is a transference-resistance connected with the feelings of refusal and rage that two days ago were still able to enter consciousness and now fall prey to repression: had anything come to the analysand's mind, it would have been aggressive ideas directed against the person of the analyst. If we follow this supposition, it would be indicated now to make the repressed aggressive impulses conscious with the appropriate interpretation. To support the probability of such a supposition, we might cite the displacement-substitute that appeared when the analysand reported how he felt defenselessly exposed to his friends' inconsiderateness. We might conclude from this that in reality the analysand feels defenselessly exposed to the analyst's inconsiderateness.

I would like to answer the question of how to evaluate this gap in associations in a different way. I do not mean to contest the notion that it is a transference-resistance, and I also think that much of the supposition I just described applies in some way. For me, in this specific analytic situation, however, the analysand's tendency to maintain a good, relaxed, conflict-free relationship with me plays a greater and more important role. This attitude on the part of the analysand, in other words, has clear priority, for I cannot see any advantage in having the ambivalent feelings the analysand carries into all of his relationships now also manifest in the analytic relationship with me. I have never yet succeeded in really remedying such an ambivalent attitude in the transference by means of an interpretation. I am also convinced that the analytic path goes into a different direction. The experience of many analysts corresponds to my own, namely that it is possible to show the analysand, by means of an interpretation, why in all other relationships he always gets caught in ambivalent feelings without his having to reactivate this attitude in the relation with the analyst. I am also of the opinion that it is precisely the experience the analysand has in the analytic relationship – namely the experience that such an ambivalence of emotional impulses does not inevitably have to occur – that in the first place creates the preconditions for finding a meaningful interpretation and for being able to utter it and formulate it effectively. For me, my analysand's gap in associations is a transference-resistance that is connected not with repressed aggressive but with repressed *positive* feelings.

What counts now is not that the analysand, torn back and forth in his feelings, experiences his ambivalence, in just the way he has always and everywhere experienced it, in the relationship with the analyst as well. What counts now is that he has a new experience. A new experience, at all costs. Everything that is lurking in the background here and that has to do with his ambivalence, I want to remember and take seriously, for I will incorporate all of this into the work of interpretation exactly when the analysand has finally, in the evolution of his transference, had the novel experience that, at least in his relationship with me, he does not have to endure the psychic hot bath of his ambivalences. Did not Freud say, decades ago already, that neuroses melt away in the fire of transference?

I'd like to return to what my analysand put forward. He lay there quiet and relaxed and felt an emptiness. Nothing came to his mind. I herewith encounter something that he cannot say. I must not make things too easy for myself and suppose that he simply does not want to say anything. Rather, and even if that were the case: he simply can't.

Now a physical restlessness sets in that is accompanied by an inhibition. This is clearly evident when he begins reporting his experience from the night before. The story aims at showing how inconsiderately he feels himself treated by his friends. We very quickly recognize that the analysand thereby also describes what he experiences in his family. Yet although, from a simplistic psychological point of view, such an observation seems to be useful and correct, it does not really lead anywhere. What could an interpretation of these connections, at precisely this time, offer the analysand? He would probably see that it is correct. Such insights often produce in the analysand the justified question put to the analyst about what he can do so things will change.

It is much more helpful to follow the sequentiality in the course of associations here as well. For then I reach the plain observation that the story about the friends and the evening they spent together, during which he was treated so inconsiderately, contains the thought in need of repression that immediately before that had gotten lost in the emptiness he felt. We might also say that the story about the friends is the consciously accessible expression of exactly that which he cannot say.

What, then, is it that he cannot say? I ask conversely: what was it that he could communicate? And I answer: he *was* able to express that his friends behaved inconsiderately because this sensation was able to enter consciousness. That is what he knows. And that can never *simultaneously* also be what is unconscious, for the unconscious is characterized by our not knowing it. It follows that the conflictual inclination that has been actualized in the transference in this very specific situation can never be what the analysand consciously expresses. What is able to enter consciousness is not also simultaneously an expression of what is unconsciously actualizing the transference-conflict. For that would be a contradiction in terms.

To advance appropriately at this point, I apply one of the concepts of the theory of technique in a way that initially seems hardly sensible and appears nonintuitive. I try to understand the contents that have been brought forward in associations as, in their sequentiality, causally mutually dependent manifestations of unconscious stirrings in the cognitive domain, and I refrain from giving the analysand interpretations that would allow him to compare everything with everything else and, rationalizing, to realize that he reacts the way he reacts everywhere.

Such comparative observations would, namely, easily lead this patient to think that he had analogous sensations toward his parents, had transferred these onto his friends and probably also onto the analytic relationship, and that the whole thing was possibly connected with his relationship with his father. He, the analysand, after all, had already reported before on how his father at home behaved quite similarly to the way the friends behaved toward him, for the father usually remained seated at the table and let his wife and children do all the work. The analyst could then continue and say something to the effect that the father's behavior had already very much disturbed him, the analysand, as a child, which was understandable, really, because it was connected, was it not, with the feelings of rivalry aimed at the father that he could never show. The father always had seemed to be the dominant one. Last night, the group of his friends turned out to be dominant, and he experienced the analyst in a very similar way.

If the analysand sees all this, which happens not infrequently, a situation easily arises that I would like to call a kind of fraternization between analyst and analysand. Our analysands are only all too ready to throw themselves into the arms of such an interpretational schema. They then make an effort to reinforce it by reporting some additional examples from their childhood history that come to weigh in as great confirmations and strengthen the analyst's assumption of being on the right track. The analysand basically acts as if he wished nothing more than to avoid the analytic process with the help of the weapons he draws from the armory of his past and thereby to resist the development of the transference wherever he can.

What remains is an unsatisfying feeling. I conclude this chapter without showing what the consistent application of the concept of sequentiality has contributed to clarifying what the analysand recounts. Everything for now remains in suspension. There are deeper reasons for this. I must ask for indulgence for not spelling them out here. For the analytic process never unfolds linearly. The consistent application of the recommended concepts does not lead further. For the moment, the enormous multiplicity of what may have been consequential in the pasts of our analysands, from birth through to the analysis, is too vast to grasp. In the analytic process, we as analysts are always the belated guests of our analysands.

Note

1   To be clear, these were not Morgenthaler's own views about this woman. Rather they are Morgenthaler's summary of the stereotypical – indeed misogynistic – interpretations set forth by the original analyst in this case.

Chapter 5

Identification

As a general rule, consciousness is characterized by reason. In the analytic process, the work of interpretation follows rational lines. It puts together meaningful, intelligible, and reasonable connections. Only then is there a chance that analyst and analysand will understand what is going on in the unconscious. Only then is insight possible.

The unconscious, however, is not rational. It does not follow the rules of thinking and of making connections that generate wellbeing. The unconscious is absurd.

The principle of consistently and imperturbably following sequentiality in the course of associations seems to combine the absurd with the reasonable. The absurd predominates. It is important to be aware of this so as to avoid prematurely building in rationalizing stopgap ideas, which is something we are inclined to do, because it is unpleasant to get stuck in the absurd.

I would like to bring back the example of the 28-year-old analysand who exhibited disruptions of his ability to work prior to the analytic sessions and apply the concept of sequentiality in the course of associations in the way that the theory of technique suggests. The principle, which comes from the technique of dream interpretation, is based on the premise that things that from the rational, secondary-process perspective just look like an additive string are, in fact, and however artificial it may seem, ordered in a sequence of causally dependent phenomena.

What is actually motivating me to propose such a nonsensical principle?

I answer: in this way, the unconscious happenings become visible in their primary-process nature.

What gives me the right to make what seems so nonsensical a claim?

I answer: the experience of psychoanalysis.

Does such an approach lead us forward?

Psychoanalysis never leads us forward. It usually leads to something entirely other than what we thought. With psychoanalysis one cannot make any form of progress. There are only transformations. In the analytic process things transform slowly and we encounter obstacles. But: obstacles are not annoying disruptions, for in them the unconscious motivations are also contained.

- Because the analysand was affected by disruptions of his ability to work, he was looking forward to coming to the analytic session . . .
- because he was glad to come to the analytic session, nothing came to his mind . . .
- because nothing came to his mind, he told the story of his friends . . .
- because he told the story of his friends, he developed the feeling that these friends were being inconsiderate toward him . . .

I go one step further, even, and follow this series into the past of the experiences made so far in this analysis:

- because the analysand was willing in the first place to enter analysis, he also accepted continuing this analysis so far . . .
- because he persisted in it, it was also possible to convey the insight to him that he takes a protective attitude toward the members of his family . . .
- because he was able to gain insight into this compulsion to which he is subject, disruptions of his ability to work arose before the analytic session . . .
- because these disruptions occurred, he felt anger rising . . .
- because he was angry, he reported in the analytic session on his inability to work and on his anger . . .
- because he reported on it, he was able to relax affectively, without conflictualizing the analytic relationship . . .
- because this relaxation set in, disruptions of his ability to work arose again before the next analytic session . . .
- because these disruptions arose again, he was looking forward to the analytic session with an almost longing expectation.

It is now becoming obvious, however, that the attention I am paying to the sequentiality in the course of associations is not helping to move things along. I am forced to introduce something new.

Is there a new concept of the theory of technique that offers itself at this point?

The analytic process, I said, is never linear. It is characterized by the fact that everything I communicate to the analysand in the interpretive process is the result of reciprocal relationships. These reciprocal relationships are determined on the one hand by the emotional movements and on the other by the contents of both the analysand's and the analyst's ideas. Looked at in isolation, the attention I pay to sequentiality in the course of associations leads at best to rationalizations and fallacies. The new concept I must introduce here is an abstraction, and with it the analytic process in its current state can no longer be understood from a linear perspective but only from a dialectical one.

This abstraction derives from a principle that psychoanalytic theory has considered to be significant since its earliest beginnings and that was introduced both in libido theory and in ego psychology to be able to depict processes in psychic development. It is grounded in an intrapsychic dynamic that is described by the term *identification*.

Identification is a psychological process through which a person takes on an aspect, a characteristic, or an attribute of another person, and in so doing changes. The change based on the model of another person can be complete or partial. The ego is built to a great extent out of such identifications.

Use of the term identification refers either to a process that is ongoing or to a state that has set in after a process has concluded. When I say *I identified with my father*, that means either that in the course of my psychic development, I have made attitudes, opinions, and character traits of my father's an integral part of my person, or it means that a part of my person has become like what I experienced certain attitudes or opinions of my father's to be, as I either consciously or unconsciously perceived them.

In these forms of identification, the one who identifies changes. That is why we speak of *autoplastic* identification. A second form of identification is characterized by ascribing to another person attributes or characteristics of one's own. In that case, the other person is completely or partially experienced and treated like oneself. In such circumstances, we speak of *alloplastic* identification, which is close to the mechanism of projection.

The difference between projection and identification lies in their contents. Projection designates everything that is experienced internally and attributed to another person or to the external world. I can say, for example, that I project my father's severe strictness on all authorities. In that case I ascribe to other persons an attribute of my father's that I experienced as severe strictness. Yet if I ascribe my own suspiciousness to my wife, I project my own image into the perception I have of my wife. I may then speak, instead of projection, of alloplastic identification because I am ascribing an attribute of my own person to another person.

Identification is used to designate very different processes, and I highlight here those aspects that are of particular consequence for the theory of technique. One of these aspects concerns identification as a form of relationship to the object. Identification is a preliminary stage of the love relationship.

The relationship starts, perhaps, with my turning to someone else because I recognize in him characteristics I have myself. Later, when the relationship deepens, the situation changes because I now love the other because he possesses characteristics I miss in myself but would like to have. The capacity for entering into and maintaining very specific identificatory relationships is developed early in childhood and makes an important contribution to ego formation.

Often when an object relationship ends, an identification with the lost object sets in. Freud wrote in "Mourning and Melancholia" that objects may possibly never be given up on but always leave their traces in the ego as identification.[1] Because the ego develops in its relationships with objects, we may say that the ego is built from the identifications with earlier love objects.

Yet all identificatory processes can also be described under the aspect of defense. In the frustration of libidinal needs and in response to every unbearable claim from a drive, an identification may be erected in the ego that temporarily silences the conflict between ambivalent strivings. The ambivalence that provokes the conflict emerges from the claims of the drives on the one hand and the demands of the superego on the other. These identifications as defense play a great role in the development of the analytic process. They often serve to deepen the analytic relationship and have, from a technical point of view, a progressive significance. Yet the defensive character of this identification is by no means always the first thing I highlight in the interpretive process. For what counts is that, in a given situation, an interpretation allows for an insight in the analysand into intrapsychic processes – and not that I now especially emphasize some complex conflict of ambivalence in the analytic relationship that might stand behind the identification.

Because, as a fundamental matter, my stance toward my analysand is such that I take him, with all his troubles, inclinations toward conflicted-ness, and symptoms, to be as healthy as possible and not as sick as possible, I also assume that he identifies with me when he gets involved in the analytic process. This identification results from the emotional resonance that accompanies the analysand's train of thought as well as everything I am telling him. The gradual deepening of the analytic relationship may be described as follows: the relationship initially begins with the analysand discovering in me properties he knows in himself; later, the relationship develops such that he recognizes properties in me that he misses in himself but would like to have. That is the result of the seduction, which plays so great a role in every analytic process. As I've already said: there is no analytic process in which the analysand doesn't try to seduce the analyst into being taken in by him and recognizing him, the analysand, as an especially love-worthy partner. Nor is there an analytic process in which the analyst does not seduce the analysand into getting involved in a deepening relationship with him, that is, into getting as well as keeping an emotional movement going. A rightly understood analytic assessment of the seduction thematic shows that ever more effective identifications progressively arise, which on the one hand accompany insight in the interpretive process and on the other contribute to the cathexes in the relationship between analysand and analyst remaining congruent rather than evolving in polar opposite ways.

That identifications always come about when a relationship is deepening in the course of analysis and that they precede insight in the interpretive process is a baseline concept of psychoanalytic technique. Every insight into any kind of behavior or into any connection – however inconspicuous or superficial such an insight might be – follows identifications that have already arisen before. This is also the means by which every analytic process, at the beginning of an analysis, is first set in motion.

The intrapsychic dynamic that is connected with the identificatory happenings is particularly apt for complementing the concept of sequentiality in the associative process. That is why, wherever the observation of sequentiality alone is not sufficient for understanding the connections resulting from the contents of the associations, I consider the analysand's possible identification with me.

I'd like to return to the example already cited and apply this new concept in conjunction with what is already known.

For reasons I don't want to go into here, let me suppose that prior to the two analytic sessions I described, the 28-year-old analysand I briefly presented has already gained an important insight thanks to an interpretation I gave him in the analysis. Through this insight, he understood that something is going on in him about which he previously knew nothing specific. The precondition for this insight also lies, among other things, in the analysand's identification with me, the analyst. This identification with the analyst effected the disruptions in his ability to work which the analysand had formed before the analytic session. For that reason, he got angry about the upcoming analytic session, in which he then spoke so freely and openly about his anger and his trouble working. I had ensured that the analysand's nonconflictual attitude would now not be transformed by some kind of intervention into a conflict in our relationship but that the relaxation and the conflict-free situation in the emotional domain of the relationship was maintained. Interpretive steps that might have suggested themselves, to promote an insight in some kind of direction, would merely have been expressions of a misunderstanding. If the analysand is able to keep the relationship with me conflict-free, then it is imperative that I not act as though I was compensating, as it were, for that absence by creating conflict myself. If I nonetheless did so, I would not only be restricting the autonomous functions of my partner in analysis in a way that would seriously compromise our relationship but I would be inhibiting the development of the analysis itself. The analysis only continues if something new can emerge – something that previously was not graspable.

I would like to try and show that in this situation with my analysand, a link was demonstrably missing that was important for recognizing the connections that were psychodynamically essential. The meaning of my detailed and seemingly complex reflections in this and the preceding chapter becomes clear only when I can make evident that we cannot here precipitously recognize connections that are not yet visible. I must wait until the things that are still confused clear up. That they are still confused has nothing to do with any lack of empathy or intuition on my part but rather with the fact that something decisive is still missing from what the analysand is offering that will lead to a clarification of the transference-resistance.

Why was it possible for the analysand, despite his anger and trouble working, to remain conflict-free during the session in which he recounted them?

He was able to remain conflict-free because in this phase of the transference, the analysand's inclination toward identification had developed unhindered. That is not always the case. Much more often, the analysand cannot initially identify with the analyst. In such cases, defense manifestations appear that are connected with early experiences in childhood and bring attitudes into the analytic relationship that appear as foreign objects and make the identification with the analyst more difficult. In my example, on the contrary, the identification with me was so strong that the effects of old defense mechanisms could not yet appear because the analysand did not want his good relationship with me disturbed.

From the point of view of technique, it is important to follow the material presented by the analysand pragmatically and not in some affective way to influence the analysand in a direction that could conjure up a disruption of the relationship.

Since in that situation, I did not act restrictively but respected the analysand's emotional readiness to maintain his identification despite all disruptive influences, this identification strengthened as a matter of course. On the day of the next analytic session, the disruption in the ability to work manifested yet more intensely. The analysand felt joy and an almost longing expectation directed at the session to come. This was an indication that he felt the identification with me and my function even more strongly than before. It was because the analysand had identified so intensely with me that nothing came to his mind. He felt an emptiness and finally told me the story about his friends and about the feeling of inconsiderateness. At this point, I did not offer some interpretation about the identification but rather noted what I have deduced so far:

> The inconsiderateness the analysand mentioned could not correspond to the unconscious impulse that became effective in the transference. I cannot, in any case, interpret it as a conflict in the transference as long as I do not even know yet in which direction this transference is developing.

How am I to interpret this situation to the analysand? I quite simply derived my interpretation from the material the analysand brought forward and contented myself with an observation that might be put as follows: "The events and feelings you associate with last night and which you just talked about cannot be the cause for your being even less able to work this morning than you were two days ago." The reason it cannot be the case is because what he talked about was conscious. It cannot be the case that something that plagues him as much as the disruption of his ability to work could be explained by something of which he is conscious.

In such a situation I can expect the analysand to engage the analyst's remarks. He cannot simply ignore them. He continues to identify with me. He feels prompted to engage with the connections more closely.

To preempt misunderstandings, let me emphasize that it is by no means mandatory to address the analysand in the way I have just suggested. One may proceed differently. One might say, for example: "The events you talk about cannot be the cause of what troubles you so." Or: "You laboriously brought in the story with your friends so you don't have to talk about something else that preoccupies you to a far greater extent."

The analyst should say what suits him. The only important thing is to show the analysand in some way that what really moves him cannot be what moved him the evening before – even as the story just told must contain the kernel of the unconscious motive for that which so bothers him in his experiencing.

In every case, the analysand will react to such a merely observing, situation-summing remark on the part of the analyst in some – definitely not haphazard – way.

What is the sense and the purpose of such a remark by the analyst?

My intent is to effect in the analysand what I tried to show in the example of the young man who believed me to be hard of hearing. The issue is to bring about a polar contrast in the conscious ideas of the analysand. He must be made aware that there is a polar opposition between what he is feeling and what he experiences in the reality of the analytic relationship. How the analyst proceeds in detail in order to achieve this is up to him.

At this point I would like to take the opportunity explicitly to articulate a dialectical concept of psychoanalytic technique that appears significant to me and that was already implied when I was setting priorities that I subsequently relativized (Chapter 3). It refers to the processes I associate with polar, opposingly oriented cathexes.

Polarizations arising from modalities of cathexes have a progressive character, one that promotes the analytic process, when they refer to intrapsychic cognitive processes that produce a disconcerting impression in the analysand because old, fixed ways of experiencing enter into an entirely different current relationship. They are of a detrimental character, one that inhibits the analytic process, on the other hand, when they arise in the relationship between analyst and analysand. That is because in that case old, fixed modes of experience easily enter the current analytic relationship in their original form and reactivate the inclinations toward conflictedness that have always already been the way they now manifest in the analytic process. Under such adverse circumstances, the analysand's and the analyst's neurotic modes of experiencing are reproduced in their relationship. Polar opposite attitudes arise toward the goals to be reached, and a more or less open combat situation easily arises, in which each partner seeks to convince the other of misunderstandings that no longer derive from contents capable of being consciously cognitively accessed but rather from affective dynamics.

When in the analytic situation I am confronted with a transference-resistance, what counts is that my analysand perceives the contrasts in which he can gain insights thanks to the way something emerges in his ideas that is irreconcilable with what he is feeling at this moment in this session of his analysis. He notices an inner contradiction. That is always the first step in the awareness of the unconscious. I do not provide any interpretation of the content of the transference-resistance before a perception of such a polar contrast has become palpable in the analysand's realm of experience. For this, the analysand needs time. Often, I have to try repeatedly to achieve this polarizing effect. If, emotionally, the relationship between me and my analysand is congruent, if, in other words, no false notes are struck in our relationship, if, in short, the relationship is not dishonest, the matter can be cleared up from one instant to the next.

Things are different, from the point of view of technique, when in the analytic situation I am confronted with a repression-resistance. Usually, a feeling of disconcertedness arises in the analysand such that he begins to perceive that he is repressing something. The gap in his thinking or feeling contains what is unconscious. When I then give him an interpretation, there must be a meaningful content ready to fill the gap.

In my example, the surprising turn came immediately after my interpretation that the events and feelings of the evening with the friends could not be the cause for the exacerbated inability to work. The analysand said: "The story with my friends certainly has nothing to do with my trouble working before our session, this morning."

The analysand spoke with a slightly contemptuous tone of voice, as if he sought to express that he considered it entirely absurd to establish a relationship between these two events at all. Then he continued:

> If there is anything specific that might be related to my trouble working, it would more likely be what happened to me this morning at the store. I sat in my office and tried to work. I made no headway. I felt an inhibition and an inner tension. Suddenly my colleague came into the room and said that he didn't have anything in particular to do right now and was going to stop by the restaurant to have a coffee. If the boss were to call for him, which certainly was not going to be the case, I should make up an excuse for him. Laughing and convinced nothing would happen, he left my office. He was hardly gone and a phone call came from the boss. My colleague was to come up and see him immediately. I was searching for an excuse and said my colleague had just gone to the restroom. I would tell him the moment he got back. Although I wasn't making any headway anyway, I was being disturbed now even more and had to run down with the files and look for my colleague at the restaurant to notify him. When I was back at my desk and wanted to continue working, I was gripped by anger. I thought my colleague ought to have to sit in his office just like me and not just run to the restaurant whenever he feels like it. I was particularly angry at him for also having distracted me from my work when I was having such great trouble concentrating.

This new episode from the analysand's current realm of experience decisively expanded my field of vision for deeper connections that I had not been able to recognize previously. Once more, I am following the two analytic rules I have to heed. On the one hand, I pay particular attention to the sequentiality of the associations and to a possible summation effect that might arise in me from the course of the things being recounted. On the other hand, I hold on to the second concept and remember that the analysand identifies with me.

As a result of this stance, it emerged that I told him the following:

> Quite evidently, you put yourself into a contradictory situation at the store this morning. First you told your boss your colleague was in the restroom to cover for him. Then you ran to the restaurant and quickly

notified him so he wouldn't get into trouble. As soon as you were back in your office, your attitude changed. You suddenly identified with your boss. In a pedagogical way, you want to reproach your colleague and get him to behave in such a way as to fulfill his duties.

With this interpretation, I was now positioned very closely – with my thesis about identification – to the material the analysand had brought forward.

The analysand reacted to these connections with understanding. He had to admit that the conclusions I laid out were already contained in everything he had reported. After this insight, he continued and said:

It really is a serious problem for me, because I am constantly afraid the boss could reproach me. I have often protected my colleague in just this way and every time I am afraid the boss might catch me when I put forward a white lie to cover for my colleague. I always imagine the boss suddenly coming to me and asking me uncomfortable questions.

I: "You're afraid the boss might reproach you."

Analysand: "Every time I meet the boss, I have the impression he will confront me about leaving the store early to come to you. It's absurd because I have so much overtime that nobody can reproach me."

I: "Your boss might also feel that you are being inconsiderate toward him and the interests of the business."

I am very close to the reproach he made to his friends the night before. This reproachful attitude evidently goes back to an identification with someone who might reproach him and of whom he is afraid.

Analysand: "Matters with my friends are basically such that I cook for them and take care of everything for them to feel at ease and to not reproach me. But it always ends up with them reproaching me all the more for spoiling the evening by doing so many things and doing the dishes, drying them, and trying to get everything back in order. They say that that is so very tiresome and arduous for everyone who has anything to do with me. Of course I then get angry at them and find them to be inconsiderate."

I: "So you are doing so many things because you're afraid you might be reproached. I suspect that today, too, during our session, you told the story of last night because you were afraid I might reproach you."

Analysand: "When I came to the session two days ago and was angry about the analysis, I expected you to yell at me and throw me out. I was surprised how friendly you were to me. When today, at the beginning of the session, I lay down and said to you how much I had been looking forward to coming to analysis, that came to my mind again. Then suddenly nothing came to my mind anymore."

I: "Nothing came to mind because you expected that it was now my turn to say something. You expected me to reproach you."

Analysand: "Because I know that you wish me to tell you something. That is why I made every effort to find something. Finally, I then reported on last night."

I want to investigate the identifications that appear in this phase of analysis more closely. The story with the work colleague whom the analysand had to go get from the restaurant points to an identification he has entered into with his boss. This means that, in this phase of the analysis, the analysand has become the way he has experienced and consciously perceived certain of his boss's opinions and attitudes. This form of identification now stands in contradiction to the analysand's anxiety that his boss could catch him leaving the store early to come to me for the analysis. The contradiction is connected to the fact that the analysand has identified with me as well. This form of identification is much more similar to the one he has entered into with his colleague whom he looks for at the restaurant and for whom he seeks to provide cover. The conflict of ambivalence that develops from these mutually contradictory modes of experiencing does not now, however, lead to a conflict in the transference but rather to a projection: the analysand transfers the boss's possible reproachful attitude to me, that is, he now expects the reproachful attitude from me. Then suddenly nothing comes to his mind anymore. There is a gap in associations that he perceives with disconcertedness. Because the identification with me is much stronger than that with his boss, he cannot maintain the projection. In the story with his friends, he once more becomes the one who wants to please everybody and who is being reproached in an inconsiderate way. He thereby expresses that he always wants to please me in the analysis but that I am just waiting for the moment when I can reproach him in an inconsiderate way. Such an absurd supposition that does not correspond to the analytic relationship in any way has made itself noticeable in the analysand's experiential domain as something disconcerting that now must be lifted into consciousness by interpretation, so that the connection with the unconscious drive-needs that have developed in the transference can be recognized and also so that the drive-impulses themselves can become conscious.

I: "You have identified with the ideas you ascribe to me, in your fantasies. In these fantasies, you experience me as someone who demands things from you the way your boss does. You are quite simply afraid I might shower you with reproaches the way you are always afraid your boss might."

From the point of view of technique, it is important now not to stop halfway but to finish the interpretive step that has been introduced. The criteria for a complete interpretation lie in considering and capturing all the stations encountered in tracing the sequentiality in the course of associations.

I: "The disruption in your ability to work that is so incomprehensible to you represents a disruption of my ability, fantasized by you – which you believe occurs when you are with me. You experience me as if I were inhibited and disrupted in doing what I ought to do. First you had that anger which you believed I had when you come here. Then you made the experience that I am not angry, and you identified with me. In the next session, today, you felt the joy you fantasize me to have when you come here. That is what caused the lapse of thoughts in you. With the notions about the story with your friends you showed how you experience as inconsiderate the people who turn to you. Here, in our relationship, you assume that I think you to be inconsiderate when you expect me to be glad when you come here. Just as you cannot bear that your friends expect you to be glad when they are with you, so you cannot bear your own feelings that demand of me to love you. To deny that, you perform in your own person how I would have to defend against you. I should become angry, disrupted, and inhibited in my analytic work and develop a defense against you. You do all of this only because you cannot bear the intensity of the feelings that move you here, in this analysis. You displace the defense that you can no longer put up yourself onto me."

After this interpretation, the analysand was able to see that the positive feelings he had developed in our relationship had become so very strong he could no longer bear them. In his unconscious fantasies, he had to task his analytic partner with tempering and rejecting these feelings. The insight into these connections triggered in the analysand a disconcerting feeling. On the one hand, he agreed, since everything contained in the interpretation seemed inexplicably already familiar to him. On the other hand, he revolted against it, since he was no longer able to harmonize his own feelings with the image he had of himself. In such a development in interpretive work, it is crucial to point out to the analysand that what is now going on within him is not haphazard but has precedents in his life story.

I: "It cannot be otherwise than that you have had such experiences in your life, probably already in your early childhood."

Thus I prompt the analysand to connect the peculiar fantasies that he has developed about his otherwise good and relaxed relationship with me, and which in no way agree with what he really feels, with memories from his life story.

With this example of an interpretive process that builds on the application of two important concepts of technique, I want to show that a methodological-technical procedure is necessary in order to recognize in certain situations that for understanding a transference-resistance something decisive is missing, something I cannot discover by my empathy alone. I might feel that something is off. It is difficult for me to grasp it, and the danger is that I might tend to supplement what is missing with stopgap notions, that in this way, unnoticeably and subtly, rationalizations and intellectualizations could slip into the interpretive process.

In my example, the methodological-technical approach helped me to limit myself to pointing out a contradiction and to refuse to give an actual interpretation. Because this sent the problem back to him, the analysand was prompted to rethink the connections that were bothering us both, and a currently pertinent experience came to his mind that showed connections that were new and surprising to me: the confrontation with his boss and his anxieties connected with that.

Only in working through this new episode did it become possible to understand and interpret the actual unconscious impulses that motivated the lapse in associations and the transference-resistance. In so doing, it turned out that the analysand could not bear the intensity of his positive feelings because drive-wishes in need of repression were connected with it.

The task of the analyst is above all to follow such processes with very close attention so as to avoid overlooking these kinds of developments, as they occur quite often. He is likely to overlook them, for example, when early on he thinks he recognizes resistances directed against the continuation of the analytic work or when he interprets aggressive impulses that he suspects are being projected onto him although their original target was one of the significant figures in the analysand's childhood. Such and similar fallacies then easily lead to reconstructive interpretations being offered much too early and in unuseful ways. These sorts of interpretations, concerning the relationship with the father or mother, are being connected with the role of the analyst in the transference-occurrences before the relationship has even become clear and deep enough for it to be possible to speak of such a meaning at all.

The instruments of technique – in my view, these are the concept of sequentiality in the course of associations and the concept of the analysand's propensity toward identification – put me in a position to organize and understand the analysand's messages, ways of reacting, and means of expression. However, it is also possible that I could continue this organizing and understanding in a continuous, that is to stay stepless, gradual descent, without recognizing the boundary at which all my understanding and interpreting almost imperceptibly slides into rationalizing. Here the great danger inherent in all technical concepts and their application becomes apparent. Analysts who consciously refrain from using technical aids advocate, often without saying so explicitly, the view that it is better to pull back from this danger from the very beginning. In so doing, however, they overlook that they are thereby also refraining from aiming, with their analysands, for an analytic process that goes beyond what alleged healthy common sense is able to guess by means of empathy and comparison with oneself.

As analysts, we must not try to circumvent the dangers that come with a methodological-technical procedure. Rather, it is necessary to move on two levels simultaneously. We must perceive the signals that indicate when and how the *quantitative* collection and organization of observational material can undergo a *qualitative* transformation in an emotional movement that concerns both the analysand and the analyst. In my example, the signal was my analysand's report about the confrontation with his boss and his illusory anxieties. The point had thereby been reached at which the collection and organization of observational material could and had to be transformed into a particular qualitative experience.

The two levels at which one moves in the psychoanalytic process are the level of the methodological-technical procedure on the one hand and the level of the dialectical interplay of dynamic intrapsychic processes on the other. The one can never be smoothly reconciled with the other. If one tries, a closed loop of rationalizations is created. Psychoanalytic technique only ever leads so far that the level of methodological procedure can be left and the level of dynamic interactive effects is attained. We must have no illusions: there is only this possibility, that of methodological-technical procedure, to be able to reach the level of dynamic interplay in the sense of the analytic process at all. Only when this detour is made is it possible to incorporate metapsychological knowledge into the work of interpretation.

I do not sit down with my analysand at a table set for us both where we could now enjoy together the meal we've ordered. But neither is it the case that at this table we're being served, instead of well-cooked dishes, nothing but trash, refuse, or pebbles. I am always the belated guest of my analysand, and I sit with him among half-empty bottles long after the meal has been served and eaten. No one has been sitting at the table like this before. It is a new experience for us both.

With this metaphor, I'm describing nothing other than the emotional content that so lastingly characterizes the analysis. In the analytic relationship, the emotional offer of the analyst always prompts an emotional echo on the part of the analysand. This emotional echo contains the leftovers and bears the traces of the guests who have convened, dined, gorged, raged, fasted, scorned, devoured, spat, stolen, and imbibed at the once freshly laid table of the child that the analysand once was. That all is now submerged in the past. As analyst, I am the belated guest who knows nothing and understands nothing of all that once took place there. I start with taking stock of what I can observe. But this stock-taking is accompanied by the analysand with ever more intense feelings. He enters into an emotional turbulence that I cannot understand and that I cannot empathize with. I do not understand him and cannot intuit empathically because I wasn't there when those things happened that the analysand, too, no longer knows of. I have in any case shown up late. I can only pause in my stock-taking and respect my partner's emotional turbulence.

If I do not recognize the boundary where it is no longer a matter of collecting further material but rather the moment at which I should restrict myself to what has been investigated so far in order meaningfully to connect it with the emotional substance, the emotional movement will inevitably subside or be absorbed, distorted, and warped, in the impenetrable tangle of the neurotic mode of experiencing. When that happens, every interpretation becomes a rationalization that is incorporated merely intellectually. Such rationalization severely constricts the development of any new emotional movement in the analytic relationship.

In an analytic process, the emotional engagement is always the first thing to emerge. Resistances, symptoms, aggressions, erotic wishes, and fears – in short, all of human beings' neurotic means of expression that get reactivated in an analysis – must, for reasons of principle, not be understood as what they are as long as they are solely serving to prevent or restrict an emotional response to the analyst's emotional offer. If an analysand only shows enough compliance that he respects the conditions of the analysis, Freud says, he cannot but respond – emotionally, I would add – to the developing relationship between himself and the analyst. This is so even if, one by one, he takes his weapons from the armory of the past to defend against the continuation of the treatment.

The weapons of the analysand must, in the process of interpretation, be neither challenged nor tackled as resistances until, in the deepening of the relationship, a transference has developed that shapes the emotional turmoil into the specific form that in the first place creates the conditions in which the metapsychological aids to the work of interpretation can be meaningfully applied.

Note

1 Morgenthaler here directly references Freud's essay on "Mourning and Melancholia," and indeed Freud there observes explicitly that the ego is "altered by identification" (1917a, p. 249). Yet no less relevant is Freud's later text, *The Ego and the Id*, where he suggests that identification with the parents "is apparently not in the first instance the consequence or outcome of an object-cathexis; it is a direct and immediate identification and takes place earlier than any object-cathexis" (1923, p. 31).

Chapter 6

The transference-resistance

What counts, at the most fundamental level, is that the analyst addresses his analysand as if the latter, in entering an interpersonal relationship, did not manifest neurotic symptoms, inhibitions, difficulties, and conflicts. The example I cited was meant to show that it is possible to combine certain reactions, ways of behaving, and emotions that move the analysand with the contents and the sequentiality of his associations in such a way that thanks to the appropriate interpretations, insights into deeper, unconscious connections emerge. As we saw, the emotional commitment the analysand brings to the analysis is not necessarily hindered by the transference-resistances directed against the work of analysis.

It was by design and not by chance that I started by introducing an analytic relationship in which the transference proceeds smoothly. This simply means that the work of analysis does not run counter to the analysand's drive-wishes or emotional offer. The work of interpretation develops in the direction the analysand is expecting. In my example of the young man who suffered from pronounced trouble working before the analytic sessions, the remarkable thing was that during the sessions, he did not suffer from anything that would have corresponded to these disruptions. Nor must I overhastily consider the moment of emptiness this patient felt when nothing came to his mind during the analytic session to be something that would mean he was resisting the analytic process.

The analyst's task – and this is what I wanted above all to show – consists first of all in supposing that his analysand takes a positive attitude toward the analyst's activity of understanding and interpretation, that is, that from the start he cooperates willingly, with interest, and with affirmative feelings. We are not entitled to suspect from the beginning something to be developing within the analysand that resists the goals of applying the analytic method.

This principle, however, must not be pursued one-sidedly because the person with whom I am getting involved by no means reacts one-sidedly. Yet for the concepts of the theory of technique, there is no way around the need for a pragmatic segmentation of the modes of reaction. This aspect, precisely, is what makes of the theory of technique a theory. I have tried to show that the existence of a transference-resistance can never be derived from the analysand's remarks alone. If the analysand reports, for example, that he was angry about the analytic session coming up, this is not sufficient for assuming any resistance against continuing the work of analysis. And even if the analysand makes derogatory remarks about the analyst or the course of the analysis, this does not yet mean that he is obstructing, or recoiling from, the analyst and the analysis.

As an analyst, I as a matter of principle assume an attitude as if the work of analysis was progressing well and not as if I constantly had to fight tendencies on the part of the analysand that put up obstacles on the analytic path.[1]

Although what is essential is to trigger in the analysand a movement that brings drive-wishes into the relationship, it cannot be avoided that there are constantly obstacles being placed in the way of this process. To delimit these inhibitions and disruptions, two aspects must be emphasized.

The first aspect concerns the ideational contents that fall prey to repression. Repression is connected with the drive-wishes that in childhood get connected with particular corresponding ideas and that, for certain reasons, are no longer accessible to consciousness. Repressed ideas cannot become conscious simply by the analysand saying everything that comes to his mind: resistances appear that are called repression-resistances. It usually is not particularly difficult to alleviate repression-resistances if within the framework of the analytic situation, an unhindered emotional exchange between analyst and analysand is possible.

The other aspect concerns drive-impulses. Disruptions easily arise when drive-wishes surface in the relationship with the analyst. If early on, for example, wishes for tenderness are directed at the analyst who is still a stranger, the analysand feels a painful embarrassment that by no means has to be neurotic. Possibly, the analysand is ashamed of having such sensations at all. Such modes of experiencing have an entirely different significance than that which I have called the emotional movement in the analytic process. They bring defensive elements into the transference that have not arisen from the drive-impulses – that is, from the id – but are formed by the ego. They are thus not derivatives of wishes and drive-impulses but rather are expressions of defense directed against these wishes and drive-impulses that arose already earlier in life, in childhood. Achievements of the ego that make their appearance in the form of defensive elements then show themselves as contents of the transference. In such a situation, therefore, the elements that characterize the transference are derivatives not of the id but of the ego. That can lead to the analyst's activity in the analytic process being felt and experienced as something hostile. Under these circumstances, we may speak of transference-resistances properly so called. The same can of course be said of negative attitudes.

A young girl suffering from severe anxiety attacks refuses to see a physician. Finally, she is persuaded by her mother and enters analysis. In the analytic sessions, she tells her life story in a calm, friendly, and collaborative way. She talks about her conflicts and about her sexual life, does not shy away from revealing intimate feelings and embarrassing experiences. But about her anxieties she does not say a word.[2]

If, now, the analyst very carefully interprets that he suspects that lying behind all of the patient's experiences there might be secret fears or anxieties, it may happen that the analysand immediately assumes a different attitude. She laughs at him and says, for example, that her mother probably influenced him and told untrue stories about her. She might also say that the analyst must certainly be particularly interested in anxiety attacks and now tries in this way to get the analysis going. If the analyst attempts in such a situation to connect the patient's remarks with her real problem, anxiety, he soon has to learn that everything he puts forward on the subject of what the analysand has reported is rejected with scornful remarks.

If in such a situation I as an analyst were to assume that my analysand's obvious defense were directed against unconscious wishes to be loved by me the way she as a child was loved by her father or had wished to be loved by him, a possible interpretation could be one that refers first of all to the repressed or denied anxieties. Such an interpretation might sound as follows: "You must react to everything I say to you with mocking remarks because you cannot admit to yourself and because you cannot show me that you have severe anxieties."

To this, the analysand might reply, say: "What you impute to me seems very peculiar to me. I believe you do not understand me at all."

It is obvious that in such situations, the analysis easily turns into a combative engagement that usually ends with the analyst coming to his wit's end.

Where is the mistake?

What's at issue here is not how to articulate an interpretation, but rather the connections that are eminently significant for a theory of technique.

In the face of such a transference-resistance there is no use in addressing the expressions of the id, of the drive-impulses, of the wishes, to stimulate the analysand to cooperate better, motivate him more strongly emotionally, the way it was the case for the 28-year-old man who was suffering from trouble working before the analytic sessions. What counts in the case of a transference-resistance is always to address the *ego* because scorn and derision are expressions of an ego activity and quite obviously represent a defense. From the point of view of technique, it is of the greatest significance to understand that the expressions of the transference-resistance in the first instance have nothing whatsoever to do with the relationship that has developed between analysand and analyst.

A transference-resistance is an expression of the analysand in the analytic situation that basically is absurd. It is absurd because it corresponds to a repetition compulsion and is brought into the relationship with the analyst as a foreign object. This foreign object is an ego activity that was deployed at some point in the analysand's life, usually already in childhood, against certain drive-wishes, and now has acquired transference-character. Now, instead of drive-wishes, it is those achievements of the ego that are being reactivated and offered in the analytic situation.

For, in the example of the young girl it turned out that she by no means reacted with scorn and derision only to the analyst's remarks. She reacted in just the same way to her own feelings, her wishes, and the stirrings of her self-esteem.

The background to these intrapsychic dynamics can be found in her life story. With pedagogical intentions, her father, long dead, had reprimanded the girl's impulses, and because reprimands alone did not lead to the submission he expected, he heaped scorn and derision on his little daughter.

In my earlier example of the young man who succeeded in obtaining an insight after identifying with the analyst, I sought to show that thanks to the identification, the analysand felt equal to the analyst and that this identification was responsible for the fact that even in periods during which transference-resistances surfaced and intensified, the analysand's attitude toward the work of interpretation was not essentially disrupted. He was able to experience the expression of his resistance as something that disconcerted him.

In the case of the young girl, who also developed a transference-resistance, we may not speak of an identification with the analyst. Yet that does not at all mean that no relationship had developed between the two partners in analysis. An identification with the analyst had so far not been possible for her because the relationship that had arisen had not yet been sufficient for it. The identification with the aggressor, with the father from childhood, turned out to be much stronger. The analysand had accordingly brought the image of the internalized, scornful, and deriding father into the analytic relationship. She was no longer herself but rather a substitute image of the frustration-inducing key character.

Such and similar phenomena characterize what we call transference-resistances. It is of course in no way the case that they develop only in the context of processes of identification. Yet identifications, especially those with frightening, frustrating figures from childhood, play an outsize role in developing such resistances.

It would be misguided to interpret this scorn and derision as an expression of aggressions against the analyst, or any depreciation of his person, or any sign of the analysand's unwillingness to continue coming to analysis. These expressions accordingly do not characterize the analytic relationship in any way. Instead, they are a foreign object, one that is built up from past ego-achievements and now becomes noticeable in the analytic relationship as something disconcerting. The disconcertion is perceived by the analyst. The analysand does not notice it. In her experience, this scorn-and-derision foreign object seems to be integrated as something that belongs to her. An interpretation would have to refer to the disconcerting matter which in the girl's experience has fallen prey to repression. Put differently, an interpretation would have to refer to the fact that this stereotypical scorn and derision neither accords with the image I have of my partner in the analysis nor can it accord with the image the girl has of herself. Such an interpretation might look something like this:

When you tell me about your life and tell me what you feel and think, I can understand everything you say very well because it entirely accords with the image I have received from you and also because I sense that it accords with the image you have of yourself. When then you suddenly scornfully laugh about your mother or find ridiculous everything you yourself feel or I say to you, it seems to me as if you are no longer yourself. Something peculiarly disconcerting that does not suit you at all then seems to push its way to the foreground. I believe you sense this and that it is something you also often suffer from a lot.

Such a transference-resistance has quite specific peculiarities that are characterized primarily by the affects that become manifest in the analysand. Affects are not to be equated with drives. Nor is the nature and direction of affects to be confused with drive-impulses. Drive-wishes aim at a wish fulfillment and are experienced pleasurably. Affects, by contrast, can be pleasurable or unpleasurable, depending on how they are expressed: hatred, love, shame, anger, revenge, etc. These affects, which also come out quite clearly in scorn and derision, are connected with an old ego-achievement. From the point of view of technique, this ego-achievement must under no circumstances be devalued – whether by assuming it to be an acting-out, or an infantile, undisciplined behavior, or an undifferentiated expression by an uneducated or ill-mannered person. These affects, which stem from an early ego activity, instead must be conceived of as what they are, namely the best the patient has to offer. That is why initially the analyst must fully respect these expressions.

To understand in what way they are the best the analysand has to offer, we must associate the affects he displays with the relationships that originally, usually in childhood, led to these affects. In doing so, we will recognize this ego-achievement to once have been erected to avoid a severe disturbance in psychic experiencing, to protect oneself against deep regressions, to preserve the ego in its functioning as a whole.

The connection between experience and affect that expresses itself in the course of the analysis as a transference-resistance is – in the case of such an identification – the characteristic fate of identificatory dynamics, which can now be uncovered. Only once this clarification is possible in the analytic process, and the connection between experience and affect can be interpreted, is it also possible for the analysand to now identify with the analyst. Then – in our example – the old, fixed identification with the frustrating father dissolves and a new identification forms, an identification with the person of the analyst who was able to give the analysand an insight into what was going on within her.

This is the path by which such a transference-resistance can be interpreted.

We can distinguish several steps in the formation of a transference-resistance. The simplest form roughly corresponds to what I presented in the example of the young girl reacting with scorn and derision.

A more complicated form of transference-resistances takes shape where fixed character attitudes influence the analytic relationship. In such cases, a patient would no longer respond with scorn and derision but take up a distanced attitude and position himself as if he were entirely uninvolved. This of course is but one example from a great variety of analogous phenomena. Common to all these forms of character resistances is the uniform tendency that finds its expression in such an attitude. This uniform tendency can show itself for example as contempt, or as arrogance, as authoritarian seeking-to-intimidate, as embarrassed avoidance of entering into physical and emotional contact with the partner, and many more of that kind.

I would like to take a closer look at one possibility. Let's say I assume the uniform tendency points toward contempt. Everything the patient expresses in his attitude then serves the unacknowledged contempt. Here I must not let myself be deceived and assume that the partner expresses other feelings in addition to his contempt, simply because I do not yet understand the inner connections. Of course other feelings can be discerned in such developments, for example tendencies that solicit tender attention or feelings of being moved. From the point of view of technique, however, it is important that I do not at first grant these attendant feelings the significance they may possibly have in later phases of the analysis. Here, too, it is decisive to give priority to the main tendency – in my example, contempt – because this trait is what determines the current transference-resistance. The tendency that lies at the basis of the character-resistance is unconscious. That is crucial, because the patient simply can never openly talk of feelings which are repressed and which, precisely because they are repressed, must find expression in this attitude which is so typical of him. Here, too, then, I must not let myself be deceived and assume the analysand could quite openly give voice to the contempt he expresses in his attitude. For if he did that, it would be a rationalization that would serve to distract me.

Under such psychic preconditions, to which also belong tendencies arising from the compulsion to confess, patients are usually afraid of the analysis. Often, they react much too intensely to the person of the analyst from the very beginning and in the analytic relationship get into an emotional turmoil that they cannot bear. The analyst must then ensure that the relationship relaxes. I never achieve that with silence. In such cases, I must address the patient. I can interpret later, and I am only ever allowed to remain silent when the patient's emotional situation permits such waiting and silence. Often it can take many hours or even weeks until the analysand allows me to listen to him and to remain silent.

The most difficult forms, by far, of transference-resistances show themselves where they begin to present no longer in expressions of affect or character attitudes but rather in actions proper. Patients then act out the transference-resistance. Ideas, affects, and attitudes are then expressed in heightened activity and pull the emotional turbulence the analysand has developed in his relationship with his analyst into the acting-out, which easily renders the analytic process chaotic.

I emphasize again that these excurses only describe the general laws that are significant in the development of transference-resistances. Of course the mechanisms of defense – denial, displacement, reaction formation, projection, ego restriction, etc. – can be deployed in developing and forming transference-resistances.

I will try to say what I find most crucial here once more in different terms.

When the development of a transference announces itself, the forces that deepen the relationship and lead the analysand to collaborate in the work of the analyst are id-impulses, drive-wishes, the intensification of urges. When a disturbance occurs, the analysand perceives it as something disconcerting. Generally, such disturbances have their source in the consequences of repressed ideas.

Yet if in the development of the transference there appear defensive processes that the analysand has not developed only in the analytic relationship but that he brings along from the past of his realm of experience, then we are dealing with ego-achievements. The disturbances that these carry into the analytic relationship make their appearance as transference-resistances. The analysand does not experience these ego-achievements as something disconcerting but rather as something belonging to him – something that suits him and is adequate to him. A transference-resistance is always an expression that the patient's ego experiences as something belonging to him. It is the analyst's task, in the interpretive process, to show the analysand what is inadequate, that is to say, to show him what about that which has been experienced in earlier life does not at all fit into the relationship between him and the analyst.

From the point of view of technique, and this is what is decisive, what counts in the case of transference-resistances is to arouse in the analysand a disconcerting feeling – whereas in the case of repression-resistances, what counts is alleviating the analysand's disconcerting feeling. These goals should always be met first before the analyst can even take on his role as an important transference-figure of childhood. To give, in the case of a transference-resistance – for instance in the case of the girl who reacted with scorn and derision – interpretations that aim at equating the role of the analyst with that of the frustrating father would be to mistake the unconscious tendency for reality. That would in turn mean nothing other than that the analyst, in his countertransference, is joining in the acting-out.

A transference-resistance initially feels congruent and not self-contradicting to an analysand. If that were not the case, it would not be a transference-resistance. That is a definition. Such a definition can provide an essential orientation in the work of interpretation. For if disconcerting feelings make their appearance in the transference-resistance, these signs may count as signals that insight is increasing and resistance diminishing. Simultaneously such signals are an indication that interpretations of meaning can be given.

If the patient says, for example, that he experiences an oddly disconcerting feeling during an analytic session, then the possibility already exists that the neurotic synthesis between behavior and emotionality can no longer be maintained, the synthesis that once, in an irresolvable situation of conflict, had to be, as it were, produced artificially. It would thus be overly hasty and premature to assume that the analysand has a negative sense of the analytic session solely because he associates his experience of disconcertedness with some displeasure that he has had on this day in anticipation of the analytic session.

I now notice increasingly, however, how my explication of the dynamic of resistances, as I have developed them here, begins to take a direction that could lead to misunderstandings. For one could get the impression that what counts in the analytic process of interpretation, in the case of a transference-resistance, is waiting for so long or prompting the analysand in a certain direction by means of "appropriate" interventions until his own feelings and behavior disconcert him. And in the case of a repression-resistance the inverse would then be recommended. There, the analysand would primarily experience disconcerting impulses that later, through insight into his unconscious stirrings, would become ego-syntonically congruent. Both of these conclusions would be too simplistic. The psychoanalytic theory of technique cannot progress in this way because its decisive features are not logic and causal thinking but rather its net of contradictions that, following along the primary-process-based connections, creates consciousness where previously a lack of understanding reigned.[3]

Notes

1 Again, this is a key moment in which Morgenthaler, emphatically, provides an alternative to Freud's image (1914) of a resistant analysand with whom the analyst must do battle.

2 As Morgenthaler will note in the chapter that follows this one, the discussion here of the case of the anxious but scornful girl is taken directly from Anna Freud's *The Ego and the Mechanisms of Defense* (1937, pp. 35–37). Morgenthaler expands on Anna Freud's discussion and uses the case to clarify further issues of identification first explicated in Chapter 5, and to illustrate larger points about how transference-resistances are experienced by the patient as ego-syntonic and are indeed the product of long-ago self-protective ego-achievements. These long-ago ego achievements should neither be devalued nor misunderstood by the analyst as aggression directed at him- or herself. Indeed, in his supervisions of analysts in training, Morgenthaler also described the dynamic discussed here as a "projective identification." In other words – as it will turn out – the girl in the case projectively identifies the analyst with the child she once was, devalued and scorned by her much-revered father. The dynamic in question is also a transference-resistance. As Morgenthaler will indicate, if an analyst can manage the tightrope task of freeing himself from the position of the devalued child while simultaneously conveying respect for the patient's long-ago ego-achievements, he can become a positive figure of identification for the analysand.

3 As with the loose ends left hanging at the conclusion of Chapter 2 (which will be taken up again in Chapter 8), this too is a deliberately discomfiting ending. Precisely the potentially ensuing confusion will be addressed in the next chapter.

Chapter 7

The dynamic of contradictions in the interpretive process

Mechanisms of defense do not have the same significance in the analytic process as they do in metapsychology. For the psychoanalytic theory of technique, everything connected with defense is shot through with contradictions. The contradictions that show themselves are welcome. They are a component of the analytic process.

For metapsychology, contradictions are disruptive. They get eliminated by the introduction of different points of view under which one and the same process in the psychic domain is investigated and described theoretically. From a metapsychological point of view, defense can be understood sometimes as an integrating component of healthy ego functions, at other times as an expression of psychopathological occurrences. The explanation for this is simple. With defensive maneuvers, the ego protects itself from overwhelming influences from the sphere of the drives and from the environment. In psychopathological developments, by contrast, repressed drive-impulses, for example, which in and of themselves do not represent any danger for the ego, are treated as if they were such dangers. That is what produces a neurosis.

One may describe matters in this way if one chooses an economic point of view and also considers genetic aspects.[1] In other cases, however, this way of looking at the matter does not suffice. Especially when quite complex disorders are at issue, contradictions can no longer be resolved by looking at individual phenomena from different perspectives. A synthesis cannot succeed. An example here could be the developments of severe psychic defects of the kind clinically described in the case of narcissistic neuroses. In this instance, unresolvable controversies arise, among the most prominent researchers, about how to evaluate the function of defensive processes.

On the one hand, there are those who say that the visible symptom formations are expressions of pathological defensive processes. These researchers always speak of defensive processes whenever feelings of care and tender impulses in interpersonal relationships are blocked; or when adaptation to the partner's needs is lacking or insufficiently developed; or when a particularly remarkable lack of understanding of what is going on within oneself is manifest.

On the other hand, there are those who say that having a capacity for defense at all requires an internal organization in the ego. According to them, symptoms appear so dramatically in developments of severe defects precisely because the entire defense has collapsed or was so poorly developed that the defense organization needs first to be built up in the analytic process so that a better-functioning ego can emerge with which it would be possible to work analytically.

The psychoanalytic theory of technique orients itself in accordance with other perspectives. It does not foster understanding but formulates concepts – concepts with whose help something can be effected that only then leads to understanding.

For decades, there has been a basic technical rule that directs analysts always first to work through the patient's mode of behaving, the transference-resistances, before giving any interpretations of meaning. By interpretations of meaning, we mean reconstructive interpretations that call attention to connections with historical experiences in the life story. With the example of the scorn-and-derision girl – taken from Anna Freud's book on the mechanisms of defense – I pointed out that the scornful behavior goes back to an identification with the strict father who once frustrated his little daughter with scorn and derision: the young girl identified with the aggressor and has since been treating her own feelings with scorn and derision. One could now say that she heaped scorn and derision on the analyst the way she herself had found her father heaping scorn and derision on her. Identified with the father of her childhood, she took on the role of this father in the transference and thereby developed a transference-resistance that made her experience the analyst the way the father had experienced his little daughter. If we sought to follow the basic technical rule just mentioned, we would have to work through the transference-resistance in such a way that the connections become clear. Only then would interpretations of meaning be appropriate.

I ask: is revealing the identification with the father stemming from childhood an interpretation of behavior or an interpretation of meaning?

Perhaps I could answer this question by saying that working through the transference-resistance contains an interpretation of meaning. Yet although this statement does not express anything that is incorrect, the question is not being answered clearly. This is so because in evaluating the dynamics of interpretive processes, contradictions appear whenever connections with the historical experiences in the life story are relevant. There are those who say that uncovering historically created connections in the analysand's life story is primarily responsible for something unconscious becoming conscious and thereby for changes in the analysand's experiential domain to occur that alleviate the existing neurosis. There are others who say that the decisive changes in the experiential domain on the contrary have to do with developments in the transference and the corresponding interpretations of the transference-resistances; the historical connections within the life story here serve to shed light on the dynamic background that makes a particular development of the transference understandable in the first place. And there are others again who say that there is no contradiction between these conceptions because the one is evidently related to the other. The analytic attitude, they say, demands that all these aspects are constantly taken into consideration and that, in accordance with whatever conditions emerge, now the reconstructions of historical modes of experience, then again the transference-reactions connected with these are to be interpreted. Essential in any case would be the so-called timing, that is, to give the right interpretation at the right point in time.

But how am I to know what's right? And if I know what's right, how can I then know when the right moment has come to communicate this right interpretation to the analysand? The answer to such questions is often vague. When I was still young, an analyst I admired once explained to me that it was a matter of acquiring experience – that with time one could sense the right moment. Supervision, he said, would help the inexperienced beginner to, in due time, learn the "timing." Another analyst, who was listening to our conversation, added, to the contrary, that what counted was talent. Those sufficiently talented could simply do it.

Much of this may be correct, but such a conception is blurry. The theory of technique should be able to formulate concepts that make it possible to grasp what seems to be ungraspable here. The process of interpretation should acquire an ideational content that allows me to understand it appropriately and to apply the necessary technical means.

In my view, the ideational content that must be concealed in all these at times inconsistent and vague conceptions puts the focus on the inner contradiction that exists between what is conscious and what is unconscious.

The unconscious is not conscious, but it expresses itself in everything that is conscious. The conscious does not know the unconscious, but it is codetermined by it. We can derive something unconscious from what is conscious, even if that which is conscious is precisely that which does not have access to the unconscious. If you listen to this naively, the contradiction is apparent.

In psychoanalytic technique, I look at things naively.

I ask: what kind of concept can I now derive from all this?

The interpretation of a connection between a specific affective content and a historical happening or a certain realm of experiencing from the past, like any interpretation, does have a meaning. But it is not a reconstructive interpretation of meaning.[2] In the interpretive process, the connection of the affective expression with the historical experiencing is circled, as it were, for so long until an interpretation hits upon the connection. That can often take weeks. If only I follow the principle of closing in on the connection between affect and ideational content in ever tighter circles persistently enough, it cannot be otherwise than that the affective connection suddenly dissolves thanks to one of the many interpretive attempts I make. The affect thus liberated now communicates itself to the ego and effects on the part of the ego a more drive-friendly attitude toward the unconscious impulses. This new manner of the ego becomes visible in the transference. The transference acquires a new coloring although its structure does not change. This effect in the transference process is unmistakable. If it does not occur, the interpretation was wrong. If the effect does occur in the transference process, the precedent interpretation was correct. In the work of analysis, I take such verifications seriously. I depend on them. For otherwise, there is nothing to signal to me that my interpretation was not just an expression of my own fantasy.

If it has come so far that my interpretation has hit upon the core point of the connection between the affect and the old idea from the past experiential realm and that a new coloring of the transference furnishes proof for it, then I know that I have given the right interpretation at the right time. I can never predict the "timing" in advance. Nor do I want to find myself in the position of illusorily interpreting my analytic labor as if it were even possible for me to foresee or to predict in advance what would be the right interpretation in the right moment.

Now the question poses itself how a reconstructive interpretation of meaning differs from the interpretive process just described. To really answer this question, I would like to try, in a short summary, to give a new turn to my way of looking at matters: I speak of a transference-resistance as long as a pathogenic connection continues to exist between an expression of affect and this – and no other – aspect of the realm of experience. In most cases, this realm of experience lies in the past, in the analysand's childhood. The interpretation of the connection of the affective content with the fixed idea that dissolves the transference-resistance and transforms it into a new coloring of the transference effects the continuation and deepening of the analytic process. This interpretation has a progressive character.

The reconstructive interpretation of meaning, by contrast, is fundamentally of a stabilizing character. I give reconstructive interpretations of meaning only in a de-stressed phase, a phase of relaxation in the emotional process of the transference. For in this de-stressed, relaxed phase, memory-material offers itself that fits the new emotional coloring, the rearticulation in the transferential happenings. These memories fit with the pattern of the entire realm of experiencing of the past life. The insights collected so far and the analyst's understanding of that which fate has sedimented in the analysand out of the relationships with the major figures of childhood determine the priority now given to all those memories and associations that, linking up to form a circle, result in a reconstructive interpretation of meaning. The analysand thus obtains a deep insight into the connections within his realm of experience, and this insight has the purpose of stabilizing what the analytic process has achieved thus far. Such stabilizers are important so that the analytic process can continue. Phases in which what has been achieved so far – that is, a bit of transformation in the dynamic sense – can be stabilized, are usually introduced by the patient with recapitulative associations and reactions. These must not be confused with affective connections. Recapitulative series of associations and reactions generally go hand in hand with a relaxed emotional movement in the analytic relationship, while affect fixations that are connected with specific memory traces are in most cases accompanied by tensions in the analytic relationship.

Progressive interpretations – interpretations that advance and deepen the analytic process – effect changes in the ego, because progressively acting interpretations are directed at changes in the affective economy. They have an economic character: they refer to patterns of cathexis that exert decisive influence on the psychic equilibrium.

Stabilizing interpretations have the purpose of extricating processes closely tied in with the reorientation of certain modalities of cathexis from the current association with the analytic relationship and of putting them in connection with drive-impulses, that is, in connection with the id. The stabilizing character of these reconstructive interpretations of meaning lies in the way in which the transformations that have emerged in the analytic process can, without conflictedness, be extended to other experiential domains outside the analytic relationship.

The rearticulations of tendencies toward conflictedeness within the ego acquire a connection to reality in the analysand's experiential domain that goes beyond the experiences in the analytic relationship. The analysand's new experiences are the experiences of his ego of having succeeded in an at least partial reconciliation with his id. The influence that such processes have on self-esteem and on the autonomous functions, on the flexibility and the elasticity that is acquired in the assessment of one's own possibilities and limitations, can be seen and felt everywhere in the subsequent course of the analysis. If the analytic process continues, the transference is restructured and takes on new forms that indicate that in the course of these transformations a new kind of relationship between analysand and analyst develops that corresponds to a different model from among the great figures of childhood than was the case in the earlier phase of the analytic process.

What becomes significant for me at this point are the insights of metapsychology into the transferences that emerge on the model of the relationship in early childhood with the father, the mother, one of the siblings, or another important figure of the life story. These insights facilitate my orientation in the manifestations of the repetition compulsion I can anticipate, and they are helpful and valuable for the adjusted stance of the analyst in the phase of analysis that now follows.

The psychoanalytic theory of technique builds its theses on the vital relationship of the two partners in the analytic process. In all its assertions, however, it makes use of metapsychology. It cannot forego the insights that metapsychology provides. Metapsychology, with all its at their basis unchangeable, inflexible laws, states that of which human psychic life consists. This is how it's always been, this is how it goes on, as if nothing ever changes. Of course the forms change, and other people have the same experiences in all the diversity of their manifold possibilities. There is something conservative about metapsychology. But that is the case only if we think of it as an ideology. For as a precondition of psychoanalytic technique, metapsychology is an instrument. And instruments are good instruments if – like tools used to take mechanical pieces apart and put them back together again – they are inflexible and silent. Often the oldest and most conservative tools are the most useful.

Notes

1 When Morgenthaler refers to "genetic aspects," he means genetic not in the sense of anything related to genes, but rather in the sense that one is asking after the *sources* or *causes* of a phenomenon; another definition of "genetic" here would thus be "etiological." When Morgenthaler refers to an "economic point of view," he means "economic" in Freud's sense of a distribution of energy. For instance, in the "Introductory Lectures to Psychoanalysis," Freud explains: "In order to appreciate the full significance of the difference which I have pointed out between the two groups of instincts, we shall have to go back a long way and introduce one of those considerations which deserve to be described as economic. . . . It seems as though our total mental activity is directed towards achieving pleasure and avoiding unpleasure – that it is automatically regulated by the pleasure principle. . . . An examination of the most intense pleasure which is accessible to human beings, the pleasure of accomplishing the sexual act, leaves little doubt on this point. Since in such processes related to pleasure it is a question of what happens to quantities of mental excitation or energy, we call considerations of this kind economic." Moreover: "It is immediately obvious that the sexual instincts, from beginning to end of their development, work towards obtaining pleasure; they retain their original function unaltered. The other instincts, the ego-instincts, have the same aim to start with. But under the influence of the instructress Necessity, they soon learn to replace the pleasure principle by a modification of it. For them the task of avoiding unpleasure turns out to be almost as important as that of obtaining pleasure. . . . An ego thus educated has become 'reasonable'; it no longer lets itself be governed by the pleasure principle, but obeys the reality principle, which also at bottom seeks to obtain pleasure, but pleasure which is assured through taking account of reality, even though it is pleasure postponed and diminished" (1917b, pp. 356–357).
2 Morgenthaler's use of the terms "reconstructive interpretation" or "reconstructive interpretation of meaning" (*rekonstruktive Deutung* or *rekonstruktive Sinndeutung*) will become clear in Chapter 9, where the phenomenon is discussed extensively.

Chapter 8

The working-through of a transference-resistance

The attempt to organize psychoanalytic technique in the sense of a theory, into a uniform and summary account, fails constantly because the path taken does not lead anywhere. Detours allow us to go back to the starting point. That is what I would like to do now, taking up the first detailed example that at the beginning served to show that not everything that develops from the analyst's well-meaning care leads to an analytic process in the analysand.

At issue is the analytic treatment of a man who for 180 sessions maintained a distant attitude toward the analyst. Every remark by the analyst, for example with respect to the possibility that the analysand had left something unsaid, was answered with irritation. The patient then emphatically insisted that he was communicating everything that came to his mind.

I reported on a particular session where the patient had recounted a dream in which he had a discussion with a woman about the Latin word *agricola*. The dreamer had added that the woman could have been the analyst. The dreamed discussion was concerned with whether the dative or the accusative of the word was to be debated. The dreamer preferred the accusative, his dreamed female partner the dative. From this dream, the analysand woke up with an ejaculation. When the analyst wanted to say something in response to the remarks of the analysand, the latter cut him off and reported on an experience from the day before – a Sunday. He had visited a childhood friend and experienced a great disappointment because he no longer managed to really connect with his friend.

I tried to show that in this analytic relationship, a confusion in the transference had emerged. I would now like to discuss this confusion in more detail and begin by noting that in the analysis, a transference-resistance had developed that led to a combative situation between analysand and analyst. It was evidently not possible for the analyst effectively to confront this transference-resistance. We may also add that in this transference-resistance, fixed character-attitudes played a large role such that matters were not nearly as clear as they had been in the case of the young girl expressing derision and scorn. The confusion in the transference was in the case of the *agricola* dreamer the result of a transference-resistance that had become chronic, encrusted. It had blocked the analytic process for a very long time.

The distanced behavior of the analysand existed from the beginning of the analysis. In such a situation, one cannot expect this attitude to change in a brief time. Nor was it certain that the distance the patient expressed in his relationship with the analyst was from the start a transference-resistance. Possibly, it became such only in the course of time. One could take the view that precisely this attitude of the patient belonged to the transference. Because the analyst should not reject the analysand's offer of transference, he must accept the stiff, distanced attitude.

Of course this attitude belongs to the transference, but I must point out the possibility of a misunderstanding here. Every transference-resistance belongs to the transference. The transference-resistance is an expression of a compulsion to repeat that concerns specific ego-achievements and that surfaces in the much more general process of repetition that I conceive of as emotional repetition, and indeed it does so in the interest of the analytic process. The theory of technique always constructs its concepts in such a way that their application leads to a promotion of the analytic process.

One can of course disagree and say that it is just particularly interesting and instructive when old ego-achievements manifest in the transference.

Such ego-achievements can indeed be stimulating. This would be the case, for example, when I am invited somewhere with friends and acquaintances. I might meet a musician there, a banking specialist, and a mathematician. We discuss with each other a controversial theater piece. Here and there, in the reciprocal relationships, reactions occur that do not fit with the current situation at all. Old ego-achievements are suddenly reactivated by emotions in one person or another. The banking specialist with his cigar burns a hole in a lady's billowing dress, the musician pours a glass of champagne on the carpet, and on our way home, I'm yelling at my wife.[1] All these are things I could work through analytically. Perhaps they are very interesting. But for an analytic process, they are fundamentally uninteresting. This is because the development of the relationship, its deepening, and the direction it takes cannot be measured by the ego-achievements. I cannot take the ego-achievements as my guide to come across what is important. Instead, I turn to the transference from the vantage of the emotional movement and try to understand and mobilize it in this sense. That is the royal road of analysis. The point is *not* that the analysand should simply adapt to the ego-achievements, attitudes, and convictions of the analyst. If that were to happen, a compromise would have been produced in the analytic relationship, one that acts like a symptom.

An example for such a compromise would be an agreement between analyst and analysand that the latter write down all his dreams and give them to the analyst to study. Another example would be the analyst's recommendation that a perpetually silent analysand should start every session by presenting the thoughts he had after waking up in the morning.

Such instructions restrict the analysis. One operates then with both conscious and unconscious ego-achievements. The analytic process, by contrast, strives for something else. It operates with the emotional movement – with forces, that is, that maintain the self-esteem and the coherence of the image the person has of himself.

The example I mentioned presents a transference-resistance. This transference-resistance brings certain of the analysand's ego-achievements into the analytic relationship in a way that disrupts the emotional movement of which this relationship consists.

Something alien has thus crept into the analytic relationship. That which is alien is an old defense that the analysand has carried within him for a long time already and which he always reactivates whenever he enters into a relationship. These ego-achievements express themselves in his distanced manner, in intellectualizing, and in anticipatory reactions of disappointment. The entire mode of reaction does not fit at all with the emotional investment the analysand displays in the relationship with the analyst, for he has been coming to analysis persistently and regularly four times a week for more than a year.

We could say that behind this defense, there must lie wishes he probably voiced in childhood and that were rejected and refused. He now brings into the analysis not his wishes but rather his defense against them.

The analyst joins in the acting-out of the transference-resistance. He behaves exactly as if what the analysand is offering was the expression of id-wishes, parts of drive-needs and drive-tensions.

Shared acting-out in the transference-resistance means assuming, suspecting, thinking, interpreting that something has id character when actually it is an ego function.

This circumstance marks the essential point at which the analytic process was blocked. The constant back and forth in the analyst's attitude toward what the analysand presented of the id and what he presented of the ego brought on the confusion. What came from the id and promoted the analytic process disappeared from view because what came from the ego overshadowed the entire relationship. What came from the ego was understood as what fit the analysand; simultaneously, it was responsible for the analyst's activity being experienced as hostile.

From these foundational technical principles, we can derive the dynamics of the transference-resistance and of this analysand's entire defensive psychology.

As an analyst, I need not reproach myself if I confuse id activities with ego-achievements because in our behavior, each of us finds himself time and again in situations where we confuse our own ego-achievements with activities of the id. Precisely because all people and also all analysts have this propensity, it is particularly important to understand these matters. The better we understand them, the better we can monitor and structure the interpretive process.

In my example, the analysand's ego-activities, which the analyst (mis) conceived of as impulses from the id, were determined by emotional preconditions entirely different from those that existed in the actual analytic relationship. The fact that in the analytic relationship everything got repeated in exactly the way it had once been in childhood meant that what came about was not an analysis but an intensification of the symptomatology.

It is very well possible to treat patients psychotherapeutically this way. There are widespread forms of psychotherapy that conduct the treatment in such a manner that the patients' symptom formations are mobilized in a way that they finally fall victim to repression. Thanks to such a procedure, the patient can feel subjectively better, even if there appear new symptoms which, however, from a social point of view seem less bothersome than the earlier symptoms. Such therapies serve above all the interests of the dominant societal morality. Many forms of short-term and group therapy easily lead to developments in this direction.

Psychoanalysis takes different paths. Genuine analysis is indivisible and cannot be replaced by other procedures. In the analytic process, the key is to treat those ego-components that appear in the analysand as a transference-resistance in such a way that the affect-repressions or affect-fixations resolve and that the energy that lies in them – as aggression or libido or whatever else – joins the transference-offer in the emotional domain. Then the analytic process can continue.

In my example, how did the analysand react to the attitude of his analyst who had (mis)understood the ego-achievements from long-ago childhood days as an expression of id impulses?

To answer this question, I must first sort out and clarify how the transference is to be understood. In other words: what exactly was the emotional offer this man brought to the relationship with the analyst?

Undoubtedly, the patient's emotional offer was extremely strong. When I say of a transference that it has been positive or negative, I am already talking about the coloring of the emotions, and this coloring results from the energy of the affects. Positive or negative feelings already have something to do with the ego-reactions that surfaced so long ago, in childhood, when the wishes associated with the emotions had been frustrated.

The investment of this man who had always expressed himself and behaved in a distanced way was great, for he persistently held on to his analysis and constantly struggled with the analyst. That does not mean, incidentally, that another analysand, one who repeatedly does not come to his sessions and, during sessions, seems to be uninvolved or uninterested but constantly complains about how badly he is doing, does not display any or only little emotional involvement. Matters are never this simple and linear.

The patient in my example displayed a massive transference-resistance. The analyst joined in the acting-out. This behavior of the analyst disrupted the analysand in what he was able to offer emotionally – in a serious way. The analysand now did something. I want to express this with a parable, so as to point out the unconscious tendency in effect here: the analysand as it were takes the uncomprehending analyst by the hand and almost seeks to guide him, the way one guides a blind man, in order for the analyst finally to do what he must do. Analysands are under an emotional pressure – the pressure of the transference they have formed – and this prompts them to do everything and anything so that the analytic process will progress.[2]

When an analysand shows this much readiness to pursue the conditions of the analysis, it has basically already happened: the analytic process must get going, even if – as Freud said – the analysand now piece by piece draws from the armory of the past the weapons to inhibit and block the analytic process.

In these unfolding events, the greatest disappointments always arise if the analytic process exhausts itself and fades out because of the way not only the analysand but the analyst, too, draws his weapons from the armory from his past to resist, unconsciously of course, the continuation of his patient's analysis.

It is a concept of the theory of technique that the analysand's expressions should, as a matter of principle, be comprehended along the lines of the conditions just described. That means: if an analysand is ready to come to analysis, and if he comes regularly, he has in every case claimed the right to have a tendency acknowledged – and be that tendency ever so much concealed and unrecognizable – to, as it were, take his partner by the hand and make him his analyst. If I as the analyst, because of my own conflictualness or for other reasons, cannot live up to this demand of my analysand's, I am still left with the curiosity to find out how my analysand will proceed to achieve his goal nonetheless.

How can we recognize this unconscious tendency in the analysand of my example?

When I heed the sequentiality in the course of associations, the question arises why the analysand in the session described first recounted the dream, then the ejaculation, and then the experience with his childhood friend the day before.

This sequentiality is linked with the expectation of disappointment. In 180 sessions, this very intelligent man had already gained a lot of experience with his analytic partner. He expected with certainty that the analyst would respond to the communication of the disappointment-reaction to the childhood friend with the interpretation that he, the analysand, was not disappointed in his childhood friend but in him, the analyst.

We should never underestimate analysands. They know much more than we suppose, and they often know their analyst better than the analyst understands them. The analysand rightly feared that his analyst would give the same interpretation he had already given so often. That was the reason why the analysand on Monday did not want to begin by talking about his experience with the friend. As preparation, he brought in a dream. In this dream, a discussion about the declinations of the word *agricola* played a central role. In the manifest content, the analysand advocated for the accusative, that is, for accusation (because of the acoustic association with *accuser*).

Was this a sign of the dreamer's wish to accuse? No, certainly not, for what was expressed in so explicit a manner in the manifest dream was capable of becoming conscious and thus could not represent the latent, unconscious content. This dream had nothing to do with an accusation.

From the point of view of technique, another aspect is important. The analysand had to recount the dream and report the ejaculation that had awoken him from the dream so that what came from the id could be accommodated in the dream and the ejaculation *before* he recounted the experience from Sunday.

When I imagine what was going on inside this man on Sunday, I may assume that his disappointment in his friend left an impression on him and he was resolved to recount this experience in his analytic session on Monday. Having had this idea, he could also anticipate that the analyst would point out to him that he, the analysand, was disappointed in him, the analyst. The analysand, preoccupied with the expected interpretation, was fully aware that he was indeed constantly disappointed in his analyst. He remembered that he had been reproaching him for months and told himself that the analyst had nonetheless always kept the upper hand. That is how the preceding session I recounted had ended.

What is decisive in all these events is that the analysand was disappointed in his analyst because he always said the same things and was unable to recognize his real feelings of caring. This made him in part sad, in part angry. He had wanted to confront his analyst combatively. In expectation of the Monday session, something in him said: no. That was unconscious. On Sunday, he fell asleep with a preconscious tendency to want to meet the difficulties in the analysis effectively. This tendency extended the dream with a discussion about a linguistic question. The analyst became the woman and the conflict presented itself in a debate centering on dative and accusative. From that, the dreamer awoke with an ejaculation.

With the dream and the ejaculation, he showed up for the Monday session. With these symbols, he placed the emotional content of his unpronounceable feelings in the hands of the analyst. Only then he did he tell his story. When the analyst now spoke of satisfaction and triumph, the analysand answered in the language of his emotionality as if he were saying: "But do keep quiet, everything you say is all wrong." When the analyst spoke about him possibly being disappointed in him, the emotional language answered again in the same way.

Dream and ejaculation had inserted themselves between the Sunday experience and the analytic session because the patient keenly sensed that he could not bring in the emotional movement associated with this Sunday experience because he knew that the analyst would only ever interpret that he, the analysand, wanted to reproach him.

What lay in dream and ejaculation was the preparation of the resolution of the transference-resistance. And what has to be stressed here especially is that it was the *patient* who took the first step, not the analyst.

It was the unconscious ego-components that began presenting the transference-resistance in this and no other possible sequence of things – in order thereby to defuse it.

It was the unconscious ego-components that entered into action, for this process was certainly not conscious. It was ego-components and not id activities that became effective, for what counts is how these phenomena are being dealt with. The analysand, after all, could have forgotten the dream and the ejaculation and during the analytic session simply reported on something inconsequential, something that would not have allowed for recognizing the emotion. Instead, they appeared so strongly that they would have been impossible to overlook.

In the sequentiality of the connections being associated, the recounting of the dream, the reporting of the pollution, the excessive reaction of wanting to keep reporting no matter what without letting the analyst get a word in edgewise, I recognize the analysand's unconscious ego-activities that, steered by id components, attempted to give the decisive unconscious needs a form that could no longer be denied in the analytic relationship.

It is interesting to observe what the analyst answered in this situation. His answer was guided by unconscious impulses that exacerbated rather than alleviated the polar opposition in the modalities of cathexis in the analytic relationship. The analyst intensified the resistance by mobilizing a combat situation.

These reflections, which can be derived from a consistent application of the concepts of technique, could show the analyst what, precisely, would have to happen next in the interpretive process at the instant when he himself, influenced by his own unconscious conflictual impulses, risks succumbing to a tendency that runs counter to the analysis.

It is not, at this point, about formulating a recipe for an interpretation. Each of us would proceed interpretively in the way that befits us. What counts here is only the principle – one that can be contained in innumerable possible interpretations. I can indicate the outlines of this principle by saying that the analyst must, in every case, accept what the analysand with his manner of presentation is aiming for. For me personally, the most appropriate way of formulating the interpretation to him would be something like this:

> Today, you first recounted the dream, then spoke of the ejaculation that woke you up, before you were able to report the disappointment in your friend. You've chosen this succession in order to prevent me from intervening and telling you that basically you are disappointed in me, your analyst, for that is not the case at all. In the dream, you represented the argument with the woman because you very much feared there would be another argument with me.

I would like to stress once more that what counts is not which words are chosen for which interpretation. The only thing that counts is making the insight possible for the analysand that what he is bringing is not in the service of any resistance. Then he can understand that in the actual relationship with the analyst, he is constantly letting himself be determined by the ego-achievements of his past and that it is this propensity, precisely, that disrupts his relationship.

In my example, the analysand began to reflect on and relativize his impulsive reactions. That became apparent when he said: "Actually, it isn't at all true that I was as disappointed in my friend yesterday as I thought at first." With this insight began the rearticulation of the manifestations that had made themselves felt in all of his relationships with human beings in such conflictual and painful ways.

He developed new possibilities of assessing the relationship with the analytic partner. He said:

> That really is something that doesn't belong in our relationship at all. It is as if something alien and disconcerting had crept in. I already had this feeling as a child when I went walking with my father and in the forest he gave the names of all the trees to me and then tested me to see whether I had remembered everything well. In such conversations

it happened again and again that we would start arguing about trivialities. I recall one discussion that was about whether the small spots on the leaves of the oak tree were normal natural phenomena or morbid changes. I liked the spots but my father insisted on their being ugly.

Now the analyst recognized the connection with the dream image. The debate about the dative or accusative of the word *agricola* contained a condensation and reactivation of old childhood experiences with the father. Such an interpretation would almost have produced itself. It is not a rare occurrence that in a phase of affective relaxation, the analysand uncovers such a connection by himself. The analysand said:

I think that with the word *agricola* I summarized all the observations of nature I experienced as a child with my father. The woman in the dream could be my father . . . or perhaps I myself appear in the dream as the person of my father. Then the woman would be in my place and prefer the caring dative. The accusatory accusative means conflict.

When matters had progressed thus far in the analytic process, the analyst added: "Perhaps all of what you have felt in our sessions here was also connected with the experiences you had with your father."

Is that already a reconstructive interpretation? No, definitely not. This interpretation merely connects specific expressions of affect with memories the analysand brought forward exactly then, and not at any other point in time, and that were associated with his father. With his insight and with the relativization of his feelings, he had rearticulated the relationship in the transference, and in so doing, the foreign object in the transference process, taking the form of actualized affective expression, became conscious.

With this step his conscious awareness of what was going on within him expanded. In the transference, the emotion previously bound to the affects of the defensive reaction communicated itself in its original, drive-derived form. Thanks to this expansion in the transference-occurrences, the transference-resistance expired. The analytic process got into a situation comparable to the one I described in my example of the young man who thought I was hard of hearing. When I was reporting about that patient, I spoke of an important reference to the father having become effective in the transference. This reference was interpreted, and this interpretation seemed to contradict the warning I had voiced immediately before that one should not, in the midst of the transference-happening, prematurely interpret the role of a figure from childhood.

Only now, in the broadened context, it seems to me, does it really become comprehensible that it is imperative for me to distinguish whether in the emotional instinctual happening, that is, in the totality of the analysand's mode of experiencing, I directly represent a father figure or whether, as the object of a current confrontation, I prompt in my analysand ways of reacting that represent expressions of affect in connection with specific memory traces.[3] For in that latter case, everything that becomes visible in the happening of the transferential process centers not on a person at all, but on an experientially distinct, very specific, isolated stereotypical conflictual tension that got fixed in the long-ago past. Because of its irresolvability and overwhelming intensity, this conflictual tension had once, in childhood, rent the situative and the emotional asunder. The consequence was that the one was repressed, the other displaced, and they both were artificially recombined in a new, neurotic manner.

These two modes of reaction that must in the analysis fundamentally be distinguished – the totality of the way of experiencing the world in connection with an important figure from childhood on the one hand, and, on the other, the affective expressions in connection with specific memory traces that get actualized in the confrontation with a present-day object – are, in life, constantly coupled. They blend, they interpenetrate, they do battle with each other in polar opposite motivations to act. They suppress and they transform each other. And together they largely determine those components of experience that are characterized by the compulsion to repeat. In these two modes of reaction lie the crucial means of approach to everything with which the psychoanalytic theory of technique is concerned.

Notes

1 Morgenthaler is being absurdist and satirical here. But he does so in order to make a serious point about not getting distracted by the *content* of a particular set of events, and instead focusing on "the emotional movement" in the relationship between analyst and analysand.

2 This metaphor of the analysand taking the blind and uncomprehending analyst by the hand would in later years often be elaborated by Morgenthaler to include the idea that the analysand leads the blind (or blindfolded) analyst by the hand into obstacles, so that the analyst stumbles, and the scales fall from his eyes. The idea, again, is that while Freud had emphasized that the patient resists the continuation of the treatment by taking his weapons out of the armory of the past one by one (and Morgenthaler had supplemented this by contending that

often also the *analyst* takes his own weapons out of the armory of the past to resist the continuation of the treatment), here now Morgenthaler stresses that within the analysand there are not just resisting forces but also forces that move the analysis onward.

3 Here, finally, with this concrete example, Morgenthaler demonstrates the importance of distinguishing between an, on the one hand (all too often problematic) tendency of analysts to rush to assume that they are, in the transference, playing the role of a particular family member of the analysand – what Morgenthaler elsewhere mockingly referred to as the rush to the mommies and the daddies – and, on the other hand, the often delayed but then highly useful recognition of a particular connection between a patient's long-ago experience with an important figure of childhood and the patient's more general "ways of reacting." But then again – and this too is classic Morgenthaler – in the paragraph that follows he relativizes this argument and admits that, frequently, a blending and blurring occur between "the totality of the way of experiencing the world in connection with an important figure of childhood" and "the affective expressions in connection with specific memory traces that get actualized in the confrontation with a present-day object."

Chapter 9

Function and structure of reconstructive interpretation

A 37-year-old musician, who has been engaged for eleven years, has been in analysis for 150 sessions. When he was born, his father was already rather old, his mother still very young. The analysand is their only child. The relationship with his girlfriend, a musician, is severely disturbed. There is no age difference worth mentioning. The two practically lived together for many years, for although they had separate apartments, these were often in the same house. The analysand loves this woman. He has always loved her. But he cannot express himself. He can neither talk to her about things that preoccupy him nor can he establish a relationship with her in which he would be able to show his feelings. He says that he lives in an inner tension, as if any and all making of contact were prevented by a wall in him and around him. His girlfriend has left him. He now lives by himself. In his profession, he is diligent and successful, but he is easily irritable, inward-looking, filled with compulsive ideas and feelings of self-denigration. He still loves his girlfriend. They meet often. They do not argue, but he remains at a loss when he is with her. He feels restricted in his life and disturbed in his capacity for expression.[1]

The analysis begins with great difficulties. The analysand lies silently on the couch and has trouble talking about himself. He hesitates at every attempt to articulate an idea. Over several months, nothing changes in his behavior. The analyst has taken an attitude toward the analysand as if all of that was completely understandable. The patient, who in every session gives the impression of a man at a loss, desperate, and who makes every effort to speak, yet without success, feels somehow good. He cannot understand this positive feeling during the analytic sessions. When, full of inner tension, he tries to put something into words, the analyst adds something to supplement or associates the patient's train of thought with another one he had communicated earlier. The analyst is always there and never leaves the analysand alone with his troubles. The tensions are reduced. The analysand seems calmed, remains silent, and wonders why he cannot speak. The analyst does not push the patient. Nor does he let him remain silent for a longer period of time but rather says, when a new state of tension begins to form from the silence during the session, well, this is this and that is that.

I want to use this example to explicate the structure and function of a reconstructive interpretation, which is why I will not here go into the details of the gradual development of the transference.[2]

After a year, the point has been reached that the patient during the analytic sessions begins to speak freely without inhibitions and disruptions. He reports on dreams that make an impression on him, about his relationships with other musicians, and about much that is going on within him. The emotional readiness he has brought with him from the start now becomes visible. He stands in an intensive relationship with the analyst. This phase in the analysis has been lasting for a while already. He regularly meets his girlfriend. They go to the theater or make music together, as they have done for many years. Until now, however, nothing has changed about the inner wall that stands between the two. The situation seems to be hopeless.

On a beautiful summer evening, they meet again. They decide to go to the girlfriend's apartment to play music together. The analysand suddenly, out of the blue, suggests playing a relatively unknown piece neither of them had ever practiced but both of them knew. The woman hesitates a little. The analysand practically throws himself into a virtuoso presentation of the piece and with grand gestures encourages his girlfriend to let herself be carried away with him. With great skill, the girlfriend accepts the musical invitation. Now comes a solo part that the analysand uses to improvise. He plays brilliant runs into which he weaves trills. The solo part becomes much longer than the composer intended, but everything fits together into the whole as if this were just how it should be. Now he gives a sign. His girlfriend joins in and they both finish the first movement with the few bars that remain. Then the girlfriend says to him: "You don't have to play like that on my account."

This is the first time the analysand does not react to a remark of this kind with silent sulking, a withdrawal, the embittered feeling of not being understood. He stands up, steps toward his girlfriend, and says: "But I play like that to give you joy." The woman almost startles, her expression is one of surprise. She says: "You know, I only said that because I could never play like you. I would like to be able to play like that." After these words, both sit down on a sofa and everything is completely different from what it has ever been before. The woman turns to him: "I want to tell you something I have never been able to say out loud. When we slept with each other, I only ever pretended I felt something. In reality, I never felt anything."

After this episode, the analysand goes home. Psychically, there is nothing special going on within him. He is calm and composed, as always. He takes care of some work. Then he lies down in bed and fantasizes. The fantasy moves him, and he recounts it first thing in the next day's analysis.

> It was very dark. I had my eyes closed. An image appeared to me from my childhood. I saw my father and approached him. I tapped him on the shoulder and asked him: "But do tell me how it was between mother and you when you slept together." At that moment, my mother appeared in my fantasy and implored my father: "Don't say anything, please, don't say anything!" I was shocked and affected very unpleasantly. I turned on the light and wanted to read something. It didn't work. I turned the light off again, but I couldn't fall asleep for a long time.

Pause.

"I met my girlfriend yesterday and everything was completely different from before." He now tells the story of their making music the night before.

The analyst interprets the connection between the nightly fantasy and the experience with the improvisation. He says:

> After the secret of your girlfriend's frigidity was revealed and you had understood that your girlfriend could not feel anything when you slept with her, the fantasy surfaced in the night in which, probably for the first time, you felt yourself to be your father's equal. You tapped him on the shoulder and asked him a question that must have quite preoccupied you in your childhood.[3]

I interrupt the course of interpretation here to provide some information about the analysand's life story.

The father had wanted a girl and was disappointed when the analysand was born. The mother loved the boy. When he was 5, he had a serious accident. At first he had to stay in bed at home but after two weeks he was brought to the hospital and had surgery. After that, he was in rehabilitation centers for many months and recovered only slowly. When the analysand entered adolescence, mother and son were time and again mistaken for siblings. He had a seductive way of interacting with his mother. With his father, he was never able to develop a real relationship colored by feelings of care. All of this is now brought into speech in the interpretation.

After the analytic session just described, the analysand is occupied with his past. He fantasizes about his sexual curiosity in early childhood and reports these fantasies in the following session.

"I remember playing doctor with little girls. I looked underneath their skirts and wanted to know what little girls looked like." He recounts a number of events from his childhood that are connected with his sexual curiosity.

While the analysand thus puts forward memories, a state of excitation arises, completely unexpectedly, which the analyst does not understand. The analysand is agitated, tossing back and forth on the couch, but is silent. Suddenly he raises his voice and says: "I will now tear myself open and show you everything." In saying so, he moves his hands and claws at his clothes. The analyst remains unclear about whether the analysand is in the process of tearing open his clothes to exhibit himself or whether he would really like to tear open his own body. It is almost a bit uncanny because one doesn't understand what is going on. The reaction of the analyst is, for the first time, inadequate. He stutters in embarrassment and does not know what he should say although he believes he absolutely must say something now.

A pause ensues. Then the analysand shouts: "I could scream at you." Nothing else. The analysand lies on the couch, relaxed. Some time passes like this. The session is over. Both get up calmly and composedly. The analysand says goodbye, inconspicuously as always, and leaves.

He comes to the following session, lies down, and is silent. A tension becomes palpable. He is struggling for words now. Finally, with a lot of effort, he manages to express that it is impossible for him to say anything. He feels disturbed and boxed in like never before, he says, and as if paralyzed and incapable of giving voice to any idea. Now there is another pause. The patient once more enters into a state of excitation. He says: "I must leave now. There's nothing else I can do, it doesn't work anymore."

The analyst gives a reconstructive interpretation:

> The feeling of being boxed in that torments you and the impossibility of doing anything but running away is connected with your childhood accident. Back then, you were forced to leave home because you had to be brought to a hospital. At the time, you had engaged in the sexual games with the girls and were full of curiosity to experience, to see, and to understand what sexuality means. You wanted to know what happens when your father and mother sleep together. You wanted to watch your parents in the bedroom. Back then, you also wished to put your hand on your father's shoulder and to tell him that you love him and that you want to be loved by him. The question you asked your father in the fantasy, after all, means nothing but this: "If you love me, you'll tell me everything." That is exactly what it was like when you were beginning to improvise while making music with your girlfriend. First you said to your girlfriend: "But I love you." It was as if you lovingly tapped her on the shoulder the way you did with your father in the fantasy. Then the woman, too, could open up and make you understand that she loves you. It is important to understand, after all, that you experienced your girlfriend telling you that she has always been frigid with you not as an insult but as a proof of love. That is quite understandable, too, since your girlfriend was always disturbed in her love by not being able to tell you everything – and that made her sad.

At this point, the analysand interrupts the interpretation and says: "A week ago it was still as you say, but now everything's lost. Now I can't see my girlfriend again. I wouldn't be able to say a word to her. I am disturbed like never before." He begins to cry softly.

The analyst interprets:

> Now you're in despair because you're sure that the love you and your girlfriend experienced in your shared exchange has been extinguished and buried again. That is connected with you having regained, in the course of the deepening of our analysis, your ability to love and with you having expressed this love to your girlfriend. Everything now seems lost to you because this love once, in your childhood, was

directed at your father. Back then, as a little boy, you wooed him intensely and received no reply. Your father could not express his love for you. It was his secret of which he was as unable to speak as your girlfriend was of her frigidity. In the last few days, you were entirely occupied with the memories of your childhood. The despair mounted in you again because you think you must once more experience all of the pain you suffered when you didn't feel loved by your father. But you could remember this and relive it because you felt, here in analysis and with your girlfriend, that everything has become wholly different. In our analytic relationship, above all, everything is wholly different from the way things used to be in the relationship with your father. You often wondered here why you feel so good despite your difficulties. You feel good because you have learned to love me the way you secretly loved your father. That, however, is possible only because you feel that I understand you, that I do not reject your caring, and that I show myself to you in such a way that you feel loved.

The analysand is no longer crying now. He has relaxed somewhat. He says softly, almost shyly: "Everything has become different. I don't understand what's been going on within me the last few days. After the last session, I was ashamed because I shouted at you."

There is a pause. Then, suddenly very lively, he continues and says:

And what was that supposed to mean, in my fantasy eight days ago, when my mother said so idiotically: "Don't say anything, please, don't say anything"? My mother was never like that. She was always on my side and liked going on walks with me much more than with my father. She also often told me how difficult it was for her to understand my father. He was too old for her and could not understand young people. What was this fantasy supposed to mean: "Don't say anything, please, don't say anything"?

It is not easy to answer this question of the analysand. The first remarkable thing is that he has recovered from his crisis and now begins to investigate with curiosity. In the current transference development, might this be the expression of a repetition of his infantile sexual curiosity? Does he want to study his fantasies the way he, as a small boy, investigated the girls? He

wants to understand what the mother meant in his fantasy the way he once
wanted to understand what the difference between the sexes means.

Those are the fantasies of the analyst. The associations of the analysand
are more instructive. We therefore follow the sequentiality in the course
of associations and look at what has played itself out, one thing after the
other, in the last several analytic sessions.

> A week ago, you first recounted your fantasy and only then spoke
> about the change in your relationship with your girlfriend. In reality,
> however, you first played music with your girlfriend and thereafter,
> late at night, had that fantasy. In the analysis, you first reported your
> mother's strange remark: "Don't say anything, please, don't say any-
> thing." Only after that were you able to tell me that your girlfriend had
> revealed to you the secret of her frigidity. All through the past years,
> your girlfriend constantly said to herself: "Don't say anything, please,
> don't say anything."

Now the analysand laughs for the first time. The analyst continues:
"During our session, you put the 'Don't say anything, please, don't say
anything' in your mother's mouth before you recounted to me that your
girlfriend had told you everything."

Now the analysand laughs out loud. The analyst laughs with him and
says: "I believe you were afraid I might suddenly have become angry and
could have shouted at you had you told me at the beginning of the session
what happened with your girlfriend as you were making music."

The analysand rebuffs this: "That cannot be. I was looking forward,
after all, to telling you how lovely it had been with my girlfriend. I have
always loved her, I just wasn't able to show her."

The analyst:

> You are right. What I just said is absurd and in no way suits our rela-
> tionship. We must understand, however, that since that session, a good
> number of things have happened that are entirely absurd and do not
> suit our relationship. When you spoke about your childhood, you sud-
> denly grew very excited and said you would tear yourself open and
> show everything. I did not understand that. Then you shouted that you
> wanted to scream at me. That seemed absurd to both of us. You were
> ashamed. Today, you were disturbed and inhibited the way you always

used to be in the past and wanted to run away because you could no longer bear yourself. All of that is absurd and does not suit us.

Ever since we're talking calmly with each other again, everything has normalized. I believe we should try to understand what appears to be absurd. For it belongs to what you fantasized and experienced in your childhood. I suspect it is connected with your mother. As a little boy and above all later, you again and again identified with your mother. I think that if we grasp the full significance of this identification with your mother, we will also understand all the seemingly absurd things that have taken place in the last few days and today.

Whenever you are not doing well, you react the way you experienced or fantasized the feelings and reactions of your mother. Your mother was afraid of your father. She feared he would scream at her when he noticed how tenderly and intimately she was interacting with you, her son. When you came to me on the Monday after making music, you took toward me the attitude your mother would have taken toward your father. You too said to yourself, "Don't say anything, please, don't say anything," and first recounted the fantasy as if you wanted to pass over the story with your girlfriend in silence. That, however, was only the case until you in your fantasy got rid of your mother and you could be yourself again. When you are yourself, you are able to speak quite freely and without anxiety. When in the following sessions you were talking about your childhood, you were suddenly again in your mother's skin. You were excited and wanted to tear up your clothes or your body the way you fantasized as a little boy your mother did in front of your father in the bedroom. Then you suddenly wanted to scream at me because you fought back against falling into the woman's role toward me. You were afraid of being raped by me the way your mother was raped by your father. Your wish to scream at me corresponds to your wish to be a man. Then you were ashamed and came to today's session disturbed. Your despair expresses your conviction that, despite the changes you feel, nothing can help you and that the analysis appears meaningless and powerless to you. That stems from your childhood experience. Back then, your father seemed so powerful to you that you had given up on yourself – somewhat like today, at the beginning of the session. I believe your despair is connected with the terrible despair of your childhood when, severely injured, you were brought to the hospital by your helpless parents. I must have appeared as helpless to you as your parents were back then. Only that way is it understandable why you believed your analysis could not lead anywhere and that there was nothing else to do but run away.

When you came to the hospital, you were horribly afraid. The surgery was something uncanny, inescapable, coercive. How can a little boy understand that? He fantasizes and experiences his illness as a punishment. He feels punished for his wishes to love and to be loved. He is not being allowed to be a man. He is not being allowed to be like his father.

You told me that you were released from the rehabilitation centers after a year and returned home and that, according to your parents' statements, you were an entirely changed child. From then on, you were always shy and well-behaved. You no longer wanted to play with little girls but studied diligently in school. You became hardworking the way you still are today. Since then, too, you are extremely sensitive. If your father merely looked at you or said something to you, you ducked and were unable to utter a word. That's how it was throughout your youth. In puberty, you had anxieties and had to submit to all authority figures. Something in you was as if broken. You felt that you were sick. You could not express yourself to anyone. To your girlfriend, too, you were unable to show your feelings.

This interpretation comprises the connections in the traumatizing influences of a very specific phase of childhood and it effects an enduring relaxation in the analysand. In the following sessions, he speaks coherently and calmly about what is going on in his current life. In the course of his narrative, he suddenly says: "From now on I can say everything that comes to my mind. Up until now, I have never been able properly to participate in the analysis at all."

The relaxation leads, in the subsequent course, to a deepening of the analytic process.

Quite evidently, the analysand has undergone a negative-oedipal movement in the development of his libido. What I mean is that, in a characteristic way, he has failed in the confrontation with the Oedipus conflict. In the phallic-narcissistic phase, castration fears had thrown him back to a sado-anal position. In other words, he had identified with the mother instead of competing with the father. He had submitted to the father and had remained fixed in the retentive attitude that accompanies the negative-oedipal constellation.

The negative-oedipal tendency had also determined the transference up to this point. When he began to talk and, finally, to improvise in music and speak with his girlfriend, and when in his fantasies he patted his father on the shoulder, the negative-oedipal position in the transference was given up under the pressure of the emotional upheaval. Because he identified with the analyst, he could now open up and show his feelings, that is, he could develop phallic-narcissistic, exhibitionistic activity. This new position he now assumed was unconflicted and represented a starting point for new experiences.

It was a beginning, a first possibility of behaving phallic-exhibitionistically without fear in a relationship. This new possibility of experience entered into the good, conflict-free relationship with the analyst. The phallicity that showed itself was supported by the transference. Borne by the current, intensive analytic relationship he could look back, unconflictedly, at the desperate struggles of childhood in which he had failed. The look back focused on the negative-oedipal drive-vicissitude that had been reactivated in the analysis. But this reactivation was not a process that specifically colored the transference as had been the case when I spoke of the releasing of the connection of an affect fixed to specific memory-traces. There, it was a question of a change in the transference after the dissolution of a transference-resistance. Here, rather, it was something that had become possible in the first place only because the transference had so enduringly been colored phallic-narcissistically. The early-infantile, sado-anal fixation typical of the negative-oedipal drive-vicissitude was reactivated and actualized in a way one might compare with the screening of an exciting movie. Similar to the way the moviegoer is frightened when he sees someone on the screen frozen with terror or to the way he grabs the armrest when someone in the film threatens to crash from some great height, the analysand joins in the affective movements that communicate themselves to him in a true-to-life way from the experiential domain of his childhood.

To make these matters even clearer, I want to compare them to a different example. Let me remind you of the young man who in a near-hallucinatory way experienced his analyst as hard of hearing and, in a certain phase of the analysis, began to speak ever more loudly until he was shouting his words. When the analyst asked him why he was speaking so loudly, it turned out that the young man had experienced him as hard of hearing because his father had been hard of hearing. This process aimed at completing a developing transference. Traits of the once-frustrating father are being projected onto the analyst. What is to emerge – steered in this way by the unconscious – is a synthesis between the father from childhood and the person of the analyst. This dynamic follows the pressure of the compulsion to repeat. The contrast-experience that the young man perceives in the analytic situation when he becomes conscious of his projection produces a feeling of disconcertedness. Thanks to the connections becoming conscious, the affect that finds expression in speaking loudly and in shouting at the partner thought to be hard of hearing becomes free-floating and makes the ego more drive-friendly and amenable to the unconscious impulses entering into the transference. The contrast-experience I was just talking about captures only one, initially small, part of the conflictual experiential domain of early childhood. The ideas, memories, and experiences that play a central role here are and have always been conscious: the young man was always clearly aware that his father was hard of hearing. To this conscious knowledge, he connected pieces of the inclination toward conflictedness whose most important sources, however, had been unconscious, that is, repressed, already in childhood.

I would like to point out once more the fundamental difference between the two processes. The metaphor of the movie being watched in the theater lends itself well to this purpose. When in the transference-development, the young man forms a definite conviction that his analyst is hard of hearing, the reactivation may be compared with a movie that had once been made of the viewer himself and that he is now watching. He recognizes himself, for example as a 15-year-old playing with his dogs. He experiences these movie scenes as if for a short time he was the 15-year-old again. Then the lights go on, the movie is over. He gets up and looks at himself in the mirror. And there it may well be the case that he has a disconcerting feeling when he now sees himself aged to be 50 years old and recognizes that he has just fallen prey to an illusion.

In the case of a reconstructive interpretation of meaning, the analysand does not register what once had been as he was back then, but rather registers it the way he is now; he is already changed and looks back to understand what was going on within him when he was still the way he now no longer is. Here is an antithesis within the dynamic that is so crucial. It is a decisive one, because only under these conditions do the unconscious impulses and ideas lose their repressing power. The analysand who believed his analyst to be hard of hearing takes cognizance of the interpretation of his projection the way he has since his childhood taken cognizance of, for example, his father's being hard of hearing. What disconcerts him is not at all the practical experience that he is no longer the same way he used to be but rather that he erroneously assumed his analyst, too, to be hard of hearing, as if all older men were hard of hearing. For he knows full well that most men he encounters hear well. This analysand thus looks back and understands what is going on within him and that what is going on within him is still the same thing that has always been going on within him. He gradually recognizes that he is just as full of conflict as he already was as a child although he no longer is a child. Therein lies the dynamic's synthesis. It leads the analytic process onward. It finally gets to the point where the analysand recognizes that alien influences from past experiencing are entering into the current analytic relationship like foreign bodies.

The antithesis in the dynamic of a reconstructive interpretation stabilizes an intrapsychic transformation that has come about in the analytic process. Now the infantile conflict-filled forms of experiencing have become truly alien and no longer belong to the present experiential domain. They appear like an echo from early times and, typically, no longer have any influence on the transference. The early conflict-filled forms of experiencing do indeed momentarily cover up the transference, comparable to clouds that cover the sun. But the interpretation of this disruption in the relationship immediately effects a clarification. The analyst must know this, for what counts is that in such a development everything has to be interpreted. No disruption of the transference must now be left uninterpreted. Sometimes the alleviation of such echo-influences does not succeed quickly and easily. Perseverance and comprehensive interpretations of meaning of infantile modes of experiencing are then decisive in the work of analysis.

I want to return to the example. The interpretation the analyst has given concerned the experiential domain of a very specific time in the patient's childhood. The connections that are being clarified now no longer have the character of modes of experiencing that seem familiar and appropriate to the ego. The experiential domain of childhood seems alien because within the transference, the phallic-narcissistic position is experienced as syntonic and ego-adequate and belongs to the image of the self. The patient senses that something has become different when he is able to speak freely and without disturbances in the analytic sessions and is able to enter into a genuine, open relationship with his girlfriend. These new modes of experiencing the phallic-exhibitionistic tendencies are now experienced as authentic and as suiting the ego. The offer that had stemmed from the fixation of the sado-anal position, and which remains as the legacy, as it were, of that phase of neurotic development, is caught like a foreign body in the analysand's transference. This is the precondition for the reconstruction of the childhood conflicts getting connected with the real circumstances of which one has become aware, along with the memories that belong to them, which the analysand has brought up in the course of the entire analysis thus far. At this point, the interpreting becomes comprehensive and draws on everything that has become known, in order to complete the reconstructive interpretation.

In this phase, the analysand is quite cooperative and generally brings up massive additional memories and supplements that deepen the insight into the infantile mode of experiencing. *This* is what we then call the phase of working-through. It can take a long time and is carried above all by the analysand himself. He associates and brings up ever more material. He extends the reconstructive interpretation. The analyst with his thoughts and ideas contributes to an ever-clearer image becoming conscious of the original position of the analysand that had been so pathogenic. This insight is only possible if in the transference precisely this position that had been captured in the reconstructive interpretation has been overcome. For then the reconstructive interpretation has a stabilizing effect on the new phallic-exhibitionistic mode of experiencing that has just been initiated immediately before.

In the important session, when the reconstructive interpretation reached its climax, the patient displayed a very intense reaction. He said he had to run away; he could no longer bear the entire situation. Were those oedipal castration anxieties?

One could say that the analyst now found himself in the role of the frustrating father who exudes a threat of castration. That would be why the analysand felt horribly boxed in and felt an urge to leave. In accordance with this view, castration anxiety had been a pertinent element in the transference.

That, however, would be an erroneous assumption since the analysis has not progressed that far. While undoubtedly castration anxiety has been mobilized, it is a castration anxiety in sado-anal garb, that is to say, in its negative-oedipal, regressive expression. The real activation of the oedipal conflict situation will be able to develop only later.

In my example, the analysis is in a phase in which the analysand only begins in the first place to adjust phallic-exhibitionistically. The further analytic development will probably lead the analysand to enter into rivalry conflicts with the analyst that will then indeed have oedipal character. It is not sufficient to say that an analysand develops anxieties in the transference and then suppose these anxieties to be oedipal castration anxieties. But it is not sufficient either to say that in the transference this patient stands in a phallic-narcissistic position and develops anxieties of an oedipal nature. Rather, it is correct to say that he has developed a phallicity toward his girlfriend and feels phallic in the transference as well. In this, he is characteristically *free* of anxiety. After all, he was quite relaxed during the musical evening and was quite calm and equable when he formed the night-time fantasy as well. In such a development, one may certainly not speak of oedipal castration anxiety. It is instead a stage of the analysis in which he enjoys the phallic exhibition in much the same way a small boy out walking with a dog bigger than him enjoys the mastery over the animal. In the analytic relationship, too, in the transference, the analysand enjoys the calm and de-stressed emotional situation in which he can, without anxiety, feel himself as phallic-narcissistic.

It is nonsense to speak in such a phase of the castrating father who in the transference threatens the analysand's phallicity. One should rather be clear that anxieties arising when a reconstructive interpretation is due do not represent anxieties in the transference. When in the transference a certain libidinal position is supplanted by the next-higher position (according to the libido's hierarchical developmental schema), a transformation of the transference takes place that gives the signal for a reconstructive interpretation. It is then that symptoms appear that seem alien to the analysand although the tendency is experienced the exact same way as earlier. The disconcerting feeling comes from the way the experience that everything has become entirely different is still so fresh in the memory. The analysand could then say: "I don't understand at all what it is with me now. It was so lovely with my girlfriend when we were making music together, and now I am again in the same desperate situation as earlier." Now we must not underestimate the significance of the real and new experience the analysand has made in the analytic process. In our example, he has been engaged to his girlfriend for eleven years and has never been able to enter into a free and open relationship with her. Now he has had the new experience. It is a phallic-exhibitionistic activity he has experienced in himself. He is surprised at the effect his new behavior has had. He does not underestimate the importance of his girlfriend's statement, speaking about her frigidity with him for the first time. Nor does he underestimate his new ability not to have to react to a remark by his girlfriend by sulking.

The decisive questions thus pose themselves: why does the analysand now cramp up again? Why is he full of tension and plagued by violent states of anxiety?

One cannot respond here that that's just the arduous way the analytic process advances – or that the analysand is regressing anew under the pressure of the castration anxieties, or that he is behaving neurotically again because the fixations are so strong, or suchlike.

Matters are different. The recapitulation of the symptoms has now attained a new meaning. The symptoms are felt to be disconcerting, as something that no longer suits the image of his person at all. The whole thing seems like a pantomime. It is as if expressions free of affect, like gestures without words, were presenting something. The analyst cannot here say that his analysand is always presenting the same thing, for he now presents his symptoms in such a way that they can be understood in their entire early-infantile significance. In the new transference-position, in our example the phallic-narcissistic position, the recapitulation of symptoms represents a rearticulation. The disconcertedness the analysand experiences is the same disconcertedness he felt as a child when he, without understanding it, had to react in a specific way. As a child, he had this enormous desire to express himself phallic-exhibitionistically toward his father and his mother, to please them, to go proudly walking with his father's large dog. This desire and this joy taken in his own beauty was suffocated in a disconcerting and incomprehensible way and crushed into a negative-oedipal submission. He suffered an accident and had to go to the hospital. The neurosis was fully formed.

This is the story the analysand presents as if in a pantomime and he thereby exhibits himself before the analyst in his newly-acquired phallic attitude. The analyst is a spectator and understands the presentation by saying: "Now we understand the story without words, this violent urge to run away no matter what. That was already the case once before in your life, namely when after your accident you were being sent to the hospital."

The analysand reacts with amazed understanding. He recognizes that back in his childhood it was exactly this event that had been particularly painful. He can recognize this because everything has become different since he has phallic-exhibitionistically made music and then was able phallic-exhibitionistically to respond to his girlfriend's dismaying remark. As a child he had to give up passively. Now he enters his surroundings actively, penetrating the obstacles. These contrast-experiences, which the analysand is ready to feel in the course of a reconstructive interpretation and which intervene profoundly in the experiential domain of his childhood and lead to there being ego where previously there had been id: these contrast-experiences yield the stabilizing effect. They are the pillars on which the next "storey" of the building that the analytic process represents will be erected. These pillars must be solidly anchored, for in the further course of the analysis, ever greater emotional movements will seek to shake the ego because ever deeper tendencies toward conflictedness are being reactivated. Gradually, the analysis approaches the main conflict, the failure in the oedipal struggle.

The free unfolding of human beings' emotional readiness to get involved with all kinds of things, new objects, other people, new interests, which change in the course of life, encounters the resistance of the compulsion to repeat. One must again and again do the same thing, must again and again invest the same things that were invested before when the child first encountered a conflict it could not manage and that was then submerged into repression. In its place, a defense was erected, a defense that determined the cathexes. The compulsion to repeat follows these cathexes. Emotionality then constantly crashes into these obstacles, in all the rest of the life that follows. In the analysis, the same cathexis compulsions appear in the transference. The concept of transference comprises everything that flows into the analytic relationship from the past of what has been experienced.

The compulsion to repeat is a compulsion because in the developmental steps the child takes, the most important figures leave impressions so definitive and durable that no later influences will be capable of matching them. That is because the psychic functions become ever less plastic the more they are formed.

It cannot be a matter of indifference whether the child who is engaged in developing autonomous functions – holding on to this, letting go of that, and moving independently – is constantly being frustrated and forced to submit or not. Let's take another child for a comparison, for example a toddler of the Dogon people in West Africa who passes through the anal phase completely without conflict: this Dogon child in its later life displays no sado-anal fixations. It does not, in a compulsion to repeat, constantly have to hold everything back when certain wishes express themselves in impulses. It will not develop greediness in dealing with money or food.[4]

In the case of a sado-anal fixation, the child during the anal phase of defiance had to let go of everything when it wanted to hold back absolutely everything. It has been defeated in the fulfillment of its wishes. Later, as an adult, the person feels strong enough belatedly to fulfill the wishes of the phase of defiance. The tendency has made itself permanent, as it were, and manifests wherever demands signal themselves or tasks emerge. At school age, the "I did not want to but I had to, now I don't have to" shows itself in not doing homework, later in not wanting to spend money on others or in being sexually ungenerous. These are examples of repetition-stations of a sado-anal fixation that has decisively influenced a person's emotional capacity.

The compulsion to repeat is the compulsion again and again to operate the same cathexes that were internalized in an important phase of development. Let's take as example a process of learning. One can learn from a carpenter how to saw wood, for example how to shorten the four legs of a table in such a way that afterward, the table is steady, something an expert does effortlessly. Those who have really mastered such a procedure will in similar situations automatically repeat the required movements. That is the manifestation of acquired experience. When we learn something nonsensical, without noticing that it is nonsensical, the same repetition automatism emerges. It, too, is built on experience. Only when the nonsensical nature of such actions becomes conscious, when the contrast-experience becomes reality, does a new way of experiencing emerge that interrupts the compulsion to repeat. In the psychic domain, the nonsensical is not as easily recognized as in the sawing of wood. The nonsensical seems to be in agreement with the image we have of ourselves. That is because of its primary-process – that is, unconscious – nature. It is made accessible to and acceptable for the ego by means of rationalizations.

The reconstructive interpretation is characterized by the particular junction at which it is located, so that the compulsion to repeat can be broken through. The ideational contents that anecdotally connect the various experiences are only stations along the lines that finally meet at this junction. The meaningful connections to these contents in the childhood experiences are important. But it is interesting to register, for example, that the proposition – that the feeling of suffocation and the inner urge immediately to need to run away had something to do with the accident the analysand suffered at the age of 5, which for so long had been conceived of as something entirely inconsequential – could suddenly have a never-suspected effect in the patient's experiencing. What is decisive in this transformation in experiencing lies in the transference-process, namely where one position gives way to another. Nonetheless, we must not believe the reconstructive interpretation to be the locomotive that pulls the analysis from one transference-position to another. Rather, the transference transforms, and therewith the meaning of what is subject to the compulsion to repeat changes. This is the occasion at which the reconstructive interpretation is given. If it is missed, the analysand in most cases regresses to the infantile position of his pathogenic fixation.

The compulsion to repeat is resolved in a new constellation of cathexes. This reconfiguration of cathexes is the consequence of tracing, in the emotional economy, the affective cathexes of the processes of defense back to the originally decisive childhood event or experience. In our example, it was the accident and the surgery, which resulted in the separation from the family.

The process of reconfiguring cathexes succeeds only within the dynamic of the transference-occurrences and is made possible by the reconstructive interpretation that is given when the libidinal cathexes in the analytic relationship change *qualitatively*. In our example, the qualitative change was recognizable in the realm of phallic-narcissistic experiencing.

Notes

1 In the audiotaped version of the seminar delivered in 1974, this patient had been married rather than engaged, and later – instead of being, as he is here, a musician who subsequently, as the story unfolds, plays his instrument with virtuoso skill – he takes his wife out on a lake in a rowboat, and rows with remarkable proficiency. In addition, the patient in the audiotape version had tuberculosis as a child; here, he was in an accident and required surgery. All the other parts of the story remain the same. It is irrelevant which details are "correct"; presumably both versions protect the former patient by hiding the "real" story. But the interchangeability of the details also underscores that these details are not the point of the tale. Rather, the dynamic essence of the tale remains the same and, as always with Morgenthaler, the drama lies in "the emotional movement" and – not least – in how, as gradually becomes clear, the (long-unrecognized) salience of a particular experience-content in childhood will ultimately provide the basis for a crucial reconstructive interpretation of meaning.

2 As the second half of the sentence indicates, although he has been deferring a reconstructive interpretation, Morgenthaler has already provided this analysand with interpretations of the transference. The reconstructive interpretation will build on these prior interpretations.

3 Although Morgenthaler uses the word "frigidity" (*Frigidität*) here and throughout the rest of the story, Morgenthaler is fully aware that the problem in the
   couple's sexual life lies not with the woman, but rather with the neurotically
   inhibited man.
4 Morgenthaler here is referencing the "ethnopsychoanalytic" studies he conducted together with his close friends and fellow psychoanalysts Paul Parin and
   Goldy Parin-Matthèy from 1960 on among the Dogon in just-then-decolonizing
   Mali. The results – centering the subjectivities of their informants – were published in numerous articles and also in the book, *Die Weissen denken zuviel*
   (Whites Think Too Much), which, after a short delay, at the turn of the 1960s
   to the 1970s became an enthusiastically received counterculture sensation for
   the West German New Left in particular (Parin et al., 1963; cf. Herzog, 2017,
   pp. 193–199).

Chapter 10

Many paths lead to no destination

In my discussion of psychoanalytic technique, I have tried to speak in a way that befits me. I did not describe psychoanalysis in its totality but talked about psychoanalysis as I understand it. I wanted to show that as an analyst, I do not approach the analysand as if he were full of pathological defense. It has been important to me to stress that what is at issue in the analytic process is a liberation and expansion of emotionality and that in the course of the transference-development, analysis leads to a profound emotional turbulence: only the turbulence is capable of loosening neurotic fixations.

The analyst and the analysand are each conflict-filled partners in the analytic relationship. I regard both as personalities that are as healthy and as well-functioning as possible. The emphasis is always on those emotional parts of the psychic systems that promote the analytic process and keep it going. This holds as much for the assessment of the analysand as it does for the assessment of the analyst, for example when the analyst goes to an experienced colleague to discuss the analysis he is conducting with a patient. Only if the analysand brings the readiness to accept the conditions of the analytic situation can an analysis be begun. That also holds for the analyst. He can work analytically only if he respects the laws of psychoanalytic technique and of metapsychology. If he is of a different opinion or if he uses different techniques, then he is doing something different with his patients. It is certainly not necessary in every case to prompt people suffering from conflicts and difficulties to enter an analytic process. There are paths other than analysis. They are to be measured by different criteria.

When I begin an analysis with an analysand, I must meet him openly and without prejudices. I approach him as if he had no neuroses and no difficulties. Above all, however, I myself must have no difficulty getting involved in a relationship with my partner.

I have stressed that long-repressed drive-impulses and ideas that surface and become noticeable in the context of the developing analytic relationship are usually felt by the analysand as something alien and disconcerting. By contrast, old defense-achievements that usually were erected already in childhood against unacceptable drive-impulses or against frustrating outside influences appear in the analytic relationship as attitudes and modes of expression that are felt as subjectively belonging to the ego. Although they are reaction-formations that only ever were really appropriate within the experiential domain of childhood, they are kept into adulthood and the entire rest of one's life as patterns of experience, as it were, and integrated into the image of one's own person without a sense of disconcertedness. At base, these old ego-achievements, which have anachronistic character, never suit the experiential domain of the adult personality, and they have an essential share in the neurotic inclinations toward conflictedness. In the analytic relationship, they often appear in the guise of drive-claims and wishes.

Repressed drive-impulses, that is, parts of the id, as well as the old, anachronistic defensive achievements of the ego are often responsible for particular difficulties that appear when in the transference, feelings quickly intensify and are repressed because of their intensity. The analysand then feels overstrained without realizing it. In the emotional realm, disturbances appear in the transference. The perspectives pertaining to the analysand's emotional offer, his instinctuality and the force of his drive-impulses, along with the feelings connected with these, are much more important for me than aspects focusing on the defense and the resistances – because they carry much more weight when I orient myself in the analytic process in such a way that my relationship with the analysand is congruent. This does not mean, however, that I do not pay attention to the defense and the resistances. Rather, I can recognize and understand the expressions of the defense-organization of the analysand's ego – as they very soon and very clearly become evident – only if I have been able to adjust to my partner in a way that suits me and that corresponds to him, that is: in such a way that the relationship is congruent.

In the analysis, I must not imperceptibly become the enemy of my analysand's emotional movement. This happens among analysts much more often than one would like to suppose. Every analysand brings a great readiness to get involved in the analysis. Whether he is able to show this readiness is another question. As an analyst, I must acknowledge this readiness and must not, with a series of irrelevant instructions, steer the relationship in a direction that does not at all suit the analysand, that does not fit him, and in which he feels rebuffed. When the analysand is severely inhibited, barely able to speak, and appears warped and crippled by his symptoms, I must by no means conclude that he is not displaying readiness. As long as he regularly comes to the sessions, this readiness exists. I would then do well to go out and meet my analysand halfway, to help him, too, to sense this readiness that he brings. The analysand can do so if I, his partner, show the same readiness. As an analyst, I should therefore not be inhibited in my phallicity. What is expected of me is comprehensive drive-friendliness, not any inhibition to expose myself.[1] As an analyst, I must ensure that the relationship gets going. And for that to happen, it is inopportune to be on the look-out for resistances right from the start.

Most people want to come into analysis at the point when a conflictual situation in their life has come to a head. They offer the immediate unsolvable conflict – a marriage crisis that is no longer bearable, a despair that sees only suicide as a solution, a professional catastrophe that throws the conditions of the patient's and his family's life into question, a severe drug addiction, or a legal prosecution. Such offers are, fundamentally, nonanalytic. A psychotherapy seems more appropriate in these cases. Psychotherapy proceeds focally, with a narrow target. In the analytic process, on the contrary, the basis we start from must be broad. With an analysis, I cannot quickly find a solution, or bridge a problem plaguing a patient. Analysis is also no good for quickly reassimilating to the dominant societal morality a patient who is in a nonconforming position vis-à-vis society, helping him be a good student, a well-behaved employee, or a successful businessman. The analytic process follows transference-structures and lines of development that do not correspond to the structures of the society in which we live. The analytic process is not a means for feeling ever better and ever more happy in some linear manner. Those who seek these things will not find them in analysis. Nor is the fulfilment of such expectations the criterion for concluding an analysis. When the analysis ends, the analyst and the analysand separate, but the process that has been begun continues. The analysand himself takes over the functions previously fulfilled by the analyst. That is what Freud meant when he said that analysis was both terminable and interminable.[2]

For the analytic process to be able to develop in this direction, analyst and analysand must from the beginning bring the readiness to accept difficulties that will arise. If the analytic relationship between the two partners deepens, drive-claims, feelings, and fantasies will appear that act disruptively. That is why I must ensure early on that I am ready to meet the analysand with a completely open attitude and without psychic disorders and difficulties of my own. The transference, which always grows from the sources of the emotional readiness that both, analysand and analyst, bring, emerges on the basis of this first experience. There undoubtedly are cases in which this readiness is not present in the analysand, but it is remarkable how rare they are.

Not too long ago, I was presented with a case in which this readiness was lacking. The analyst had tried everything, and drawn on everything, to get the analysis going. The patient was a woman who had worked in Vietnam, who later lived in Africa, and who stood in a severe conflict with a man who had worked with her in the tropics. She felt herself under extraordinary pressure and developed peculiar anxieties and states of exhaustion. All of her symptoms developed in the direction of an almost paranoid disorder close to psychosis but one whose effects more resembled those of a phobia. The patient returned to Switzerland, was completely spent and unable to work, plagued by hysteriform states, and depressed. She was examined thoroughly at the hospital. Nothing special was found, and the patient was referred to the psychiatrist. The psychiatrist suggested an analysis. Helpless as she was, the patient agreed and went to see the analyst, who began the analysis with her.

The analysis failed because the emotional readiness of which I have spoken so much was lacking.

When this case was presented to me, I had already reviewed the protocol. In a two-hour discussion with the physicians and analysts, I first, on the basis of the course that eight months of analytic efforts had taken, rejected all reproaches made against the analyst, since they were untenable. The analyst had very adequately adjusted to the patient. He was emotionally ready to get involved; he had in no way rebuffed or otherwise frustrated the patient. He had tried everything, and his attempts were analytically oriented in the best sense of the term. The relationship became ever more tense and narrowed down, like a funnel. The patient began bringing presents for the analyst and, during the sessions, cried quietly and shyly. She could not really understand what was actually supposed to happen in her analysis. From this contradiction, I deduced that most probably, the patient was physically, not psychically ill. I suggested she be medically examined once more and an experienced tropical doctor be consulted because I suspected a tropical disease of the kind that is often overlooked in routine examinations in our European hospitals. I was convinced that this woman was ill. My suspicion was confirmed. The patient was suffering from amoebic dysentery.

I know from personal experience how treacherous tropical diseases can be. Years ago, having returned from Africa, I suffered from hard to grasp disorders accompanied by severe vegetative symptoms. The colleagues who had examined me could not find anything and suspected a neurasthenia and connected it with my neurosis. I was already convinced myself that I was subject to a severe neurotic regression after I had been closely examined in a hospital experienced with tropical diseases and once more nothing had been found. Finally, a tropical doctor discovered the giardiasis I was suffering from. With the help of Atabrine pills, I was restored to full health within a few days.[3]

Why am I telling you this story? I want to show that it is possible within the analytic process to identify a physical illness with almost complete certainty: namely when the analytic process does not get going even though the relationship does not encounter any obstacle that could be analytically explained. Such a development is to be assessed like a signal. The analyst here is almost in a more favorable starting position than the somatic physician who can only say that there probably is a psychogenic order because he cannot find anything somatic.

I will never forget a young man who was referred to me for psychoanalysis from a hospital. He suffered from the most severe anxiety attacks. He had been thoroughly examined, to no result. I took the patient in for treatment. After five or six sessions, he suddenly began to sweat profusely during the session, developed a redness of the face all the way to the hairline, and trembled strongly. I stopped the treatment and examined him physically. He had a high fever and a suspicious finding in the lungs. I sent him as an emergency case to the radiologist, who identified a tubercular cavern. The patient entered a sanatorium the very same night. Four weeks earlier, the doctors in the hospital had not found any sign of tuberculosis because nothing could be detected yet. But the anxiety attacks quite apparently represented the forerunners of the serious somatic illness.

There can be no doubt that, within the analytic process, there are signs that make the discrepancy between certain of the patient's reactions and the expectable attendant emotional movements so conspicuous that it is possible for the analyst to demonstrate that the analytic process cannot get going because of a reason outside of the analytic encounter.

This is of course only possible if the analytic relationship is begun and developed further in accordance with the laws of the theory of technique and in keeping with what one calls the analytic situation. One may not say in all cases in which the analysis is blocked that there has to be some disorder that is not psychogenic.

Yet the really great difficulties that young prospective analysts display again and again do not lie in the assessment of the psychogenic or somatic causes of their patients' symptoms. Rather, they lie in the analysts' propensity to see, everywhere and anywhere, only defenses, and thereby not sufficiently to perceive, and also not appropriately to respond to, the analysand's fundamental emotional readiness in the form in which it offers itself.[4]

Nonetheless, if the analyst is responsive to his analysand, resistances will inevitably develop. These are transference-resistances. They are characterized by the way they tend to be felt as ego-syntonic, even though in the analytic process they act as foreign objects. Transference-resistances are by no means evident only in the defense mechanisms. The situation is not like that. To represent it, I must pay attention to the relationship that exists between the transference-resistance and the compulsion to repeat, which Freud referred to as the resistance of the id. This relationship is also the reason why I distinguish an interpretation of the transference-resistance from a reconstructive interpretation of meaning.

I want to compare the neurotic analysand with big Gulliver being tied to the ground by the Lilliputians with a thousand threads. Interpretations of transference-resistances may be equated metaphorically with cutting such threads one by one. Every time this succeeds, Gulliver moves a little more. Soon he can lift his foot and give a sign with one of his hands. His movements cannot yet be used for a coherent, meaningful action. Yet the more this process of untying progresses, the closer the moment comes when Gulliver can execute the first coordinated movement of expression. Relating this image to the dynamic course of the analytic process, I can say that at that moment, the analysand changes the meaning of the transference. The role the analyst has played in the transference up to now is superseded by a succeeding one. The connections that have resulted from the experiences of childhood determine these roles. But the point is not to emphasize these roles in the interpretive process and equate them with the significance the analyst has for the analysand. Rather, it is to recognize, to understand, and to interpret the sense of Gulliver's movement of expression, however fragmentarily it initially still presents itself. Only then can the relation to the projection, to the role the analyst has played in it, be clarified. These reconstructive interpretations describe what the already liberated emotion reveals, not what inhibited it. The further the analytic process advances, the more comprehensively Gulliver can move and the more complex and multiply revelatory are his possibilities of expression. These possibilities of expression are the language of the unconscious.

Every reconstructive interpretation stabilizes the incipient transformation of the transference and makes it possible for this new form of the transference to take firmer shape and become sufficiently robust for the next-deeper layer of psychic experiencing to be reactivated.

This is how the evolution of the analysis can be understood along the lines of transference-transformations. A transference can for example be positive and determined by tender feelings that assign to me, the analyst, the properties of a loving, understanding father. But then the relationship changes and I become a figure that corresponds to a distanced, punitive, hard, and cold mother. Finally, a new form of the transference can develop, one in which the relationship displays caringly helping traits or one in which it acquires an authoritarian-frightening coloring.

I warned against highlighting such roles too early in the interpretive process. There is no doubt, however, that they occur. After all, they practically impose themselves and lead me in my analytic reflection to what I called a summation effect. I feel prompted by the wealth of the analysand's associations to interpret the significance I take on in the transference. In the analysand's fantasy I represent an important figure of his childhood. I *interpret* this fantasy; I do not by any means confirm that this fantasy corresponds to the analytic reality.

The *effect* that a reconstructive interpretation has on the transference as it is unfolding verifies or falsifies the interpretation. If a reconstructive interpretation was correct, the level of transference changes, while after the interpretation of what had been a transference-resistance, the transference acquires a new coloring.

If after a reconstructive interpretation a regressive process sets in and intense resistances appear, the interpretation was wrong or incomplete or untimely. I was then mistaken, or I was unable to make clear to the analysand what is at issue in his experiential domain.

I am together with my analysand to try and provide interpretations of what I have come to understand. Often, that does not work and I try again and again, for weeks and months. I gradually come closer to some core occurrence that I do not recognize. None of what I say is really accurate. Reconstructive interpretations cannot be compared to Easter eggs that are hidden somewhere and that I will suddenly find as long as I keep looking attentively for them. Here, too, we are dealing with processes that are developing. Sometimes I have to start four times, five times, or ten times until suddenly something fits. These are the struggles in which I find myself, and this is the reflection in psychoanalytic technique of what Freud expressed in one of the Addenda to "Inhibitions, Symptoms and Anxiety": the resistance of the id, its compulsion to repeat, is unassailable.[5]

I cannot resolve or alleviate the compulsion to repeat by means of interpretation. Only the integration of an insight, of entire series of insights, changes the emotional scope of the relationship, and only such changes in the emotional dynamics can lead to a moderation of the compulsion to repeat. These are processes that might emerge in the course of transference, in the course of the entire analysis – but often only very late.

Anyone can see from my discussion of psychoanalytic technique that I have considered my personal vantage more than I have engaged generally valid views. This also makes it possible to see who I am, what I advocate, and who I am not and what I do not advocate. It is visible in my way of adjusting to the analysand, of trying to begin, keep up, and deepen the analytic process, of assessing the interpretive process and the verifications that confirm the interpretive process as meaningful or refute it as misleading, and finally of estimating the consequences of an analytic process.

I have wondered whether it makes sense publicly to advocate so personal a vantage and impose it on others, to pursue all of these things that might be important only for me and my individual tendencies and conflict-dispositions. My presentation of the theory and practice of psychoanalytic technique is not colored so subjectively because I was unable to express it in more objective and generally valid terms. Nor did the very personal subjective color emerge from any belief on my part that my way of working analytically is particularly recommendable, particularly effective, or something special in some other respect. My intention was to represent reality such as I experience it and assess it in my work as an analyst in as direct and unadulterated way as I am capable. For those who have followed my text up to this point, it cannot be a matter of accepting or rejecting my explanations, of being persuaded by this or disappointed by that. Those who are still hoping to find all that is missing have not understood that what counts is recognizing for themselves the reality that is decisive for *them* and that *they* experience and must assess in their own analytic work. I think that in such a process not just I but everyone says to himself: "I build the box I sit in myself, and I jump into the fire I have started for myself."

What is that supposed to mean?

It means nothing more and nothing less than that the person concerned is always the one who exposes himself. As analyst, I expose myself. The resources and devices I have to protect myself against anxieties and conflicts are the resources and devices of the analyst I described: keeping to the analytic "setting," that is, the external frame in which the analysis unfolds, knowledge of metapsychology, and knowledge of the theory of technique. My analysand sets for me the traps he must set. He watches and waits. He does not pose to himself the question of whether I will step into these traps or whether I know to avoid them. The question poses itself whether *I* know it and whether I am able to see through the unconscious motives. The traps the analysand sets are not traps aimed at me personally. They are the traps he sets for everyone and, first of all, for himself. As an analyst, I have to accept that and neither feel put to the test nor think that the analysand does this or that to hurt me.

As an analyst, I constantly find myself in midst of interconnections of motivations amidst which I do not want to go in circles but from which I do not wish to extricate myself either, for what counts is that the analysis does not fall into the water like a stone that draws circles yet sinks, and the circles come to an end and nothing has changed except that somewhere on the bottom there is now a stone. As an analyst, I do not get involved in the analytic process to prove something. Nor do I get involved to prove nothing. I go down a path with my analysand. Every analyst goes down a path with his analysand. All are different from each other.

Where does this path lead?

When methods are developed from the dialectical comprehension of happenings and are applied, methods that make something that feels foreign, locked in on itself, uncomprehended, into something familiar, opened up, and comprehensible, then what has been developed must not be lost and dissolved. What shows itself there has always been there. It was, by itself, without connection to something else. Now it is grasped by functional capacities, and although those capacities initially belonged to the analyst as well, they subsequently detach from his person and his sphere of influence and become functional capacities of the analysand and his sphere of influence.

That is where the path leads. There are no goals that I or my analysand can set our eyes on to get to that place toward which the analytic process strives.

In analysis, everything always turns around the same experiences. Goals that inevitably appear and that analysand and analyst consciously, preconsciously, or unconsciously aim for and seek to reach, that they are somehow also forced to bring in as auxiliary supports, are revealed as an illusory invention of the analysis itself and are relativized. The analytic process is without destination. Like all other developments in life, certain formations and results may be recognizable only once they have arrived. The analytic process follows lines that time and again relativize the setting of destinations. The dynamic that develops from this finally allows the flexibility and elasticity in the ego to emerge that make a rearticulation of the inclinations toward conflictualness possible. These rearticulations cannot be dictated by any system of rules. They can neither be foreseen nor can they be planned in advance. They emerge or they don't. Their actualization can be promoted, but cannot be forced, by the analytic process. Such rearticulations, moreover, can also arise in people's lives without analysis, when intrapsychic dispositions and social conditions favor developments in this direction.

In many cases, even a carefully conducted analytic process is unable to unfold far enough to reach the point where the flexibility in assessing one's own tendencies toward conflictualness I described really arises. Rather than speak in such cases of mistakes on the part of the analyst or of a premature rigidification on the part of the analysand that block the analytic process, I prefer to consider the socially conditioned constraints – to which analyst and analysand are exposed like everyone else – to be an often decisive factor. It is then that we see that the social and economic structures of the society in which we all live have had, and continue to have, so sustained a repressive influence that from a certain point onward, the shared enterprise of the analytic partners seems as if paralyzed. It is then as if the positivistic (as opposed to dialectical) models of thought – with their overestimation of goal-setting, their achievement-oriented actionism, their dichotomous valuations, and so forth, models that so distinctly characterize the prevailing social structures – dominate all facets of human experiencing. For both partners, the attempt at assuming a different attitude and acquiring greater inner and outer autonomy than societal morality grants the individual usually fails. It fails less, however, because of any real, concrete restrictions resulting from the social sphere than because of the usually unconscious demands of the superego – both the analyst's and the analysand's – that force them to renounce the continuation, which becomes ever more difficult, of the shared work of analysis.

Notes

1 This insistence of Morgenthaler's that the analyst should *not* have "any inhibition to expose [him]self" is a key point – the very antithesis of the mainstream understanding of Freud's notion that "The doctor should be opaque to his patients and, like a mirror, should show them nothing but what is shown to him" (Freud, 1912, p. 118).

2 The reference here is to Freud's "Analysis Terminable and Interminable" – often understood to be expressing late-in-life pessimism about the therapeutic efficacy of all psychoanalysis – a pessimism which Morgenthaler actually does *not* share (cf. Freud, 1937). Yet despite all the skepticism expressed in this essay, Freud does conclude in a vein evocative of some of Morgenthaler's views as well. While conceding that "every experienced analyst will be able to recall a number of cases in which he has bidden his patients a permanent farewell," Freud asserts with equanimity: "Our aim will not be to rub off every peculiarity of human character for the sake of a schematic 'normality,' nor yet to demand that the person who has been 'thoroughly analysed' shall feel no passions and develop no internal conflicts. The business of the analysis is to secure the best possible psychological conditions for the functions of the ego; with that it has discharged its task" (pp. 249–250).

3 Giardiasis is an infection of the small intestine caused by the microscopic parasite *Giardia lamblia*. It is contracted through contaminated food or water or contact with infected people. In the 1970s, the typical treatment was with the antimalarial drug quinacrine (*Atabrine*). Nowadays, a more likely treatment would be with the antibiotic metronidazole (Flagyl).

4 Again, this is a key point for Morgenthaler. In striking contrast with conventional postwar psychoanalysts' conviction that defenses need to be identified and analyzed early on, Morgenthaler insists on seeing the motive forces within the patient that seek to enter into an analytic relationship and to move the analytic process onward.

5 In an intriguing Freudian slip, Morgenthaler here has confused the resistance of the superego, which Freud had contended was, of the five types of resistance he had identified, the resistance most impossible to undo, with the resistance of the id (Freud's fourth type). In an Addendum to the 1926 essay, "Inhibitions, Symptoms and Anxiety," Freud had said: "The fourth variety, arising from the id, is the resistance which, as we have just seen, necessitates 'working-through'. The fifth, coming from the super-ego and the last to be discovered, is also the most obscure though not always the least powerful one. It seems to originate from the sense of guilt or the need for punishment; and it opposes every move towards success, including, therefore, the patient's own recovery through analysis" (p. 160). Nonetheless, the slip is quite understandable, for in the original 1926 text Freud did remark with regard to the repetition-compulsion of the id: "If, now, the danger-situation changes so that the ego has no reason for fending off a new instinctual impulse analogous to the repressed one, the consequence of the restriction of the ego which has taken place will become manifest. The new impulse will run its course under an automatic influence – or, as I should prefer to say, under the influence of the compulsion to repeat. It will follow the same path as the earlier, repressed impulse, as though the danger-situation that had been overcome still existed. The fixating factor in repression, then, is the unconscious id's compulsion to repeat – a compulsion which in normal circumstances is only done away with by the freely mobile function of the ego. The ego may occasionally manage to break down the barriers of repression which it has itself put up and to recover its influence over the instinctual impulse and direct the course of the new impulse in accordance with the changed danger-situation. But in point of fact the ego very seldom succeeds in doing this: it cannot undo its repressions" (p. 153). Only in the final line of this book does Morgenthaler return to the superego.

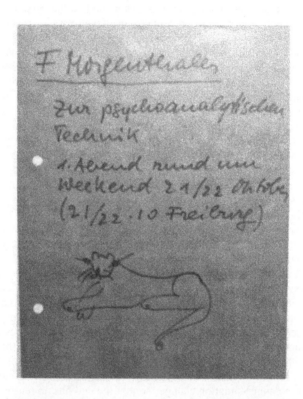

Figure 11.1 Announcement for a seminar on Fritz Morgenthaler's *Technik*, Freiburg, West Germany, October 1978. Morgenthaler frequently "signed" his correspondence with a hand-drawn lion. Personal collection, Ita Grosz-Ganzoni.

Part II

Supplementary material

Chapter 11

Review of Heinz Kohut,
The Analysis of the Self

A systematic approach to the psychoanalytic treatment of narcissistic personality disorders

The very title of the book, *The Analysis of the Self*, clearly shows that Heinz Kohut does not limit himself to presenting the application of the psychoanalytic method of treatment to narcissistic personality disorders.[1] The importance of his work goes far beyond that: it is of fundamental significance for the continuing development of psychoanalytic metapsychology. The scientific comprehension of the development of the libido (S. Freud) first led to the conception of an id analysis; the exploration of the ego and so-called ego psychology (Hartmann and his colleagues) led to an understanding of the processes that take place in the development of the ego and that are decisive for the structuring of the personality. This development led to the formulation of ego analysis. Finally, with his contribution, Heinz Kohut presents the foundations for a development of narcissism, whereby a new conception arises: the conception of an analysis of the self.

Three criteria must be stressed if we are to understand Heinz Kohut's contribution to the body of knowledge that is psychoanalysis. First, the author develops his theses with great clarity, and in accordance with the most strictly scientific perspectives, as he expands the present state of metapsychology sensibly, coherently, and without ambiguities. As second criterion, we must stress Kohut's merit in always deriving theoretical considerations, inferences, and abstractions from empirical observation. He starts from the course of the analysis as it was conducted and assesses, critically and uncompromisingly, the personal, practical experiences he uses for the verification of the theory. Finally, mention should be made of the creative impulse, which is responsible for the rich profusion of ideas and the often surprising twists and turns.

Thanks to these criteria it is possible for the reader to take the path indicated by Kohut and also to place himself in a position, as analyst, to continue developing the approach on his own, with his own analysands. For these reasons we are entitled to say that this book, which meaningfully combines theory and practice, may well represent, for today's practicing psychoanalyst, the most important work since Anna Freud's *The Ego and the Mechanisms of Defense* of 1936.

Looking at the content of the book more closely, special attention is to be paid first to the introductory considerations. The delimitation of narcissistic neuroses from the psychoses on differential-diagnostic grounds is of special significance and therefore considered in detail. But the main emphasis is on laying out the rationale for why patients who present a profound disturbance in their narcissistic development are nonetheless able to form a specific, stable narcissistic transference – indeed, one that allows for the therapeutic reactivation of archaic structures without any need to fear dangerous further regressions. In this context, Kohut calls attention to the psychodynamic factors responsible for the cohesion of the self, whereby he also underscores how important it is to heed not just the pathological but also the well-functioning aspects of these patients' psychic organization.

The book's core is dedicated to the two manifestations of narcissism, both of which Kohut derives from the – unavoidable – imperfection of maternal care in earliest childhood, and which he discusses separately. He says that the infant substitutes for the earlier perfection of the dual union between mother and child the establishment of a grandiose and exhibitionist image of its self and the ascription of the earlier perfection to an admired, omnipotent (albeit transitional) self-object. In this way, Kohut is able to introduce two new concepts to the metapsychology of narcissism: the *grandiose self* and the *idealized parent imago*. Under favorable conditions of development, the archaic grandiose self's exhibitionism and fantasies of grandeur are, in ways specific to each phase, integrated adequately into the adult personality and subsequently nourish ego-syntonic ambitions, joy taken in one's own activities, and a positive sense of the self. Under similarly favorable conditions, the idealized parent imago, too, is integrated into the total personality. Introjected as idealized super-ego, it becomes an important component of the psychic organization for it ensures that ideals of one's own are formed and that one's own ideals can be pursued.

When on November 30, 1971, Heinz Kohut gave the New York Psychoanalytic Society's A. A. Brill lecture and spoke about "Thoughts on Narcissism and Narcissistic Rage," he said the following: "If I were asked what I consider to be the most important point to be stressed about narcissism I would answer: its independent line of development, from the primitive to the most mature, adaptive and culturally valuable."[2]

Starting from this concept, the author in the book's two central chapters examines the psychopathological disturbances to be found in patients presenting insufficient integration of the archaic grandiose self or the idealized parent imago. He shows very persuasively how the symptoms of these patients can be understood, how the emptiness in the sense of self, the inability to obtain narcissistic gratification by oneself, feelings of shame or anger when encountering the slightest insult, lack of relationship to oneself and to others, present themselves from the perspective he is taking up. From here, he develops the technical concept: the therapeutic reactivation of the idealized parent imago or rather the omnipotent object, on the one hand, and the therapeutic reactivation of the grandiose self, on the other. The forms of narcissistic transference that evolve in the course of the psychoanalytic treatment of the seventeen patients presented in the book clearly and unambiguously are demarcated from the forms of transference in psychoneuroses and, further, allow for a distinctive differentiation in two additional directions. The first type relates to the idealized parent imago and strives to shape an *idealizing transference*, the second builds on the grandiose self and aims for what Kohut calls an actual *mirror transference*. From the technical point of view, Kohut's explanations are of decisive significance when we keep in mind just how difficult the treatment of narcissistically disturbed patients is. With great precision, and in a scientifically solid way, Kohut demonstrates that a welter of seeming expressions of resistance and defensive attitudes in reality cover up an incapacity of the patient to put up any kind of defense-reaction at all. He shows how momentous the technical mistakes are that we as analysts make all too easily when we do not understand the patient correctly.

The last part of the book sheds more light on precisely those sources that concern the countertransference and that are responsible for the analyst being inclined to reject narcissistic patients' needs for transference. Essentially, the difficulty with idealizing transference is that the analyst is expected to be much too much for his patient, while in mirror transference he is expected to be much too little, namely practically nothing. Both are hard to bear. Kohut summarizes the situation by explaining how, for long stretches of the analysis, the analyst is experienced not as an object but as a *function*.[3]

As is the case for all significant works, a review can convey only an indication. Thorough study of the book is indispensable today if, as an analyst, one wants to have a sense of the significance of the problematic of narcissism. One will then learn to what extent exactly Kohut's contribution to comprehending narcissism facilitates the management of the therapeutic work with serious narcissistic neuroses. Yet one will also recognize just how helpful and useful this contribution is in conducting almost all analyses, for there is hardly one among our analysands in whom a narcissistic problematic does not, sooner or later, come up at least temporarily.

Notes

1 Heinz Kohut's book was published in English in 1971 and it would soon appear in German as *Narzissmus* (1973). This review by Morgenthaler was based on the English original and was published in Alexander Mitscherlich's influential journal *Psyche* in February 1973, just in time to promote the German translation. Kohut had already presented to German-language readers on his work with patients with narcissistic character disturbances in the pages of *Psyche* in 1966 and 1969, and at the turn from the 1960s to the 1970s, a number of West German and Swiss analysts were taking up and discussing Kohut's innovative notions in a variety of venues. Morgenthaler in this review deemed the book "for the clinically active psychoanalyst of today perhaps the most important work since Anna Freud's *The Ego and the Mechanisms of Defence* of 1936." The two men had been in cordial correspondence at the latest by 1971 and the review clearly delighted Kohut. By the spring of 1973 (when Morgenthaler wrote to Kohut in April of "the friendly affection [between us], which is based on reciprocity" and reported on his recent trip to Papua New Guinea), the correspondence had become regular; Morgenthaler would also at the Paris IPA in July of 1973 prominently defend Kohut against his rival expert on narcissism Otto Kernberg. For the next four to five years, in numerous public lectures and training seminars, Morgenthaler became one of the most significant promoters and extenders of Kohut's work in the German-speaking lands – though not without qualification or criticism, as the next supplement will show.
2 This talk was subsequently published (Kohut, 1972).
3 Morgenthaler's enthusiasm for this particular Kohutian idea – that the analyst, in cases of narcissistic disturbance, often needed to serve more as a *function* for the patient than an *object* – was evident already in a paper he delivered at the IPA in Rome in 1969, and was amplified yet further in an essay of 1974 on perversions as self-healing attempts. Although in *Technik* the idea shows up only occasionally and indirectly, it is nonetheless implicit all through in the way that the analyst is encouraged to help the patient develop an expanded self.

Chapter 12

Letter to Heinz Kohut, September 25, 1977

Translated by Nicholas Levis

25 September 1977
Heinz Kohut M.D.
130 North Michigan Avenue
Chicago, Illinois, 60601

Dear Mr. Kohut,

I read your new book and then started to study it all over again. I am not yet done with this second stage of closer examination.[1] Your book is spectacular. Allow me to extend my very heartfelt congratulations for this work. You are like a pioneer discovering a territory far larger than the areas you have described.

What is fascinating for me in your discoveries is how obviously it shows that which is ubiquitous in human life, that which characterizes the emotional movement of a person in respect to the self and his or her environment. You are the first to give a name to this "self-evident" aspect, of which no one speaks. It is the unknown, even though every person carries within himself, and feels within himself, that the most important thing is to shape well the relationships with oneself and with others.

In my lectures on technique, whenever I say the relationship between analysand and analyst must always be right and congruent if the analytic process is to proceed smoothly, and when I point out that the classic metapsychology lacks the proper concepts to enable this "feeling of rightness," questions arise that demand an answer: what exactly constitutes this rightness, this congruence? Much of what I have said on this question fits into your concept, but I was missing the concept itself. You have now developed it and provided it.

I belong to those analysts who have always worked in the same way that you now articulate. I did it intuitively and with a bad conscience, because

I knew that it did not fit fully with what I had been taught. But I couldn't help myself and often doubted whether I was a serious analyst. Curiously enough my analyses went well and the supervision that I carried out proved to be very helpful to many who turned to me and who continue to do so. It was always said that I was an artist. With this label, the classicists of metapsychology and technique were able, also in the international context, to permit me to exist, as a kind of special case in the cabinet of curiosities. Now everything looks different. Your new pioneering book gives renewed impulse to psychoanalysis. It goes in a direction that accords with my own. This is why, when reading your book, I understand all of it as if I had always known it. I remember reading Freud for the first time. It was just like that. I am sure that you are setting something new in motion with your book. Much will be put in motion. There is one thing I want to say: those who have already somehow sensed all this, who already were thinking and feeling along the same lines, they will understand you and feel obligated to you. The others meanwhile will fight you. They will not be able to see that which they have not themselves already seen. While they may more or less show goodwill they will seek to place you somewhere on the periphery, so that nothing changes. But something will change. The psychoanalytic point of view cannot in the long term look away from what you are now revealing.

Your book is not easy to read. True, it is written well and clearly. The prose is light and fluent. Your language is simple, clear and does not contradict itself. The repetitions, which you use in various passages so as to emphasize important points, also help to lend weight to your train of thought where needed. Despite all this, it is not easy to gain sight of the big picture. It is hard to stabilize one's own view of your book. There is much that slips away again and again, that can no longer be fashioned into a single unity with subsequent chapters. But why is this?

I do not believe this is the case because you want to make it harder, or because you do not bring things together coherently, or because you allow your train of thought to become vague. No. The real reason is that the reader himself changes in the course of reading, or I should say in the course of study of the reading. That which one read in an earlier chapter was read by a different person. One must go back and read again passages that one had already understood. And then one reads it differently, understands it anew and builds it into a new, larger set of connections. That is the quality that makes your book a difficult book. It is also what gives your book its explosive nature.

One has the choice of either suppressing everything and pushing it aside and trying to deny that which is difficult, or else one must gradually recognize the consequences that again now go far beyond that which you describe.

It was with wise intent that you hewed closely to the narcissistic neuroses, to the situation of the ill patients, as you formulated your theses. You showed how the psychoanalytic treatment of these people proceeds differently and more sensibly when guided by your theses and concepts. From your examples, especially Mr. M., it becomes wonderfully obvious how important it is that the analysand understands what has happened to him, how this understanding then sets something else in motion, and how in turn other things can be understood. This means not simply stamping out whatever seems to be pathological so as to postulate some kind of "healing" through an illusory disposal. The dynamic that you indicate is more fundamental.

In everything that you have developed, you stick rigorously to your analytic work with patients. Only in a very few cases do you venture out onto branches. One such branch is the comparison with physics. What you say about that is beautiful and long overdue. Psychoanalysis above all cannot simply ignore these insights from physics that relativize so much.

Another branch that you barely explore is that of society and its structures. In this connection you leave it to "others" to work it out. You say you are not competent to do so. But I ask myself what you would expect from sociologists. You surely must know that these "others" will never be able to do it. How should they see that? How will they understand it?

No, it is the case that your concepts and theses must be applied to the ill society in the same way as you apply them to the ill patients whom you describe. The widening scope of your concepts is society in its structures. Basically one could say that your book provides the cornerstone for a psychology of society, a psychology of society that uses the model of the pathology of the narcissistic neuroses. You do not touch upon this at all, at least not explicitly. I think that is a good decision; you are restricting yourself. If your book were expanded to societal structures, it would no longer be your book. A similarly comprehensive view of societal structures would lead to insights that the rulers in our society would never allow. Such an insight is allowed to you as a psychoanalyst only if you keep to your corner. Anything else would be too dangerous. Your book anticipates much, it is almost mind-boggling, but I can see it clearly. Your concept is the concept of every person's experience, every person's emotional experience. Nobody may be permitted to recognize it as that which you see, even though everyone feels it in themselves – for if it were to be recognized, society with its constraints could not continue to exist as it has until now. Yes, you were right to have made your book into your book, and limited yourself to your own area. It is precisely in the focus on this area that you make clear what is urgent and necessary. That these same principles are at work ubiquitously wherever people live and experience opens a further field of unknown size, replete with shifting dangers of the crudest possible misunderstandings.

In connection with this a metaphor came to me while reading your book, and I have not been able to rid myself of the question it prompts. At the Spanish royal court, Velazquez painted Philip's court jesters and the counts, barons and court ladies. Later Goya also painted the people of Charles's court, his children and courtiers. But in addition to that he also painted ordinary people and the mass execution of the rebels and the priests as donkeys. What then is the connection of all that to you and your book?

You, Heinz Kohut, along with your colleagues who choose your supervision, all of you treat patients of elite social standing and class. You all move within a milieu of elevated prosperity. (Even the patient who was abandoned by his mother and spent early childhood in a children's home was later a speculator on the stock exchange!!) I am comparing you and the people you occupy yourself with to the members of a royal court. The mass of the people live outside that circle. Now I have always asked myself, is Kohut a minister at the court, or is he a count, baron or prince who moves within the human sphere of this elite society? Or is Kohut the wise court jester, who may live at the royal court, but does not actually belong to it, who is only waiting for the right moment, once he is alone, to whisper the entire truth in the king's ear without shame or shyness? What I mean to ask is: are you really aware where you stand in the society and that your work could be and must become an instrument of the mass of the people? In other words this is not simply about expanding the metapsychological concepts of psychoanalysis but rather a revolutionary concept of life praxis in general. Yes, one cannot ignore that a relationship between people that is not dishonest can hardly survive without your concepts. But you speak about this at best at the periphery. I am not saying you should have done it differently. And I also think that it is good the way it is. What interests me is something else. I would like to know how things look within you, deep down inside. I sense there is an inner shyness there, a tendency not to want to grapple with it, to leave it to others. I ask myself whether that is possible. I do not believe it is really possible. Others will not be able to take it up. Once again decades or more will pass until someone comes who can transform that into something that brings out the kind of profound insight that will go far beyond the psychoanalytic.

If one were to compare your work with a wide-spreading tree, I believe you stay at the trunk. Once again I believe you are right to do so. But one of the very large branches of this tree is sexuality. You deal with it only on the margins, and only bring it in where it fits into the framework of your concepts and within the circle of your interests. With respect to Oedipus, however, you then suddenly and unexpectedly go far beyond that, but only allusively. However, you speak very explicitly about the most decisive aspect, namely that the Oedipal experience as such is something fundamentally positive for the entirety of psychic development.

I liked that very much, and it corresponds to my own longstanding view. What you are expressing and developing applies without a doubt not only to the Oedipal, but also to everything sexual as such. However, you do not go this far. You stick with an image of "healthy" sexuality. Over and over again you demonstrably deploy this image as a polar opposite to "abnormal" sexuality. I have often asked myself whether that is also a function of how you first of all want to say the one thing on which you justifiably stake so much, and so you intentionally and thoughtfully limit yourself to just that – for the sake of clarity – or if instead you truly are of the opinion that, for example, the fetishist on whom you report would have to rid himself of his fetishism, as he himself believes, so as to feel well and whole in himself? At the same time you describe, so compellingly and clearly, why and how this fetishism arose. Almost everything is simply the way it is. Changes do not come about because something like the fetishism disappears. Changes can be attributed to transformations in the flexibility of the way of experiencing, and this can be understood psychoanalytically with regard to a human being with any form of experiencing sexuality. The same is true of Mr. M. with his love of the 14-year-old boy. In that case you rightly note that no coarse homosexual relationship arose between the two, and you describe how for Mr. M. it became possible, following the experience with the girl that he greeted, to use the love relationship to the boy to bring about the integrating transmutation of his failed idealization of his father into an ego ideal. Yet there you stay with a polar opposition in your observing and assessing of sexual strivings and permit the reader to feel confirmed in his prejudiced, moralizing, unarticulated attitude toward homosexuality, instead of pointing out that precisely in this development that you describe in Mr. M. something has happened that is of such decisive significance in analytic work with homosexuals and many perverts, so that the agonizing, the irritating, that adheres to the sexual practice can be relaxed, and exactly in this relaxation can lead to transformations in the sexual experiencing. For me in other words it is such that you, in this case of Mr. M., are describing exactly what is the most important step in analytic work with homosexuals, the step that the homosexual must take in the analysis so as to become reconciled with his homosexuality. Of course everything then changes, but not in a way that corresponds to the societal morality. The homosexual remains homosexual, just as the fetishist remains a fetishist, but differently. With all this I do not mean that I am not in agreement with you. I think I am more in agreement with what you say than you are yourself because in some cases I take your train of thought further than you do.

Now I wish to turn to the letter that you have sent me. Elrod in the meantime has written to me but I have not yet been able to reach him. He wants to come see me and discuss the whole thing with me. I want to read the article by Elrod and this Osterkamp first before I go ahead taking a position in the way you expect.[2] *Das Argument*, the Marxist periodical that is published in the German Democratic Republic, was in earlier times a very good dynamic leftist review. For a few years now it has become an inflexible organ of orthodox Marxists who very typically are unsympathetic to psychoanalysis. I must first see what that looks like before I obligate myself to anything. I am traveling tomorrow again to Sardinia where I want to complete my big painting that I already started there. Actually I only came back to Zurich because of my exhibition. Surprisingly I was asked if I could do this show on short notice. I accepted and am now exhibiting my South American watercolors. The opening was two days ago. Many people came. I was very happy with the reception of my pictures. Despite my painterly activities I am again booked for many lectures this coming October, and will in the course of my lectures on various issues of technique and metapsychology have the opportunity to be able to speak at length about your book.

I have reread this letter to you, surely the longest and most thorough that I have ever written. Everything remains a fragment. I see it is difficult to do you justice. It is simply the case that your book has made a very big impression on me and I feel that it will still take a lot before I have the full overview of everything that you say.

I would like it best if we could talk about this at length, whether this will be in the USA or at our own place, when you come to Europe again.

My friends, the Parins, are now on holiday. They are traveling to Spain.

Many heartfelt greetings to you and your wife.

From your

F. Morgenthaler

Notes

1 Sent in response to Heinz Kohut's second major work, *The Restoration of the Self,* published in English in 1977, Morgenthaler will note at the end that this letter is "surely the longest and most thorough that I have ever written." As it turns out, it was in this letter that Morgenthaler first formulated the eloquent defense of sexual idiosyncrasy that would two years later, in a sequence of published essays, make him the first European analyst since Freud to declare that homosexuality is not a pathology. The letter, along with further correspondence between Kohut and Morgenthaler, is from the archive of Thomas Kohut.

2 Norman Elrod was a psychoanalytically interested Swiss psychotherapist. Ute Osterkamp was a West German psychologist involved in the "critical psychology" movement who was unsympathetic to what she saw as "the scientific untenability of Freud's drive-theory" (1976). *Das Argument,* contrary to Morgenthaler's statement, was a Marxist journal published in *West* Germany. Kohut's request for Morgenthaler to involve himself came in an ongoing context of debates within left-leaning circles over whether psychoanalysis had potential value either for personal growth or cultural criticism or whether it was reprehensibly depoliticizing and adaptation- and conformity-inducing. Morgenthaler's own differentiated contribution to that question is in the essay he published in *Kursbuch* in 1977 (Supplement 3).

Figure 13.1 Cover of the special issue on "Sensualities" of the New Left journal *Kursbuch* in which Morgenthaler's essay on "Modes of Interaction in Perversions" appeared, 1977. Reprinted by permission of Rotbuch Verlag.

Modes of interaction in perversions and perversion of modes of interaction

A look over the fence around psychoanalysis

Perversions are interactions (see Figure 13.1).[1] Fetishists, transvestites, sadists, masochists, pedophiles, pyromaniacs, exhibitionists, voyeurs, transsexuals, necrophiliacs, sodomites: I won't describe them here. I don't want to try and capture them psychoanalytically; neither do I want to compile what has long been known or add something new. Perversions are modes of sexual experiencing that seem particularly disconcerting and unrelatable, not only because people's sexual development in the majority leads to a heterosexual choice of a partner but because the psychic development from the infant to the adult in the cultural and social realms of certain societies suppresses the polymorphous-perverse character of human sexual life and heterosexuality represents an ideological monopoly of societal morality.

Most of what is being said about perversions is hypocritical. What we call perverse is a myth. To experience something in a specific way, differently from others, is only a gradual difference from perverts' way of experiencing. In describing perversions, we distinguish and we distance ourselves. Every society produces the perversions and the perverts it needs.[2]

In Manhattan, I discovered the colorfulness of New York in the red-white-and-blue chimneys behind the skyscrapers' black and green facades. This colorfulness awoke in me a sensual excitation. I was fascinated. During an analysis, a fetishist reported what is going on within him when he finally finds the long-sought-for yellow boot that sensually excites him, fascinates him. Can the two be compared? T. comes to me, reads what I just wrote and asks: "Was your impression of Manhattan really so strong that you can compare it with the fetishist's impression, with erection, orgasm, and so on?" I say to T.: "Do you really know so exactly what is going on in a fetishist when the object of his longing fascinates him? Does it come to an erection and orgasm there?"

The comparison is incorrect. It contains a distortion. Seen from the out-side, there is a great difference between the fetishist and me in New York. He seeks and finally finds what he is looking for. I was surprised because I unex-pectedly saw what I couldn't have been looking for. But I say: it's the same thing. It is about access to magnificence.[3] The glow of positive self-esteem bears, in all people, the traces of magnificent omnipotence from childhood. On this level of experiences, success has little to do with reaching a goal.

When I exhibited my watercolors of American cities, a critic wrote: "He sees luminously bright colors even in the grey stone deserts of New York or Chicago." Is that perverse? No, of course not. Perverse experiencing represents a quantitative intensification and sexual coloring of the mag-nificence. The pervert has a much more direct access to sensuality. That, however, leads to a qualitatively changed interaction with sensuality that is no longer adequate to reality. Children generally have a much more direct access to the perverse than adults. Typical of this is less this or that trait in their sexual games, and more the direct, open access to sensuality, to the work of the senses.

A child-analyst, about 40 years of age, called me on the telephone, in quite some excitement. She requested a meeting with me about a peculiar case in her analytic practice. She spent five hours on the train and came to the meeting we had arranged. She cried, she was at a loss. For more than two years, she had been analyzing an 8-year-old boy, a social misfit. The boy had since stopped displaying symptoms. He was an intelligent, bright boy full of imagination, very much ahead of his age. The boy had recently come to his session and demanded of his analyst that she explain to him what is happening when the bull is mounting the cow from behind. The analyst tried offering the boy the sexual education she could provide. At the end of the session, the boy said: "If you don't want to tell me what happens when the bull mounts the cow, I'll ask the people on the street." In the following session, the same thing happened again. The analyst was increasingly at a loss, the boy increasingly defiant, almost violently aggressive. It was in that phase that the woman rushed to come see me.

I:	"Why are you crying?"
The analyst:	"I should never have been allowed to become a child-analyst. I do not understand children."
I:	"You are an excellent analyst. You just didn't understand that with his question about the bull and the cow, the boy

wanted to know whether you, his analyst, have had sexual intercourse, whether you have a man to make love with. He knows, after all, that you aren't married and that you don't have children."

When our meeting was over, the woman was anxious in expecting the next session with the boy. "What shall I say to him? Shall I tell him the truth? Is that still analytic?"

The next session with the boy took a completely unexpected course. He was relaxed and did not ask again. It was as if he had been sitting there with us when we were having our meeting. That was the unconscious.

Seriousness in playfulness and playfulness in seriousness are traits of experiencing that give magnificence a point of access to an individual's self-esteem without shame, incapacity to adapt, and torturous self-destruction needing to occur. When the boy addressed the analyst's intimate sexual sphere, the woman lost her playfulness. Everything was deadly serious now. A deep rift opened up between the playful and the serious such as it appears quite generally in our achievement-oriented society. Since people are raised to experience, in the processes of work, the seriousness of life, it cannot come as a surprise that the playfulness of leisure time can only be a forced, desperate compensation. The everyday becomes grey, sensuality is lacking. We may compare the relationship of the dominant society to perverts with that of the analyst to the bull-and-cow boy. The incapacity to approach and understand what is playful in a serious manner and what is serious in a playful manner leads to a hypocrisy that covers over a profound helplessness. Society feels threatened by the manifest perversions because they address its microstructures, which are themselves perverse, the way the boy addressed his analyst's sexual sphere. In society, the consequences are misunderstanding, hostility, and denigration in assessing the perversions.

Psychoanalysis has always tried to understand perversions in their essence, to hold childhood vicissitudes responsible for this or that sexual behavior in the adult. Psychoanalysis has contributed a lot to clarifying these questions. It failed, however, to reach the goal it pursued, to cure the psychically ill from their sexual deviations, from pathogenic sexual abnormalities. Yet it is incorrect to put it that way. For psychoanalysis does not actually have a goal. It is just that psychoanalysts pursue goals because they think in socially conformist terms. In the service of the interests of a dominant society, psychoanalysis has lost much of its real substance. It has itself taken on the modes of interaction of the society in which it developed and in which it must prove itself. It completes and renders its scientific instruments more precise with the same seriousness with which the society in which it moves enhances and diversifies the means of production without taking the psychic consequences for consumers fully into consideration. The absurdity that pervades all this striving is being denied. It is identical to the perversity that covertly pervades the interactions of "normal" people. Although psychoanalysis discovered the polymorphous-perverse nature of infantile sexuality and although it is capable, thanks to this knowledge, of revealing the drive-vicissitudes of the people it takes into its care, it became ever less capable of recognizing the absurd within itself the more it adapted to the roles society assigned to it. Anything playful in its serious pursuits seems suspect. The seriousness in playfulness garners ever less attention because it no longer conforms to social standards of assessment. Nonetheless, psychoanalysis is, after all, the science of the unconscious. The seriousness with which it pursues the scientific comprehension of its object should be pervaded by playful pleasure, so that the full extent of human beings' potential possibilities can be perceived, so that everything that previously seemed set can be put in perspective, extended, rearticulated anew, and understood differently. The results of such a process would correspond to the seriousness that is at the basis of all real playing. In the modes of interaction of psychoanalysis there is a widening rift evident between playfulness and seriousness, just as in the society in which we live. Psychoanalysis applies the same standards, scientifically and practically, to its activity that achievement-oriented society brings to the work ethic. Because the modes of interaction of psychoanalysis carry with them the myth of omniscience, its representatives enjoy great social prestige. The elitist, condescending consciousness that accompanies this prestige represents whatever is magnificent in a rigid and ritualized way, just as whatever is magnificent is hidden within the disconcertingly sexual admixture to the perverse ritual.

I compared the colorfulness of Manhattan with the shoe fetishist's yellow boot in order to wrest the perverse from our fixed ideas about fetishism. What has been fixed as an object in "the yellow boot" is a congealed emotional movement, and this congealing has a profound meaning in the experiencing of the person who has become a fetishist. Here, too, the rift between seriousness and playfulness is apparent. The ritualization in a perverse activity reflects the loss of the playful in a phenomenon that should be taken seriously. The society looking at the pervert, however, treats the human being like a play-toy it cannot take seriously.

Everyone carries within him an image of himself, and this image must be beautiful and whole for one's self-esteem to be so strong and resistant that it can bear the reality of life and the reality of the society in which one lives.[4] Now, the image we have built up of ourselves is the result of a long development that began very early in our life and that has been steered very early onto decisive, highly specific tracks. For the fetishist I spoke of, the yellow boot is a part of his image of himself. When life begins, mother and child are a unity, each a part of the other. But it cannot remain that way. Unavoidably, this dual-unionist self-conception is disrupted. Then the child's world is no longer perfect. Something is lacking. A gap, a fissure, a gaping cavity that causes anxiety leads to a greedy urgency to alleviate this disturbance, to fill in what is lacking. Fantasies of omnipotence and megalomania seek to restore the perfection of the child's world by shutting out reality. This cannot succeed. Under the pressure of reality, the fantasies of omnipotence and greatness are transformed into movement, into an energy that is put into the service of striving for the fulfilment of ideals. In the dual union, the child was only satisfied, in love with the satisfaction, as it were. Later, it falls in love with the person who brings satisfaction. The child idealizes the great figures of its surroundings. Then, it becomes more conscious of reality and internalizes the admiration that had at first been directed outwards. Now it discovers in itself things it admires. This is how the image of one's own inner person emerges, an image meant to be whole, coherent, and beautiful. But the whole, coherent, beautiful image of oneself never really emerges. Each and every one of us in this process suffers a shipwreck. In what we think, fantasize, do, and creatively produce, each and every one of us strives to fill in the gap, to round out the self-conception, to restore the beauty of the image of ourselves. When such striving becomes a conscious goal, either the most profound shame or undifferentiated arrogance arises. Both are unbearable in the long run. The tendency in any case remains unconscious, undirected. There are many paths that lead to that which only ever constitutes an approximation.

The gap in self-esteem produces in people an agonizing self-destructive tension that deprives its expression of all sensualness. Psychoanalysis sees in this a structural disturbance of the narcissistic development in early childhood that has far-reaching pathological consequences in personality formation. Psychoanalysis early on saw the significance of infantile sexuality as an expression of the polymorphous-perverse, inborn structure of the sexual.[5] In all cases, the polymorphous-perverse is built into a person's image of themselves in one form or another, and it plays as great a role in the development toward heterosexuality, so highly invested in our society, as it does in all other, disapproved-of forms of sexual experiencing.

In childhood, the traits of one's sexual disposition still participate without contradiction in all doing, fantasizing, and creating. That is why in the various phases of childhood development, some elements of infantile sexuality are always involved in the image of one's own self. Because infantile sexuality normally is structured polymorphous-perversely, we can also say that children quite generally have direct naive access to the perverse. When they become adults, this access becomes less apparent. It is quite similar with certain talents. There are children who draw and paint as if there were a secret Klee or Picasso hidden in them. With the onset of puberty, the talent fades and makes way for a different movement. We should not regret this.

There are people who discover in their childhood – somehow, at some point, always very early and unfathomably – a sharply contoured trait, or streak, of perverse fascination. They fit – with precision and at an exact spot – this newly discovered, highly valued something, like a colorful stone, into the mosaic of the image of themselves. In the further course of their development, usually with the onset of puberty, this sharply contoured trait of perverse fascination might fade and make way for a different movement.

Yet the discovery of such a clearly contoured trait of perverse fascination is not to be compared so much with a talent as, rather, with what a talent can uniquely produce. A talent is an exhilarating capacity for play that can give creative expression to what has been experienced but it never represents the only way to give expression to what has been experienced. When roles must be taken on, when institutions and formalizations begin codetermining our experiencing, in short, when heads are societally set straight, then talents can fade because people's fantasy usually cannot be set straight that easily. There is the possibility, however, that such talents can be revived under new and different circumstances.

A clearly contoured trait or streak of perverse fascination is the manifestation, the product of a creative achievement. It was accomplished in the past, very early, in a threatening situation. Distinctive traits from the polymorphous-perverse sexual disposition were emphasized, developed further, and differentiated, and, like a plug, fitted into the threatening gap in self-esteem as seamlessly as possible. With this, a void in the image of one's own self was filled so as to avoid a rupture in the image of one's own person. Such a rupture would have led to a mode of experiencing that could do nothing but oscillate between disconnected omnipotence and helpless inner emptiness. This plug-like construct in a person's experiential domain seems perturbing, like a stiff foreign object, comparable to a prosthesis. But the comparison with a prosthesis is misleading. The perverse trait is a living component of the person because it contains the sexual drivenness as such. The comparison with a prosthesis is correct, however, when we look at the social interactions within which perverts move. When roles must be taken on, when institutions and formalizations begin to codetermine the experiencing, in short, when heads are being set straight, the perverse isolated streak in these people's experiencing intensifies and becomes a perversion. The ritualization of the perverse action amplifies the sense of a foreign object. The rigidification keeps pace with the societally demanded conforming – or even partially replaces it. The taking-on of roles and institutionalizations, formalizations and societally conditioned manipulation contain the perverse microstructure of the modes of interactions among the "normal." On both sides, an amplified echo effect emerges: the pervert amplifies his perversion. Society intensifies its attitude and ritualizes its own modes of interaction toward perverts.

Things don't have to be this way. In other cultures, there are social structures that allow the development of a completely different mode of interaction in which the polarization just described is not expressed to the same degree. In Papua New Guinea, but also in Madagascar, I encountered cultures where specifically the access to animistic forms of experiencing is able to integrate the polymorphous-perverse background of human psychic life into all doing, creating, and thinking, and to express this in the most varied of forms. In these cultures rituals can be joyful celebrations that allow participation in a sensual pleasure in a playful way while the rituals of our society are usually cold and proceed without inner sensual participation on the individual's part.

In Madagascar there are peoples who bury many of their dead in a special way. One ethnic group in the southwestern part of the island maintains a custom according to which the daughters of a deceased, socially important man cut the flesh of the corpse from the bones by the river and clean the skeleton until it is white as snow. Then the bones are separated and placed in a small coffin that is buried accompanied by special ceremonies. A neighboring ethnic group buries its dead in huge piles of stones that are decorated by wooden steles and statuettes representing scenes from the life of the deceased. On the plateau in the center of the island, particularly colorful small houses are built that usually stand on the crest of a hill and house the coffin containing the dead. Once a year, the coffin is brought out and taken for a walk the whole day. Some men carry it on their shoulders and constantly trip on purpose so that the relatives and all those accompanying the walk will hear the rattling of the bones. A joyful festive mood reigns. In our society, such a way of dealing with the dead would be condemned as a desecration of corpses perpetrated by perverse necrophiliacs.

In the middle Sepik district of Papua New Guinea, numerous deep cuts are made on the backs of the young men in their initiation such that the bad blood can flow out. Such a procedure is superfluous for women because they menstruate. On the occasion of the initiation festival, which takes place once the wounds have healed, particular members of the initiate's family perform in prescribed roles that conform to old customs. Men appear wearing women's clothing and women wearing men's clothing. This institutionalized transvestism is an integrating component of the local populations' cultural and social consciousness. In our society, such occurrences would be called sadistic acts among transvestite psychopaths.

What is remarkable in both examples is how casual and playful people in these societies know how to be in dealing with perverse manifestations of doing, thinking, and experiencing. The contrast with similarly accumulated perverse modes of interaction in our own culture maybe lies less in those thematically verifiable perverse traits of this or that behavior that are found in all human societies, even if they do not present so obviously everywhere, and more in the way in which these modes of interaction are handled. In those societies, when people are confronted with their own perverse modes of experiencing and those of others, everything appears playful, casual, and relaxed. In our societies, perverse modes of experiencing lead to tension-filled and rigid modes of interaction both in the one who feels them and in all others who find themselves confronted with them. The loss of the playful that comes with this has the effect that the pleasure taken in reinvigorating childhood fantasies that powerfully expand one's self-esteem is degraded into bizarre ridiculousness.

In all perversions, the discovery of a sharply contoured streak of perverse fascination was once, in early childhood, the discovery of a splendid
possibility for powerfully invigorating a puny self-esteem threatened by
an inner emptiness. That is why it is possible to say that a perverse fascination opens up access to magnificence. In childhood, such fantasies of
omnipotence can still be combined, without contradiction, with sensual
pleasure. In the foreign cultures I mentioned, modes of interaction have
been developed that preserve and integrate this attainment of pleasure by
means of the perverse. That is why in these societies, the polar opposi-
tions between perverse and normal modes of interaction hardly appear. In
our society, the corresponding modes of interaction are rigid and lacking
in pleasure. The ritualizations are often voided of emotions. This leads to
everything perverse being devalued as laughable and weird.

This is another way of understanding the influence of societal structures
on the shape perversions take.

In this way of looking at the matter, the emphasis is not on this or that
sexual practice but rather on the sensual expression that this or that kind of
experiencing either provokes or does not provoke.

Sensuality is not identical to sexuality. Nor can we say that a specific
kind of doing or a specific choice of activity is more sensual than another
one. Anything can acquire a sensual glow if what we are doing or the way
in which we are doing it completes the image we have of ourselves, makes
it beautiful in our own sense, such that a relaxed basic mood arises in us
that is the precondition in the first place for an undulating playful eroticism
that seduces others into turning toward us.

Thanks to their socially-adequate role behavior, it may seem easier
for banking experts, car salesmen, bicyclists, psychoanalysts, vegetable
merchants, film distributors, heterosexuals, husbands, antiauthoritarian
pedagogues, and policemen to develop a good, balanced sense of self.
Whether in the process the relaxed basic mood arises that really makes it
sensual depends on how much hypocritical mendacity is blended in with
the self-assessment.

Perverts, homosexuals, rent boys and whores, drug addicts, and juve-
niles who refuse to take on a role offered by society have a much harder
time fashioning and also holding onto a complete, beautiful image of
themselves. If however they do succeed, they have achieved this success
in a much more autonomous way than their societally conformist fellow
human beings. Success in this sense is very rare. Mendacity is much more

easily visible in their case and is punished more brutally. Their despair appears as an illness.

Psychoanalysis of perverts and other social misfits can decisively promote and even prompt a development toward a stable and whole sense of self that can incorporate the sexual mode of experiencing of a perverse or other nature – on the condition that the psychoanalyst does not try to fight the perversion, the "social deviance," as something disruptive, pathological. What appears pathological here was once the "colorful stone" someone found and fitted into the mosaic of his inner image for it to shine and continue to exist. There was no choice there, and if the price to be paid for it was the rigidification of sensual experiencing, there was nonetheless the chance at some point of being able to set what had been "rigidified" into motion. Renouncing the "colorful stone" would have meant disintegration, psychic incoherence, would have meant real, perhaps incurable illness.

In the practice of psychoanalysis, we experience this in the following way: the relaxed basic mood that finally enters into the so anxiously guarded perverse structure of psychic experiencing initially and in all circumstances emerges in the context of the slowly deepening relationship between the psychoanalyst and his analysand. For that to be possible at all, the analyst must be conscious of his own profound inclinations toward conflictedness and not deny them. This is something he can have experienced only in his own personal analysis. Yet this experience showed him as well that there is no means by which his very own conflictualness, which is pervaded in its own way by perverse inclinations, can ever be eliminated. The experience of one's own analysis is the experience of being limited, of being restricted to what little one can change. The vast majority of things are the way they are. Only flexibility in dealing with them and elasticity in assessing the internal and external demands that everyone makes of themselves make rearticulations possible that put things in perspective, that expand ways of looking at things, and that allow for comprehending differently what had previously appeared settled.[6]

One of my first analysands was feeble-minded.[7] I was working in a hospital at the time. Paul L. was so feeble-minded that he was able at most to grasp a very simple linear causal connection, for example: My father was very strict. Therefore I had to work all the time. Or: The soup was too hot. I could not eat it. Paul L. was in analysis with me for three and a half years. Three hour-long sessions a week. After three years, he once showed up at the hospital for his session and sat down at my table, put his head on his arm and cried for a long time. Then he said: "Now I've got it. I AM FEEBLE-MINDED." He continued crying the entire session. I sat next to him and was speechless. After the session, Paul L. went home and said to his wife: "Me and you, we are both feeble-minded. We will not make children, or else there'll be a disaster." In the course of the following months, Paul L. became foreman in a plant nursery. He worked there the entire winter because he was so capable and prudent. He had four workers under him whom he led. He could neither read nor write. One of his workers did it for him.

With Paul L. and our shared experience I looked over the fence of psychoanalysis for the first time. How is this to be understood? Is it necessary to analyze someone who is feeble-minded in order to understand psychoanalysis? Or is the comparison intended to mean that perverts, like the feeble-minded, need to be analyzed? It's always possible to misunderstand everything.

The feeble-minded Paul L. grasped what was most improbable, that which was perfectly obvious for others but long unknowable to himself. At the same time, it was the most unchangeable; it was what it is. In the playful relationship of the analytic situation, he came to grasp what was serious. He then dealt with the fact that had to be taken seriously, his feeble-mindedness, with playful wisdom. He became someone else, although always still himself, feeble-minded – but differently. The feeble-mindedness of Paul L. in my example is merely an extreme expression of what finally happens in every case of analysis. It does not have to be a case of feeble-mindedness, where the mental vulnerability makes self-knowledge hard to imagine. It is in every case a long process until the seriousness of self-knowledge concerning one's own limitations is joined by the playful. For the activity of the psychoanalyst, this self-knowledge is a precondition. For the analysand, and quite especially for the pervert in analysis, it will be decisive to advance to such self-knowledge.

The psychoanalyst establishes a relationship with his analysand that suits himself and not primarily the analysand. Only then can the relationship really be congruent. It is congruent with what is taking place in the psychoanalyst. When that is the case, the analysand will develop, ever more comprehensively, an emotional echo – one which, borne by feelings, sets into motion everything that was once rigidified. Meanwhile, in the course of this process, the profound vitality of the partner, who in our case is a pervert, becomes the great manipulator of the other, his analyst. That is why it does not suffice for the analyst to look within himself and keep the relationship with his analysand congruent and deepen it. He cannot withdraw from the enormous seduction emanating from his partner, but he can very well become conscious of it.

The challenge here is to transform something cruel into something serious, manipulation into play. Common sense is not adequate here. Experience and a methodological bag of tricks are also not reliable supports. This is because the modes of interactions of the perverse reactivates the secret and hidden perverse traits of the modes of interaction of the normal.

As a science, psychoanalysis has created a finely organized theory with profound meaning: metapsychology. It has moreover described concepts of a theory of psychoanalytic technique. Metapsychology and the theory of psychoanalytic technique are not systems of rules that can be applied in specific situations for specific purposes to reach specific goals. It is, however, possible to misuse them to that end, if one thinks in positivistic terms. Positivistic thinking, in our society, is the basis of economic success, the ideology of performance-conscious man, the instrument of the dominant class, of power generally. Positivistic psychoanalysis wants to distinguish the healthy from the sick, wants to help the one who suffers by realizing goals, wants to cure everything that appears to it to be ill. Yet doing psychoanalysis means: thinking dialectically and dialectically understanding and applying the scientific theories created by psychoanalysis. They serve the analyst to maintain his relaxed basic mood. This is only possible if in the work of interpretation the relaxation of the analysand retroacts on the analyst. In such reciprocal interactions, the unconscious becomes conscious at the point when a quantitative accumulation of particular, situation-bound ideational contents undergoes a qualitative shift, one that unexpectedly lifts what has been understood previously onto a new level of comprehension.[8]

I won't try and elucidate the process that brings perverts to stay perverse without being perverse, the way we all are perverse without really knowing it. With a metaphor, I want to describe the perverse modes of interaction of the "normal," and thereby I am looking over the fence of psychoanalysis, over the fence of the dominant modes of interaction, over the fence that separates those manifesting perversions off from the others. The comparison I draw on really concerns everyone, irrespective of his position at work or in society, irrespective also of the forms his sexuality takes. I am not concerned with an agenda, not with a goal to be set, but with an attempt at evocatively representing a dialectical reciprocal effect.

In a psychiatric hospital, a doctor has for several months been watching a woman who has been living in the institution for more than ten years and year in, year out is unable to do anything but go to a window in the morning and stare into a courtyard all day. She does not see anything in this courtyard. She no longer experiences anything, is unresponsive, motionless, rigid, and mute. The doctor begins paying ever more attention to this woman. He circles around her, he shows up late at night, early in the morning when the patients are still in the dormitories, and he tries to establish a dialog with her. It all appears hopeless.

One evening, the doctor suddenly turns to the woman who, as always, is standing at the window and tells her insistently that he has been watching her the entire night and the entire day, without interruption. What brought him to behave this way, the doctor cannot explain to himself. The woman is completely astonished, turns around, and begins talking to the doctor. She is completely changed and begins to work in the laundry shop the very next morning.

It is not my intention to find a psychiatric or even a psychoanalytic explanation of this episode. I want to compare this vignette with the relationship society establishes with perverts. Fundamentally, society and all its members who think of themselves as normal look at perverts with the obstinate gaze of the woman staring into the courtyard of the institution. None of them see anything in the perverse. They do not experience anything in dealing with it, they are emotionally unresponsive, rigid, and mute. I want to compare the doctor – absurd as it may sound – with the pervert.[9] The pervert moves in a society that maintains modes of experiencing and interaction that are foreign to him but to which he has gotten used. I think that in this respect he may be compared with the doctor in the psychiatric institution because the doctor, too, feels the patients' modes of experiencing and interaction to be disconcerting even if, in accordance with this professional activity, he has gotten used to them. The doctor's private life follows different modes of experiencing and interaction, namely ones that suit him. Very much analogously, the "private life" of perverts contrasts with the modes of interaction of the "normal." A pervert's modes of interaction are the rituals of his sexual practices that suit him. The patients' institutional life is separated off and usually has little or, if possible, nothing to do with the doctor's private life.

In my example, something special happens. The doctor begins to take an interest in the mentally ill woman in a way that really accords with the modes of experiencing and interaction of his private life much more than those practiced in the institution by the patients. That is unusual. A playful tendency begins to invigorate the professional ritual of psychiatric activity in a special way. He circles, almost with a child's curiosity, the woman who has long been given up on and called incurable, and he develops a fantasy that mightily inflates his self-esteem. He wants to try the most improbable thing. He wants to reestablish the dialog with this unresponsive ill person. He seeks access to omnipotence and finds it by calling out to the woman that he has incessantly stared at her in just the way she is constantly staring into the courtyard. He has thereby taken up the modes of experiencing and interaction of the mentally ill in the institution without, however, giving up his own, which are entirely different, without even changing them. He has remained exactly who he has always been. Nor has he taken on a new role, has reacted neither artificially nor mendaciously. He has not taken the patient by surprise or misled her, but rather succeeded in getting into a dialog with her. He has taken the playful element of his own omnipotence-fantasy seriously and thereby eased the seriousness of his partner's illness by playful means. In this way, he finds access to the dialog, which prompts the patient to emerge from her rigidification and to make the modes of experiencing and interaction that accord with the private life of the doctor her own. In doing so, she has remained exactly who she has always been. Nor has she taken on a new role, has reacted neither artificially nor mendaciously. She feels neither taken by surprise nor misled; instead she takes up again the dialog she used to pursue with other people in the past. She has only given up the disconcerting rigid and ritualized modes of experiencing and interaction that had brought her and all the other mentally ill into the institution.

Were I to take my comparison all the way, then the pervert would be the one who seeks the dialog with the others, the normal people. He circles the normal people and tries time and again to get close to them. If it were possible for him, following the doctor in our example, to enter, with his private – that is, his perverse – modes of experiencing and interaction, into society's normal ones in a playful way, something unusual would emerge. He might succeed, like the doctor, in suddenly approaching the perverse that has become deeply embedded and rigidified within what seems the normal. In his new partner, he would sense a feeling of being moved, or a glow in the expression, that would also shift something within himself. He would be enriched, the way the doctor felt enriched by the experience with the woman.

With this provocative comparison, I want to express that in most cases something must happen within the so-called normal person, who also has a polymorphous-perverse structure, insofar as he has only been able to look at the pervert the way the ill woman looks into the hospital court-yard. What happens to him must be what he least expects, namely that he has been drawn into in an affective dialog by another person who has a playful, relaxed way of dealing with the perverse and yet does not particu-larly stand out, that he has unexpectedly taken up modes of experiencing and interaction that are simply not envisaged among the "normal" – even though these modes are not noticeably distinguished from others. Precisely by getting involved and crossing over the fence of the so-called normal modes of interaction, he finds a playful access to his own perverse traits and can also recognize them in someone else. Then he can succeed in having something take place within him that is unsettling because it may no longer appear to him as normal. Yet that is precisely what is required to transform and expand the normal, which after all contains the perverse, into something that, beyond this "normal," is actually healthy.

Nonetheless, at the end, I would also like to ask: what must happen with the pervert if he has only been able to look at his own perversion the way the ill woman looks into the hospital's inner courtyard? What must happen to him is the same thing that happened to the so-called normal person, the thing that he also expects the least, namely that he is unexpectedly being included in an affective dialog and takes up modes of interaction that are simply not envisaged in perverts. He feels unsettled, because these modes of interaction are noticeably different from those he has followed so far. Precisely by getting involved, crossing over the fence of the perversion, he finds a playful access to the traits of his own person that are not perverse at all, and he is able to compare them with similar traits in others. Then he too can succeed in having something take place within himself that is unsettling – not least because it no longer appears to him as perverse.

Notes

1 This essay by Morgenthaler first appeared in 1977 in a special issue of the New Left journal *Kursbuch* on "Sensualities" (*Sinnlichkeiten*) – which also can sug-gest associations with "The Work of the Senses" or "Sensibilities." The essayist and literary critic Hans Hütt recently reiterated what a key text this particular Morgenthaler essay became for the West German gay rights movement in the later 1970s (Hütt, 2016, pp. 124–125), and the essay does provide interesting glimpses of Morgenthaler's generous capacity to identify with sexual and social

outsiders. But it also bears emphasis how much this text incorporates many of the most essential propositions about psychoanalysis put forward in *Technik*. Meanwhile, the phrase "modes of interaction" (*Verkehrsformen*) requires some explanation. It had been a title theme in two prior issues of *Kursbuch* regarding gender relations and communal living experiments. The reference to *Verkehrsformen* was a gesture to early Marxist language, evoking as it did the notions of "exchange" and of "relations of production" (e.g. in Marx's "The German Ideology"). Yet, for the editors of *Kursbuch*, who never explicitly explained their use of the term, it was evidently intended more to signal how human beings interacted with each other in daily life within capitalist society (Niese, 2017, pp. 589–590). A good example of the emotional connotations surrounding the term at the time can be gleaned from a contemporaneous essay by the social psychologist Gerhard Vinnai (who in 1979 would also, in turn, be cited in Morgenthaler's most famous essay on "Homosexuality"). Vinnai used the term *Verkehrsformen* to denote how "the modes of interaction of human beings are, in capitalism, hardly dependent only on free will; the people interact above all as attachments to their merchandise – to which also the labor power that produced the merchandise belongs" (1979, p. 68). Morgenthaler in this essay extended his more general critique of his fellow psychoanalysts' tendencies to enforce social conformity to a critique of their tendencies to encourage also sexual conformity. But he demonstrated as well what we would now refer to as a queer eye for normative heterosexuality.

2 Morgenthaler's approach to perversions is distinctive, but there are pertinent echoes here with the work of the prominent critical West German sexologist Eberhard Schorsch, who – inspired directly by the Frankfurt School philosopher-sociologist Theodor Adorno – argued around the same time that "In perversions lies the key for comprehending the sexual immaturity of our society . . . perversions expose the narrowness, the one-dimensionality, the amputated pleasure of a solely genital, partner-oriented heterosexuality." Or again: "Perversions are not themselves deficient, pathetic forms of normal and healthy sexuality, as psychopathology and also psychoanalysis constantly suggest, but rather they are reactions and rebellions against the pathetic forms of sexuality as they are permitted by the society in the form of constrictive, partner-based genital heterosexuality." Schorsch too, like Morgenthaler, was more generally interested in the potential "theoretical significance of sexual deviations for the question of a liberated sexuality" (Schorsch, 1975, pp. 150–152; cf. Adorno, 1963). In later writings, Schorsch would also draw on the work of Morgenthaler.

3 The English word "magnificence" captures Morgenthaler's meaning, for in German the word Morgenthaler uses – *grandios* – has positive connotations; it can mean "wonderful." By contrast, "grandiose" in English has more negative valences, associated as it is with an inappropriate and overweening sense of self-importance. That was not Morgenthaler's meaning. Heinz Kohut had introduced the notion of a "grandiose self" in 1971 in his *The Analysis of the Self*. And more generally, Kohut was intent on defending as valuable, and encouraging in his patients, a feeling of healthy narcissism; Morgenthaler greatly appreciated this perspective of Kohut's and built it into his own work.

4 Note here the echo with the letter to Kohut written in the same year. It was, clearly, not least in his interaction with Kohut that Morgenthaler worked out his own touchstone ideas. Also the paragraph which follows this one echoes numerous Kohutian points, and simultaneously articulates a radical position on the place of "the sexual" in the life of all people.

5 In this essay the terms "the sexual" and "sexuality" are used interchangeably. However, Morgenthaler subsequently came to make a distinction between, on the one hand, "the sexual" (*das Sexuelle*) – which he understood as the vital, unruly, creative, undirected forces of the primary process – and, on the other, what he called the "dictatorship" (and at one point even a "military junta") of already-formed "organized sexuality" (*organisierte Sexualität*) – whether that organization turned out to be homo or hetero or perverse or pan (1984, pp. 23–24). Morgenthaler's version of "the sexual" is not to be confused with the French psychoanalyst Jean Laplanche's version of *le sexual* (2011). Whereas Laplanche stressed, as a kind of anthropological universal, the way "enigmatic messages" from the caretaking adults (including unconscious sexual elements) need to be translated by the child and forever after shape the organization of his or her sexuality – indeed the interactions with the caretakers "implant" sexuality in the child – Morgenthaler was more inclined to see repressive, "drive-hostile" forces in society constricting human beings' access to emotionality, sensuality, and capacity for love.

6 This passage expresses the core of Morgenthaler's convictions about psycho-analysis, and it is one which shows up as well in the first chapter of *Technik*. It also, again, echoes a passage in the 1977 letter to Kohut, demonstrating once more the importance of the engagement with Kohut for Morgenthaler's ability to articulate his views on this central set of concerns.

7 Morgenthaler's humane and generous perspective is yet again evident in this case example of a patient who is (in the terminology of the time) "feeble-minded" (*debil*). For aside from a handful of exceptions, psychoanalysis, in its long history, has been generally problematic on the phenomenon of cognitive disability (Herzog, 2019). Morgenthaler, by contrast, as he notes in the next paragraph, was himself transformed by the experience with this patient.

8 Though Morgenthaler does not refer to the term "summation effect" here – more extensively discussed in Chapters 3, 4, and 5 of *Technik* – this is an espe-cially succinct and apt description of what he means by the term.

9 Note that the metaphor usage is this section of the essay is inconsistent. At one point, the doctor helps to heal the mentally ill woman staring into the courtyard simply by persisting in concerning himself with her. But at another point, the pervert is the doctor, while the normal society is the mentally ill woman staring into the courtyard.

Bibliography

Adorno, T. (1982 [1951]) Freudian Theory and the Patterns of Fascist Propaganda. In: A. Arato & E. Gebhardt, eds., *The Essential Frankfurt School Reader*, pp. 118–137. New York: Continuum.

Adorno, T. (1998 [1963]) Sexual Taboos and Law Today. In: *Critical Models: Interventions and Catchwords*, pp. 71–88. New York: Columbia University Press.

Adorno, T., & Horkheimer, M. (1969 [1947]) *Dialectic of Enlightenment*. New York: Seabury.

Aron, L. (1996) *A Meeting of Minds: Mutuality in Psychoanaly*sis. Hillsdale, NJ: The Analytic Press.

Bergmann, M. S. (2000) *The Hartmann Era*. New York: Other Press.

Binswanger, R. (2003) Zur Praxis der Dialektik in der Psychoanalyse. *Werkblatt – Zeitschrift für Psychoanalyse und Gesellschaftskritik* 51.2: 3–23.

Binswanger, R. (2005a) Diskussionsbeitrag zu den Hauptreferaten. *Journal für Psychoanalyse* 45–46: 417–419.

Binswanger, R. (2005b) Lesehilfe: Fritz Morgenthaler, "Technik. Zur Dialektik der Psychoanalytischen Praxis." *Werkblatt – Zeitschrift für Psychoanalyse und Gesellschaftskritik*, www.werkblatt.at/morgenthaler/lesehilfe.htm.

Binswanger, R. (2012) Erinnern – Rekapitulieren – Durcharbeiten: Psychoanalytische Deutungsmuster am Beispiel des 9. Kapitels von Morgenthalers *Technik. Werkblatt – Zeitschrift für Psychoanalyse und Gesellschaftskritik* 68.1: 49–75.

Binswanger, R. (2016) Dream Diagnostics: Fritz Morgenthaler's Work on Dreams. *Psychoanalytic Quarterly* 85.3: 727–757.

Deserno, H. (2005) "Handhabung" oder "Analyse" der Übertragung? Zur Differenz von Technik und Methode der psychoanalytischen Therapie. *Journal für Psychoanalyse* 45–46: 100–130.

Engels, F. (1877) *Herrn Eugen Dührings Umwälzung der Wissenschaft*. Leipzig: Genossenschaftsbuchdruckerei.

Fehr, M. (2005) Die Welt anschauen. In: F. Morgenthaler, ed., *Löwen zeichnen. Vögel zaubern: mit Fritz Morgenthaler verreisen*, pp. 52–56. Giessen: Psychosozial.

Forrester, J. (1988) Translators' Note. In: *The Seminar of Jacques Lacan: Book 1, Freud's Papers on Technique, 1953–1954*, pp. vii–viii. New York: Cambridge University Press.

Freud, A. (1937 [1936]) *The Ego and the Mechanisms of Defence*. London: Hogarth.

Freud, S. (1900) The Interpretation of Dreams. In: *The Standard Edition of the Complete Psychological Works of Sigmund Freud, Volume IV (1900): The Interpretation of Dreams (First Part)*, pp. ix–627. London: Hogarth.

Freud, S. (1912) Recommendations to Physicians Practising Psycho-Analysis. In: *The Standard Edition of the Complete Psychological Works of Sigmund Freud, Volume XII (1911–1913): The Case of Schreber, Papers on Technique and Other Works*, pp. 109–120. London: Hogarth.

Freud, S. (1914) Remembering, Repeating and Working-Through (Further Recommendations on the Technique of Psycho-Analysis II). In: *The Standard Edition of the Complete Psychological Works of Sigmund Freud, Volume XII (1911–1913): The Case of Schreber, Papers on Technique and Other Works*, pp. 145–156. London: Hogarth.

Freud, S. (1917a) Mourning and Melancholia. In: *The Standard Edition of the Complete Psychological Works of Sigmund Freud, Volume XIV (1914–1916): On the History of the Psycho-Analytic Movement*, pp. 237–258. London: Hogarth.

Freud, S. (1917b) Introductory Lectures on Psycho-Analysis. In: *The Standard Edition of the Complete Psychological Works of Sigmund Freud, Volume XVI (1916–1917): Introductory Lectures on Psycho-Analysis (Part III)*, pp. 241–463. London: Hogarth.

Freud, S. (1923) The Ego and the Id. In: *The Standard Edition of the Complete Psychological Works of Sigmund Freud, Volume XIX (1923–1925): The Ego and the Id and Other Works*, pp. 1–66. London: Hogarth.

Freud, S. (1926) Inhibitions, Symptoms and Anxiety. In: *The Standard Edition of the Complete Psychological Works of Sigmund Freud, Volume XX (1925–1926): An Autobiographical Study, Inhibitions, Symptoms and Anxiety, The Question of Lay Analysis and Other Works*, pp. 75–176. London: Hogarth.

Freud, S. (1937) Analysis Terminable and Interminable. In: *The Standard Edition of the Complete Psychological Works of Sigmund Freud, Volume XXIII (1937–1939): Moses and Monotheism, An Outline of Psycho-Analysis*, pp. 209–254. London: Hogarth.

Greenson, R. (1958) Variations in Classical Psycho-Analytic Technique: An Introduction. *International Journal of Psycho-Analysis* 39: 200–201.

Greenson, R. (1967) *The Technique and Practice of Psychoanalysis*, vol. 1. New York: International Universities Press.

Gutherz, D. (2019) On Not Getting What You Want: Elvio Fachinelli's Anti-Authoritarianism. *Psychoanalysis and History* 21.3: 267–291.

Hamburger, A. (2017) Beziehungsanalytische Traumdeutung. *Journal für Psychoanalyse* 58: 7–28.

Hartmann, H. (1954) Problems of Infantile Neurosis: A Discussion (Arden House Symposium). *Psychoanalytic Study of the Child* 9: 31–36.

Hartmann, H., Kris, E., & Lowenstein, R. (1946) Comments on the Formation of Psychic Structure. *Psychoanalytic Study of the Child* 2: 11–38.

Heinrichs, H-J. (2005a) *Fritz Morgenthaler: Psychoanalytiker, Reisender, Maler, Jongleur*. Giessen: Psychosozial.

Heinrichs, H-J. (2005b) Die Idee der Plombe: Anmerkungen zur Fritz Morgenthalers Perversions-Theorie. *Journal für Psychoanalyse* 45–46: 322–338.

Herzog, D. (2017) *Cold War Freud: Psychoanalysis in an Age of Catastrophes*. Cambridge, UK: Cambridge University Press.

Herzog, D. (2019) Psychoanalysis Confronts Cognitive Disability. *Psychoanalysis and History* 21.2: 135–146.

Hütt, H. (2016) Angst vor der Gleichheit. *Jahrbuch Sexualitäten* 1: 117–137.

Knellessen, O. (2005) Der Tanz des Analytikers auf der Lücke: Zu den Gemeinsamkeiten von Metapsychologie und Technik. *Journal für Psychoanalyse* 45–46: 131–150.

Kohut, H. (1966) Formen und Umformungen des Narzissmus. *Psyche* 20.8: 561–587.

Kohut, H. (1969) Die psychoanalytische Behandlung narzisstischer Persönlichkeitsstörungen. *Psyche* 23.5: 321–348.

Kohut, H. (1971) *The Analysis of the Self: A Systematic Approach to the Psychoanalytic Treatment of Narcissistic Personality Disorders*. New York: International Universities Press.

Kohut, H. (1972) Thoughts on Narcissism and Narcissistic Rage. *Psychoanalytic Study of the Child* 27: 360–400.

Kohut, H. (1973) *Narzissmus: Eine Theorie der psychoanalytischen Behandlung narzisstischer Persönlichkeitsstörungen*. Frankfurt am Main: Suhrkamp.

Kohut, H. (1977) *The Restoration of the Self*. New York: International Universities Press.

Körbitz, U. (2003) . . . im Fluss der emotional Bewegung. Fritz Morgenthaler: Technik. *Werkblatt – Zeitschrift für Psychoanalyse und Gesellschaftskritik* 50.1: 49–57.

Körbitz, U. (2020) "Who Is Speaking?" Morgenthaler and/or Lacan Behind the Couch. *Psychoanalysis and History* 22.1.

Kris, E. (1936) The Psychology of Caricature. *International Journal of Psycho-Analysis* 17: 285–303.

Kris, E. (1952) *Psychoanalytic Explorations in Art*. New York: International Universities Press.

Kurz, T. (1993) Aufstieg und Abfall des Psychoanalytischen Seminars Zürich von der Schweizerischen Gesellschaft für Psychoanalyse. *Luzifer-Amor* 6.12: 7–54.

Lahl, A., & Henze, P. (2020) Developing Homosexuality: Fritz Morgenthaler, Junction Points, and Psychoanalytic Theory. *Psychoanalysis and History* 22.1.

Laplanche, J. (2011) *Freud and the Sexual*. New York: International Psychoanalytic Books.

Lenin, V. I. (1927 [1915]) Zur Frage der Dialektik. In: *Sämtliche Werke*, vol. 13, pp. 373–379. Berlin and Vienna: Verlag für Literatur und Politik.

Lewy, E., & Rapaport, D. (1944) The Psychoanalytic Concept of Memory and Its Relation to Recent Memory Theories. *Psychoanalytic Quarterly* 13: 16–42.

Loewenstein, R. (1963) Some Considerations on Free Association. *Journal of the American Psychoanalytic Association* 11: 451–473.

Mao Zedong. (1954 [1937]) *Über den Widerspruch*. Berlin: Dietz.

McLaughlin, N. G. (1998) Why Do Schools of Thought Fail? Neo-Freudianism as a Case Study in the Sociology of Knowledge. *Journal of the History of the Behavioral Sciences* 34.2: 113–134.

Morgenthaler, F. (1969) Introduction to Panel on Disturbances of Male and Female Identity as Met with in Psychoanalytic Practice. *International Journal of Psycho-Analysis* 50: 109–112.

Morgenthaler, F. (1974) Die Stellung der Perversionen in Metapsychologie und Technik. *Psyche* 28.12: 1077–1098.

Morgenthaler, F. (1977) Verkehrsformen der Perversion und die Perversion der Verkehrsformen: Ein Blick über den Zaun der Psychoanalyse. *Kursbuch* 49: 135–148.

Morgenthaler, F. (1979) Innere und äussere Autonomie. *Neue Zürcher Zeitung* (6 July), pp. 31–32.

Morgenthaler, F. (1980) Homosexualität. In: V. Sigusch, ed., *Therapie sexueller Störungen*, pp. 329–367. Stuttgart: Thieme.

Morgenthaler, F. (1984) Sexualität und Psychoanalyse. In: M. Dannecker & V. Sigusch, eds., *Sexualtheorie und Sexualpolitik: Ergebnisse einer Tagung*, pp. 20–38. Stuttgart: F. Enke.

Morgenthaler, F. (2004) Traumdiagnostik: Zur Bedeutung der formalen und strukturellen Gesichtspunkte. In: *Der Traum: Fragmente zur Theorie und Technik der Traumdeutung*, pp. 53–87. Giessen: Psychosozial.

Morgenthaler, F., & Kilian, H. (2017 [1978]) Einleitung. In: *Technik: Zur Dialektik der psychoanalytischen Praxis*, pp. 7–12. Giessen: Psychosozial.

Niese, K. (2017) *"Vademekum" der Protestbewegung? Transnationale Vermittlungen durch das Kursbuch von 1965 bis 1975.* Baden-Baden: Nomos.

Osterkamp, U. (1976) *Grundlagen der psychologischen Motivationsforschung, Band 2. Die Besonderheit menschlicher Bedürfnisse: Problematik und Erkenntnisgehalt der Psychoanalyse.* Frankfurt/Main: Campus.

Parin, P. (2019) *Beziehungsgeflechte: Korrespondenzen von Goldy und August Matthèy, Fritz Morgenthaler und Paul Parin.* Vienna and Berlin: Mandelbaum Verlag.

Parin, P., & Morgenthaler, F. (1969) Ist die Verinnerlichung der Aggression für die soziale Anpassung notwendig? In: A. Mitscherlich, ed., *Bis hierher und nicht weiter: Ist die menschliche Aggression unbefriedbar?* pp. 222–244. Munich: Piper.

Parin, P., Morgenthaler, F., & Parin-Matthèy, G. (1963) *Die Weissen denken zuviel: Psychoanalytische Untersuchungen bei den Dogon in Westafrika.* Zürich: Atlantis.

Parin, P., Morgenthaler, F., & Parin-Matthèy, G. (1971) *Fürchte deinen Nächsten wie dich selbst: Psychoanalyse und Gesellschaft am Modell der Agni in Westafrika.* Frankfurt am Main: Suhrkamp.

Parin, P., Morgenthaler, J., & Binswanger, R. (2003) Aus welchen Quellen schöpfte Fritz Morgenthaler? *Werkblatt – Zeitschrift für Psychoanalyse und Gesellschaftskritik,* www.werkblatt.at/archiv/53morgenthaler.htm.

Pomeranz, R. (2005) "Technik oder was?" Ein Werkstattbericht zum Workshop über Morgenthalers "unausdrückliche Dialektik." *Journal für Psychoanalyse* 45–46: 151–159.

Rapaport, D. (1960) *The Structure of Psychoanalytic Theory: A Systematic Attempt.* New York: International Universities Press.

Reich, W. (1946) *The Mass Psychology of Fascism.* New York: Orgone Institute Press.

Reich, W. (1948 [1933]) *Character Analysis.* London: Vision.

Reiche, R. (2005) Das Sexuelle bei Morgenthaler: Verführung, Plombe, Weichenstellung. *Journal für Psychoanalyse* 45–46: 280–297.

Reiche, R. (2009) Fritz Morgenthaler. In: V. Sigusch, ed., *Personenlexikon der Sexualforschung,* pp. 533–539. Frankfurt am Main: Campus.

Reichmayr, J. (2003) *Ethnopsychoanalyse: Geschichte, Konzepte, Anwendungen.* Giessen: Psychosozial.

Reichmayr, J., & Reichmayr, M. (2019) Einleitung. In: P. Parin, ed., *Beziehungsgeflechte: Korrespondenzen von Goldy und August Matthèy, Fritz Morgenthaler und Paul Parin. Werkausgabe Paul Parin,* vol. 2, pp. 7–18. Vienna and Berlin: Mandelbaum Verlag.

Schorsch, E. (1975) Sexuelle Deviationen: Ideologie, Klinik, Kritik. In: V. Sigusch, ed., *Therapie sexueller Störungen,* pp. 118–155. Stuttgart: Thieme.

Strachey, J. (1938) Editor's Introduction to "The Interpretation of Dreams." In: S. Freud, ed., *The Standard Edition of the Complete Psychological Works of Sigmund Freud, Volume IV (1900): The Interpretation of Dreams (First Part),* pp. xii–xxii. London: Hogarth.

Tändler, M. (2016) *Das therapeutische Jahrzehnt: Der Psychoboom in den siebziger Jahren.* Göttingen: Wallstein.

Theweleit, K. (1987 [1977]) *Male Fantasies. Vol. 1: Women, Floods, Bodies, History.* Minneapolis: University of Minnesota Press.

Theweleit, K. (1989 [1978]) *Male Fantasies. Vol. 2: Male Bodies: Psychoanalyzing the White Terror.* Minneapolis: University of Minnesota Press.

Vinnai, G. (1979) Die Misere des Kleinbürgers und ihr Niederschlag in therapeutischen Prozeduren. In: H. Nagel & M. Seifert, eds., *Inflation der Therapieformen,* pp. 54–103. Reinbek: Rowohlt.

Zweifel, S. (2019) Die Utopie vom Utoquai. *Neue Zürcher Zeitung* (18 July), p. 34.

Index

acting-out, shared (Mitagieren) 13, 58, 60, 121
Adorno, Theodor 3, 190n2
affects (*Affekte*) 45, 49, 106, 108, 122, 127
American Psychoanalytic Association 15
anxiety (*Angst*) 44, 94, 103, 137, 142–4, 153, 179
associative process (*Assoziationsverlauf*) 46–7, 87
ambivalence (*Ambivalenz*) 80, 86–7, 94
Anyi 1, 5

Black, Margaret 5

cases (briefly mentioned): the analysand trying aggressively to seduce the analyst 9, 35; the homosexual man treated by Kohut (Mr. M) 17, 169, 171–2; the man who is inhibited around all women 23; the man with compulsive ideas 32; the man with the cognitive disability 4, 67n3, 184–5, 191n7; the man with the yellow-boot fetish 175–6, 178–9; the woman staring into the courtyard 187–9, 191n9; the woman with the tropical disease 152–3; the young woman sexually attracted to older men 9, 33–4
cases (extensively discussed): the anxious and scornful girl 103–7, 109, 110n2, 112, 119; the emotionally inhibited musician 130–9; the man who cannot concentrate at work and resents his colleagues and friends 75–81, 83–99; the man with the *agricola*-dream, resolving a confused transference 41–51, 55, 118, 122–7; the man with

the father who was hard of hearing 13, 72–4, 90, 127, 139–41; the woman disappointed in both her husband and her lover 13, 68–70
cathexis (*Besetzung*) 39n2, 40n5, 100n1, 116, 145–7; and modalities of (*Besetzungsmodalitäten*) 10, 55–6, 90, 116, 125; and new constellation of (*Umbesetzung*) 147
conflictedness, conflictuality, conflictual inclination (*Konflikthaftigkeit, Konfliktneigung*) 26–7, 49, 66, 70–2, 75, 145, 150; of the analyst 8, 14, 19, 25–6, 37–8, 48, 59, 184
combative situation (*kämpferische Auseinandersetzung*) 10, 118
congruence (*Stimmigkeit*): 10, 109–10, 167, 185; of relationship 34, 87, 91, 150, 167, 185–6; of cathexes 37, 70, 78, 87
consciousness-psychology (*Bewusstseinspsychologie*) 9, 45, 55

Dannecker, Martin 5
defense (*Abwehr*) 69, 71, 86, 89, 103–4, 108, 165; and its misrecognition 38, 111–12, 120, 149–50, 154, 159n4
Devereux, George 5
disability, cognitive 4, 191n7; *see also* "feeble-mindedness"
disappointment, anticipatory 120, 123
disconcertedness (*Befremden*): 48, 150; as experienced by the analysand 72, 76, 91, 95, 104, 140, 144
Dogon 1, 145–6, 148n4
drive (*Trieb, Triebregungen, Triebschicksale, Triebwünsche*) 15–16, 36, 106, 127, 140, 173n2; and

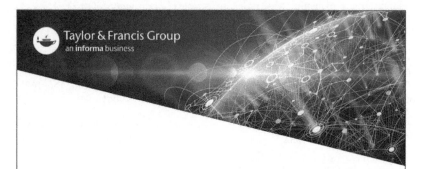